THEODOR FONTANE: THE MAJOR NOVELS

ANGLICA GERMANICA SERIES 2

Editors: LEONARD FORSTER AND M. SWALES

Other books in the series

THEODOR FONTANE:
THE MAJOR NOVELS

ALAN BANCE

CAMBRIDGE UNIVERSITY PRESS

CAMBRIDGE
LONDON   NEW YORK   NEW ROCHELLE
MELBOURNE   SYDNEY

CAMBRIDGE UNIVERSITY PRESS
Cambridge, New York, Melbourne, Madrid, Cape Town, Singapore,
São Paulo, Delhi, Dubai, Tokyo, Mexico City

Cambridge University Press
The Edinburgh Building, Cambridge CB2 8RU, UK

Published in the United States of America by Cambridge University Press, New York

www.cambridge.org
Information on this title: www.cambridge.org/9780521155038

© Cambridge University Press 1982

First published 1982
First paperback edition 2010

A catalogue record for this publication is available from the British Library

Library of Congress Catalogue Card Number: 81-21688

ISBN 978-0-521-24532-6 Hardback
ISBN 978-0-521-15503-8 Paperback

Das Lyrische hab' ich aufgegeben, ich möchte sagen, blutenden Herzens. Ich liebe eigentlich nichts so sehr und innig wie ein schönes Lied, und doch ward mir gerade die Gabe für das Lied versagt.

(I have renounced lyric poetry; with a bleeding heart, I am tempted to say. There's really nothing I love so well and so deeply as a fine lyric, and yet it was precisely a talent for the lyric that was denied me.)

Theodor Fontane to Wilhelm Wolfsohn, 10 November 1847

ACKNOWLEDGMENTS

In addition to expressing my gratitude to Mrs Kay McKechnie for her editorial expertise, I should like to thank my wife Sandra for her help and encouragement; Professor Martin Swales for invaluable advice; and Professor Charlotte Jolles and Dr Eric Dickins for their generous willingness to read proofs. Any surviving errors are entirely my own responsibility.

AFB

CONTENTS

FOREWORD

In Fontane's work there is a development from a highly-coloured poetic or balladesque mode, to a more complex, realistic treatment of social relations and nuances. The process is an exemplary one for nineteenth-century art, whose pretensions to the exact reproduction of reality culminated in Zola's famous definition, 'un coin de la nature vu à travers un tempérament'. This study of Fontane's major novels attempts to follow through a dialectic central to the discussion of nineteenth-century art in general: the tension and opposition between objective faithfulness to 'facts' and a higher or poetic truth.[1]

Fontane seems to have been instinctively aware that all accounts of reality are subjective, themselves aspects and products of that reality, and serving to make some comment upon it.[2] Among Fontane critics, it is Richard Brinkmann who has made this point most eloquently. He says of Fontane's realism that it succeeds in avoiding the dual limitations of a neo-idealist elevation of art, and of the exhaustive objectivity attempted by other realists and the Naturalists. Increasingly, in the course of his development, Fontane's fictional form rests upon an awareness that fiction presents a subjectively selected and interpreted objectivity, and that this objective reality itself exists only 'als eine, in die das Subjekt verschlungen und verwickelt ist' ('as one in which the subject is intimately involved').[3]

Brinkmann stresses Fontane's respect for 'Thatsächlichkeiten' (factualness),[4] his immersion in the tangible, everyday world of his characters, and his close scrutiny of individuals (p. 38). Fontane renounced the licence to pronounce overt judgment upon his characters, or to take up the 'high-serious' position of idealist art. Indeed, he was uninterested in the debate about the 'hierarchy of art', or the question of 'idealism versus realism' which exercised Stifter and Otto Ludwig[5] among others. To assume that the difference between serious and trivial art lies merely in the exalted nature of the subject-matter already seemed as outmoded to Fontane as the related, and equally stereotyped, assumption of opposition between innovators and exponents of tradition, locked in 'the dramatic conflicts between innovating "heroes" and academic "villains"'.[6] And Fontane would surely have been amused to read Stifter's comment in 1865 that the academic experts had not yet established how far objective reality could be allowed to go in a work of art, and since this question had been left to the discretion of individual artists, in recent years the conflict over 'realism and idealism' had ensued (Greter, p. 131).

Fontane's freedom from the trammels of theory about his own art, and his resistance to categorization, are reflected in the latitude claimed by critics in attributing to him the classical ideals of harmony and 'Maß' (restraint), on the one hand,[7] and qualities of the *fin de siècle* artists of language-conscious *Nuancenkunst* (art full of nuances) and decadence, on the other.[8] Müller-Seidel, for example, 'persuasively links Fontane with the experiential half-heartedness of Schnitzler's art' (Erika Swales, n.2, p. 121, referring to Müller-Seidel, p. 371).

Equally persuasively, Fontane's art was associated by Peter Demetz with the 'novel of society' (of which Jane Austen presents the best examples), where to travel is always to arrive safely; where crises are banished to the intervals of the story; where the social patterns of 'Diners' and 'Landpartien' (excursions) shape the fiction; and where the lower-middle classes are 'condemned by their menu'. Demetz at times makes Fontane's novels sound rather like the German equivalent of English early nineteenth-century 'silver fork fiction' (e.g. Bulwer-Lytton's *Pelham, or the Adventures of a Gentleman*, 1828), which served as a textbook in etiquette for the parvenu: 'man könnte fast sagen, Freiherr von Knigge eher als der individuelle Schriftsteller bestimme die Konturen der Roman-Architektur' ('one might almost say that Freiherr von Knigge [author of a famous eighteenth-century book on etiquette] had laid down the outlines of the novels' structure, rather than the individual writer').[9]

It is not the subject-matter that creates the distinction of a work of art, but the treatment of the subject. What is almost a truism now was a discovery in the nineteenth century. To draw a parallel with the pictorial arts, Edouard Manet's 'Un Bar aux Folies-Bergères' (1882), sharing its theme with much trivial art of the period, was an enigma to contemporaries. It presents the blank frontal view of a female, a subject well known from contemporary treatments of the 'woman in a shop-window' theme.[10] The woman on display, waiting for a buyer, reflects the marriage-market ethos. The difference between Manet's treatment of the theme and those of his trivializing contemporaries is that the attitude of *his* female becomes a metaphor of emptiness, distance and inaccessibility: the revelation of the world of cheap entertainment is raised to a poetic level. Similarly, as Ingrid Mittenzwei points out (p. 101), Fontane's use of social conventions and a conventional *affaire* in *Irrungen, Wirrungen* is a mere *Gerüst*, a scaffold. The novel is a demonstration 'daß dasselbe, von verschiedenen Leuten getan oder gesagt, keineswegs dasselbe ist' ('that the same thing, performed or spoken by different people, is not at all the same thing'; ibid., p. 103) – an epigrammatic statement that challenges Peter Demetz's reduction of Fontane's novels to their bare social structure. However, Demetz himself takes the analysis of Fontane's art well beyond the limits of the social novel, to conclude that, with Fontane, we might well reach the only *apparently* paradoxical conclusion that the status of the masterpieces of the most important German realist was defined, as much as anything, by the richness of their symbolic texture.[11]

As both Gärtner and Schuster[12] emphatically stress, concentration on details, *Thatsächlichkeiten* and social phenomena, in place of the 'higher' concerns of hierarchical or classical art, does not mean the replacement of idealism by noncommittal pragmatism: that would be the very antithesis of Fontane's endeavour. The pragmatism of his time, Bismarck's *Realpolitik* and the unprincipled materialism of the *Gründerzeit* (the boom following unification), was anathema to him. He always had 'einen ganz ausgebildeten Sinn für *Thatsächlichkeiten*' ('a well-developed sense of *factualness*'; Fontane's emphasis), but he declared, significantly: 'Ich habe das Leben immer genommen, wie ich's fand und mich ihm unterworfen. Das heißt, nach außen hin; in meinem Gemüthe nicht' ('I have always taken life as I found it and submitted to it. That is to say, outwardly I have: but not in the depths of my heart'; *Briefe an Friedländer*, p. 235). That rider – 'in meinem Gemüthe nicht' – speaks of his reservations about his age, one which is all too ready to submit to the irresistible power of 'facts', in brash over-reaction to the preceding, politically ineffectual phase of *Dichter und Denker* (poets and thinkers). In the words of a contemporary politician:

Die Zeit der Ideale ist vorüber. Die deutsche Einheit ist aus der Traumwelt in die prosaische Welt der Wirklichkeit hinuntergestiegen. Politiker haben heute weniger als je zu fragen, was *wünschenswert*, als was *erreichbar* ist.[18]

(The time of ideals is past. German unity has descended from the world of dreams into the prosaic world of reality. There is less occasion than ever for politicians to ask what is *desirable* rather than what is *achievable*.)

The role of art *was* to ask what was 'wünschenswert' (desirable) (the more so as contemporaries declined to do so), and that is – among other things – inevitably a political question, whose implications Gärtner brings out by reference to the *Poesie und Prosa* polarity in Fontane's autobiographical novel *Meine Kinderjahre* (Gärtner, p. 105).

Fontane was not the man to confine himself to registering, and thereby tacitly condoning, the *status quo*. An older view of Fontane's resignation and quietism – supposedly shared by others of his generation – resulting from a consciousness of nineteenth-century German political failure (a view still represented to some extent by Richter in 1966),[14] has not been a fashionable one of late. Its popularity began to decline with the publication of Fontane's highly political letters to Friedländer in 1954, which effectively helped to silence any remaining support for Spiero's conception of Fontane's 'kühl wägende, entherzte, alternde Welt' ('cool and calculating, unemotional, ageing world').[15] By the same token, Brinkmann's conclusion of 1967, reprinted unaltered in the new edition of his book in 1977, reads less convincingly fourteen years on: it contends that Fontane's conciliatory attitude to the individual case, the *Einzelexemplar* of society, sometimes goes so far as to permit the suspicion that 'it applies to conditions themselves, to their inhumanity'.[16]

Because Fontane fought his age with its own weapons ('Thatsächlichkeiten'), it was all too easy to interpret his closeness to the world he depicts as identification with its *mores*. But, as Aust puts it, 'Kunst kann eine positive Gegenwelt sein, wenn sie nur – das scheint paradox formuliert zu sein – tief genug mit der Wirklichkeit verflochten ist' ('paradoxical as the formulation may seem, art can represent an alternative world, as long as it is deeply enough involved with reality').[17] Schuster's formulation is similar; Fontane's social criticism and his suggested solutions to the failings of society are combined in one and the same artistic medium, yielding 'eine Faktenüberschreitung, ohne die Mittel der faktischen Wirklichkeit zu überschreiten' ('a transgressing of the facts, without transgressing the medium of factual reality'; Schuster, p. 178).

Verklärung (transfiguration) – a term Fontane applied to his own art,[18] and one which in earlier years was misapplied to it by critics who gave it the meaning of the escapist idyll,[19] of 'heiteres Darüberstehen' (serene detachment) – is a synonym for this 'step beyond factualness', a 'dimension of art that is not present in historical reality' (Aust, p. 17), 'a making transparent of mere factualness to bring out its human character' (Schuster, p. 180), an 'unaffected free humanity', 'the essence of poetry'.[20] *Verklärung* is 'a transformation...which ensures that the reality portrayed has the quality of a poem';[21] the very process that Fontane feels is lacking in the writing of

xiii

criticism of Turgenev's work.

Turgenev, which 'so grenzenlos prosaisch, so ganz unverklärt die Dinge wiedergibt' ('reproduces things in such an infinitely prosaic and untransfigured manner').[22] Fontane admires Turgenev's sharp eye and unpretentious style, but is unrelenting in his verdict: 'Ohne diese Verklärung giebt es aber keine eigentliche Kunst... Wer *so* beanlagt ist, muß *Essays* über Rußland schreiben, aber nicht Novellen' ('But without this transfiguration, there is no real art... anyone with these particular talents should write essays about Russia, not novellas'; ibid.).

Some recent work on Fontane has explored the poetic aspect very successfully; in particular that of Norbert Frei, whose monograph[23] on the poetic role of Fontane's heroines is extensively referred to in chapter 2 of this book. Others, however, have moved in a different direction. Fontane's writing (like Turgenev's) supports some fine analysis of social relations and the 'accommodations' which 'must exist within any conceivable socio-economic constellation'.[24] The point has been made above that Fontane's *Verklärung* is achieved only *within* the framework of actual social conditions: the 'world of tact' is one he understands and conveys supremely well. Some critics go so far as to deny 'the possibility of an immediate and "authentic" expression of a true personality' in *Effi Briest* (Minden, p. 871); or to suggest that 'even (Effi's) frequent moments of seeming naturalness and spontaneity are somehow a socially made version, a "Vorstellung" of the natural'.[25] However, this line of argument can lead to the problematical notion of the novel's 'divided aesthetic allegiance' (Minden, p. 869) and to the assertion that it 'tells two stories', one of which is a more or less disposable luxury offering the escape of poetry, 'the poetically necessary pathos of early death', where the young child, Effi, trampled on and brutalized by society, finds refuge in death from the world of tact. The other story, the indispensable one, is that 'not of poetic inevitability and satisfying pathos, but a much blacker one of *pure waste*'. An echo of this last comment is found too in Professor Garland's chapter on *Effi Briest*: 'the general sense of waste is tempered by numerous

818

1818

 8888888888

FOREWORD

touches and acts of kindness, compassion, or simple goodness'.[26]

Professor Garland's illuminating and highly readable book is a good illustration of the fact that it is possible to take Fontane more or less exclusively on the level of the social novel, and to make perfectly valid statements on this level; that, for example – on *Effi Briest* – 'character and social environment are the stuff of this novel' (p. 172). While undeniably true, such statements, as they stand, would presumably not have completely satisfied Fontane himself, for it is difficult to see in what way they differentiate him from his 'prosaic' counterpart, Turgenev.

The answer to the rhetorical question, 'is the undistorted externalization of personality thinkable?' (Minden, p. 872) is 'yes – to a romantic'. And it is my contention that Fontane *is* a romantic (although in the following chapters I shall limit the use of the term 'romantic' in favour of 'poetic'). However 'naive and misleading' (ibid.), quixotic or irrational it may seem, the dominant social structure of Fontane's works is in conflict with an indispensable counter-structure, what he himself calls the 'verklärender Zauber des Künstlerischen' ('the transfiguring magic of the artistic'),[27] which has aesthetic need of the 'thinkable' authentic position outside society. (As chapter 2 will argue, women often supply the need, for reasons which are not only aesthetic, but also as factual as the realist can make them.) Brinkmann deals with the point when he argues that Fontane does not deny that one's personal position and decisions are preconditioned by society in a *general* way, even before the *specific* acute pressures applied by society; yet there remains a residual freedom between this predetermination of the individual and the massive claim exerted by society (p. 107). And in that residual freedom or 'room for manoeuvre' – which may exist in truth only in the aesthetic realm, but for that very reason serves as part of the *raison d'être* of Fontane's aesthetic enterprise – lie two constituent elements of Fontane's romantic/ realist art: a 'verklärte Wirklichkeit' ('transfigured reality', the antithesis of 'pure waste') 'in which the question of the meaning of existence, the world and history is not only raised but receives a concrete answer' (Aust, p. 17); and the element of mystery or 'Räthselmacht' (mysterious power),[28] which finds its appropriate form in the 'rätselhafte Modelung' (mysterious shaping),[29] conspicuously absent, in Fontane's view, from Turgenev's art of the 'photographischer Apparat in Aug und Seele' ('photographic apparatus in the eye and the soul').[30]

The most striking aspects of this 'mysterious shaping' are at the same time devices which help Fontane to maintain the decorum of the dominant social structure: his discretion, and his symbolic allusions. Discretion is a virtue prized by most critics of Fontane. From a technical point of view it need be no more than the refined art of suggestion, whose value was known to Fontane the ballad-writer,[31] and was propounded in the 'objectivity' theory of Spielhagen, in which Fontane took an interest in the early 1880s. But technical considerations are not the whole story. According to Minden, this discretion or reticence on the part of the narrator in Fontane's novels is 'a projection of the flight into the social, the recourse to the world of tact, on to the plane of style' (p. 875). Such a view goes a long way towards implying that the narrator's silence is tacit assent to the 'accommodations' demanded by society. Although this may be true of some occurrences of reticence – Fontane accepts 'Thatsächlichkeiten', after all – in a more important sense the opposite is surely the case. The reader is invited to question the accommodations demanded of the individual: an obvious example is the presentation in *Effi Briest* of Frau Zwicker at Bad Ems. Without comment from the narrator, she stands as an awful example to Effi and the reader of the complete, cynical adjustment to the demands of the world of facts. It is not too much to say that after Effi learns of her social fall from grace through the discovery of her adultery (information she receives in the presence of Frau Zwicker), she is faced ultimately with a choice of 'Frau Zwicker or death'; that is to say, of accommodating 'facts' by shamelessly living up to her name as a fallen woman, or succumbing to the despair engendered by the irreconcilable conflict between her own subjective sense of being wronged, and the irreversible condemnation of society.

More positively, discretion is at the same time a provocation to the reader to contemplate the mysteries the author is unfolding to us, 'an invitation to...participate imaginatively in the creation of the story' (Leckey, p. 48). It is significant that Leckey is convincingly able to take this art of reticence, allusion and 'Sprunghaftigkeit' (narrative leaps), back to the romantic world of the ballad (pp. 45–51), a connexion confirmed by Fontane himself in a comment on the art of suggestion in John Everett Millais's painting 'Autumn Leaves' (1856).[32]

To return to an earlier point: Fontane's realism has the capacity to comprise a statement about reality beyond the world of facts (or tact) it presents, 'beyond the facts by means of facts precisely captured' (Schuster, p. 184). The role of Fontane's symbolism in turning *Prosa* into *Poesie* (Greter, p. 140)[33] has been exhaustively analysed, notably by Günther[34] and Thanner, and not least by Peter Demetz. To these interpretations can be added Peter-Klaus Schuster's more recent book. It is not necessary to adopt all of Schuster's startling new findings in order to concede that he uncovers a good deal of 'disguised symbolism' in *Effi Briest*. His suggestion that Effi's life is viewed in the novel in terms of parodistic versions of the 'either-or', 'Eva-or-Maria' stereotypes imposed upon the female by Prussian–Wilhelmine society in the name of the prevailing order, recalls the 'double standard' of Victorian sexual myth, under which 'the virtuous matron relies for her very existence on that spectral figure of the temptress'.[35] At the very least, Schuster's book is a powerful argument against the school of thought which denies that Fontane's heroines have any aesthetic function beyond their socially-conditioned and socially-implicated one: for example, his isolation of a repertoire of sacrifice-rituals in *Effi Briest* cumulatively exposes Effi's role as victim (see chapter 3, below).

Schuster underlines and reinforces the more well-established 'elemental' symbolism surrounding Effi in the novel, analysed in the 1960s by Dietrich Weber[36] in an article that drew attention to such irrational motifs as 'Naturkultus' (the cult of nature), 'Nachtluft' (night air) and 'der Ruf des Elements' (the call of the elemental), and demonstrated that the points in the novel where the elemental breaks in are precisely those where psychological or moral considerations are irrelevant or in some way insufficient. Weber's conclusion was that explanations of the social and psychological import of the novel, or of its events as a process of transgression and expiation, offered inadequate categories. For the novel operates on two levels, those of 'Schuldtragödie' (tragedy of guilt) and 'Schicksalstragödie' (fate tragedy). While the first is carried through with remorseless thoroughness – Fontane's sober sense of the facts does not allow him to evade the issue – it is not the full story of *Effi Briest*. The 'Schicksalstragödie' manifests the stylistic principle that 'the factualness of life, despite all the objectivity employed by the realist in depicting it, is made in the end to seem inscrutable'.

If that should seem too negative a note on which to launch a study of the ascendancy of poetry over prose in Fontane, I am happy to adopt Karlheinz Gärtner's formula (p. 197), a suitable rallying-cry: '[Fontane's writing] is essentially constructive, the overcoming of the reality that provokes it'.

1 · INTRODUCTION

'Das romantisch Phantastische', says Theodor Fontane in a letter of 1891, 'hat mich von Jugend auf entzückt und bildet meine eigenste südfranzösische Natur' ('The romantic and fantastic has delighted me since my youth and constitutes my essentially southern-French nature'; to Hans Hertz, 15 April 1891). Either Fontane was deceiving himself, an inference encouraged by the fanciful invocation of his French provenance, or Wandrey was doing him a grave injustice when he wrote in 1919 that 'das Romantische' in Fontane was a matter of external techniques, as evidenced by the early ballad-writing, and that Fontane himself was completely 'unromantisch'.[1] Wandrey is an acute and in some ways still unsurpassed commentator on Fontane, and we cannot dismiss his verdict lightly: but is Fontane's self-characterization then a distortion of the truth? Wandrey's remark was made in his chapter on 'die balladesken Novellen', *Grete Minde* and *Ellernklipp*, which he criticized as a 'wrong turning' in Fontane's development. One way to test the durability of Fontane's 'romanticism' is to compare one of these early 'balladesque Novellen' with a mature work, and for relative similarity of subject-matter the obvious choices are *Ellernklipp* and *Effi Briest*. In chapter 3 of this book such a comparison is carried out, and it seeks to show that there is a continuity within change. The survival of certain external qualities of the ballad-style is obvious evidence of this continuity; but, more substantially, it is the survival and refinement of a quality I shall more often call poetic, rather than romantic, which bears testimony to Fontane's sustained interest in something more than merely *Wirklichkeit* (reality) or *Gegenwart* (the present), 'das Phantastische' in an evolving subtlety of forms.

The term 'romantic' has a period association with the Romantic movement, and is open to confusion. What both Fontane and Wandrey seem to have in mind is not Romanticism in its Schlegel–Novalis sense, but a picturesque extension of what I have called 'the poetic'. *Poesie* in German has the connotations I wish to suggest when thought of as the antonym of *Prosa*, pertaining to the mundane and reasonable world. The ensuing interpretation of some of Fontane's novels is built on the theory of a dialectic of conflict between *Prosa* and *Poesie*.

It might be objected, with some justification, that 'poetic' and 'prosaic' are not respectable critical terms. I am inclined here to emulate the strategy of William Empson, who used 'ambiguity' to mean anything he liked, warning the reader that his distinctions between the 'Seven Types' would not merit the examination of a profound thinker.[2] The terms I have chosen seem to denote better than any others a nineteenth-century awareness of dichotomy everywhere observed. It is seen at its plainest in Fontane in a discussion of the compatibility of flannel underwear and heroism in *Unwiederbringlich* (V, 65);[3] or in the contrast between his admiration for the glories of Anglo-Scottish history and his increasing dislike of contemporary British materialism or mammonism;[4] or the debate about the relative merits of ballad as against prose at the 'Kastalia' literary club in *Vor dem Sturm* (chapter 43, I, 333–52). All three of these examples involve the heroic aspect of poetic tradition, a focus for nineteenth-century awareness of the cleavage between the banal facts of modern existence and the more inspiring world of stark conflicts and self-conquest embodied in the epic and ballad tradition. In chapter 2 of this book I discuss the confrontation of Fontane, a writer whose first love was the ballad, with this legacy, tracing here and elsewhere his typically nineteenth-century (though not necessarily very German) instinct to tolerate the ordinary while admiring the ideal, and his success in creating poetic triumph out of everyday circumstances in such novels as *Irrungen, Wirrungen, Frau Jenny Treibel* and *Effi Briest*.

Throughout European intellectual centres in the second half of the century, a purely materialistic, scientific conception of the external world was in the ascendant. For Basil Willey, it was the Positivist Auguste Comte, a thinker who commanded influence on both sides of the Channel, who was the central figure of his century, a place he gained by his attempt to reconcile all those nineteenth-century irreconcilables that fill the middle ground between the two poles of poetic and prosaic – destruction and construction, negation and affirmation, science and religion, the head and the heart, the past and the present, order and progress.[5] Writers and artists in particular were not prepared to give in without a struggle to the victory of prose. In Germany, opposition took a number of different forms, from Grabbe's unsuccessful rearguard action in defence of the heroic,[6] to Heine's combination of savage irony and bittersweet yearning for *Poesie*; the latter best seen in a poem like 'Prinzessin Sabbat', showing the magic transformation of a Jewish household, unavoidably obsessed with sordid and material things on weekdays, into a haven of peace and poetry after dusk on Friday evenings. In England, opposition to the stress on hard facts, 'Useful Knowledge' (epitomized by the Great Exhibition of 1851), laissez-faire pragmatism and a complacent belief in progress, is summed up in Matthew Arnold's *Culture and Anarchy* (1869), and his contrast, in *Friendship's Garland* (1871), between England's great moment in the year 1815 and her condition half a century later. (Dubslav's claim in *Der Stechlin* on behalf of the merits of 1813 in Prussian history is in the same vein: VIII, 283.) England, according to Arnold, has lost the aristocratic tone, and her destiny is left to a middle class which has no ideals except those of being left in peace to do a roaring trade.[7]

It is interesting – and indicative of the intellectual prestige of Germany in 1871 – that Arnold turns to the German language to supply the word he requires to summarize his opposition: national life, he says, needs a basis in some vital idea or sentiment in order to be great (a debate about national greatness is couched in very similar terms in Fontane's *Unwiederbringlich*: see p. 108 below), and *Geist* (spirit *and* intellect) is the term he chooses to employ.[8] We are reminded by

3

it of a contrast between Germany and England in their respective national and popular reactions to the onset of the age of prose, which otherwise have so much in common. German perception of change in the nineteenth century was the more acute, measures of defence against it more extreme, because of the relative abruptness of developments and the degree of shock induced by them in Germany. The 'general crisis of modernization' in pre-First World War Germany led to a refusal to modernize,[9] to the nationalistic stress on a separate and quasi-mystical German tradition distinct from the aims and values of the Western democracies. British Imperial jingoism, by comparison, lacked the intellectual pedigree of German nationalism, and was correspondingly more pragmatically inclined and thus more short-lived as circumstances rendered it outmoded. The cult of German *Geist*, however, although up to a point an understandable reaction to change and anarchy on the part of honourable men like Thomas Mann, for example (*Betrachtungen eines Unpolitischen*, 1918), or Hugo von Hofmannsthal ('Das Schrifttum als geistiger Raum der Nation', 1927), became a banner to be waved by backward-looking nationalists and rabid anti-semites, until finally National Socialism succeeded in identifying German *Geist* and culture with one political ideology to the total exclusion of all others.

Even in the Second Reich, however, these tendencies were already in evidence. A dangerous and volatile mixture had been created: a combination of high industrial and commercial development, with political and social backwardness. Germany was in a high degree what the first European Machine Age was in general: a parvenu civilization.[10] Nineteenth-century Europeans took the brunt of an expansion of physical capabilities greater than any previously known. In Germany, the task of assimilating this change, which everywhere led to a disturbance of balance, was all the more formidable because of the political instability inherent in a late and somewhat coerced unification under Prussia, and the lack of a democratic infrastructure able to deflect or absorb shock-waves. Where in

England the social circumstances of the time created a self-indulgent emphasis on mawkish sentiment and on all the aspects of life which had suffered from industrialism, in Germany, although the cult of sentimentality was not unknown, another kind of false-poetic solution was increasingly in vogue: the heroic and the monumental became the official taste of the Second Reich. The public language of speeches and the press, and the officially and popularly approved art of the period, were similarly bombastic and inflated, in a stylized attempt to convey the 'greatness' of the new Reich.[11] In Fontane's *Unwiederbringlich* the cult of the heroic and of the national past is shown up for the false-poetic and dangerous panacea that it was. Others beside Fontane identified the dangers of the heroic pose. Jakob Burckhardt, for example, saw both the break with tradition which Germany was undergoing, and the unlovable form her reaction was taking.[12]

A problem raised by Fontane was how to achieve a dissociation from parvenu materialism without either contributing to the contemporary cult of the heroic, or appearing simply nostalgic and escapist. The question is raised in *Frau Jenny Treibel* when Corinna Schmidt asks herself if there is any good reason why she should not enjoy the fruits of modernity and participate in the scramble for comfort and material possessions to which her contemporaries have surrendered. To complement and offset the modern, emancipated figure of Corinna, Fontane employed the person of Professor Schmidt, whose understanding of the decline of classical humanist education from the vision of *Bildung* (education) known to Humboldt and the German idealists, to rote-learning and Latin grammar as an end in itself,[13] fails to dispel his belief in the culture of antiquity as an antidote to modern German materialism. He is a survivor of the old Germany, a 'philosophic, a-political and unpractical' nation[14] which inspired the cliché but well-substantiated description of *Dichter und Denker* (poets and thinkers), but which was caught up by the end of the century in a process of transformation, in the course of which 'the German scale of values

5

changed; amiability and contentment gave place to aggressive and rather humourless efficiency as the national ideal [and] great significance was attributed to appearance and material possessions'.[15]

Without nostalgia, and with careful checks and balances to control sentiment, Fontane achieves the enlargement of sympathy by the imaginative heightening of the real, to comprehend his age and at the same time to formulate a poetic reply to it. In doing so he reaches back to the best classical–humanist tradition of Germany, while embracing also an Anglo-Saxon, pragmatic version of realism, not opposed to German idealism, but simply immune to its lure of the transcendental. Few of Fontane's contemporaries cared to or were able to put into practice in the novel the poetic definition of realism put forward in G. H. Lewes's essay of 1858, 'Realism in Art', which states that the true business of art is intensification, not distortion or falsification of the real, and that the common appearances of everyday life will furnish all we ask.[16]

The climate of Germany in the second half of the nineteenth century was not receptive to the *novel*, in particular, as a poetic vehicle. Both the particularly acute German desire for a poetic counterweight to the mundane present, and Germany's social backwardness, are reflected in a backward-looking preference for other, traditional genres. The popularity of the ballad-form throughout the century, and the continuing prestige of the drama as a genre, despite its decline in practice as measured by the absence of major new plays or playwrights between about 1860 and 1880, indicate that the German quest for the poetic was not generally thought to be furthered by the novelist, who continued to be seen as the 'Halbbruder des Dichters' ('half-brother of the poet'), in Schiller's condescending phrase.[17] Hegel, for whom the drama was 'die höchste Stufe der Poesie und der Kunst überhaupt' ('the highest stage of poetry and of art as a whole'),[18] agreed with the dramatist Grillparzer, who in turn not only echoed Schiller but expressed a common nineteenth-century viewpoint in describing the novel as 'halbe

Poesie' ('half-poetry'),[19] and elsewhere remarked that 'Poesie in Prosa ist Unsinn' ('poetry in prose is nonsense').[20] The prestige of the ballad, derived largely from the inspiration of the rediscovery of folk-poetry in the preceding century and the part it played in restoring pride in German national culture, has likewise been cited as a reason for Germany's failure to achieve distinction in the novel, a genre which is the glory of nineteenth-century European literature. It has also been said, and is an indication of the magnetic pull of the ballad-form, that it was the attraction of the ballad that for too long distracted the supreme novelist Fontane from his true *métier*.[21] This is only one example of a general German tendency of the time to regard a conventionally poetic form as superior to the allegedly prosaic and even trivial genre of the novel.

The inclination to regard poetry as the exclusive repository of rich imaginative content and powerful emotional impact is one that has its origins in the history of aesthetics and rhetoric.[22] It survives down to modern times in, for example, an entry in Gero von Wilperts's *Sachwörterbuch der Literatur* under the rubric *Prosa*: 'die Poesie wendet sich mehr an die Phantasie, die Prosa mehr an den Verstand...' ('poetry addresses itself rather to the imagination, prose to the reason').[23] As a case in point, nineteenth-century German suspicions about the historical novel, the preference for and success of the drama as a vehicle of 'historical, national and mythological aspiration',[24] were discussed very much in antithetical terms of *Poesie* and *Prosa*. A defensive review[25] by the major German historical novelist before Fontane, Willibald Alexis, 'aware that the historical novel is regarded by strict-observance aestheticians as a hybrid form of an already inferior genre',[26] characterizes the form, typically for the early nineteenth century, as 'zur Prosa herabgestimmte Epopöe' (Alexis, p. 31).

Even in England, in the late nineteenth century, we come across a remark such as that of the critic John Morley on a much-admired writer, George Eliot, concerning the limitations of the novelist (as against the practitioners of other literary forms) 'bound by the conditions of her art to deal in a thousand trivialities of human character and situation'.[27] But such genuflection in the direction of poetry and condescension towards the parvenue genre, the novel, bear little relation to the reality of the literary situation in England. The novel indisputably reigned supreme; as it did in Russia, too, where a striking development led in the 1840s to an almost total domination by the novel and the eclipse of poetry by the end of the century. In England, France or Russia it is inconceivable that 'a natural novelist would have been confined within the crumbling ruins of the ballad',[28] a form to which Fontane said a reluctant farewell in the shape of his balladesque Novellen, and to which he reverted later in life. It is all the more remarkable that, as the following chapters aim to show, his achievement in the novel was precisely, and almost uniquely in German letters, a successful rearguard action fought to defend poetic values against the prose of modern circumstance, through the medium of a 'prosaic' and, in Germany, relatively unsuccessful literary form.

And yet his success, though rare in German terms, is a not untypical nineteenth-century triumph; for, in a wider perspective, it is apparent for example that the history of European art and architecture of the period is the history of two opposing scales of value: the hierarchical and grandiose, and the commonplace and unpretentious, an opposition resulting in a victory for the prosaic, albeit in the form of a curious inversion whereby artists are only truly poetic where they dare to be prosaic. Ingres, for example, is less masterly when dealing with exalted themes, such as the 'Apotheosis of Homer', than with more down-to-earth subject-matter. This poeticizing of prosaic matter is above all true of the Impressionists and Post-Impressionists, of van Gogh and Toulouse-Lautrec;[29] and it holds true in the wider sense that the characteristically nineteenth-century works which fired the popular imagination, and still do, were not pseudo-Gothic products of high art, but Paxton's Crystal

8

Palace and Eiffel's Tower, the work of a gardener and an engineer respectively.

If this observation should seem to have taken us rather a long way from Fontane, the connexion is nonetheless perhaps clearer than is immediately apparent. Thomas Mann brings it out in a remark in his essay 'Der alte Fontane':

Diese so leichte, so lichte Prosa hat mit ihrer heimlichen Neigung zum Balladesken...etwas bequem Gehobenes...Sie steht in der Tat der Poesie viel näher, als ihre unfeierliche Anspruchslosigkeit wahrhaben möchte.[30]

(This prose, so light, so lucid, has in its veiled tendency to the balladesque a certain comfortably elevated quality. In fact it is much closer to poetry than its unassuming, unpretentious manner seems prepared to admit.)

I make the point in the course of this essay that Fontane, too, becomes most truly lyrical when he looks beyond the ostensibly more colourful, balladesque subject to explore the poetry of the prosaic. To establish this is to show that the line of Fontane's poetic development is unbroken, that poetry is refined, not rejected.[31] The victory of prose, in visual terms so hauntingly captured in that quintessential nineteenth-century canvas, Turner's 'Fighting Téméraire', in the contrast of the graceful, heroic but superannuated man-o'-war from the age of sail, bathed in the golden glow of sunset as it is ignominiously towed away to its death by the grimy, parvenu steam-tug, practical product of the machine age – the victory of prose, at least in the major novels of Theodor Fontane, is after all not complete.

2 · *POESIE* AND *PROSA*

The antithesis *Poesie–Prosa* as applied to Fontane is not one
which rests solely upon intrinsic analysis of his works: it is a
pair of terms within which he himself was accustomed to think,
and which accompanied him throughout his life. In his autobiographical novel, *Meine Kinderjahre* (1894), Fontane recalls
his formative years in the 'poetic' Baltic port of Swinemünde,
in contrast to the 'prose' of his next place of residence,
Neuruppin in Brandenburg. 'Alles [in Swinemünde] war
Poesie. Die Prosa kam bald nach' ('Everything [in Swine-
münde] was poetry. Prose soon followed'; XIV, 184). Reuter,
in his literary biography of Fontane, makes out a case for the
dialectic of Swinemünde versus Neuruppin – parallel to that of
Fontane's *Prinzipienreiter* (fanatic for principles) mother and
Prinzipienverachter (principle-hating) father – as an antithesis
of cosmopolitan, naturally democratic openness to the world,
and narrow, stifling Prussian insularity. Confirmation of this
view appears to be supplied by Fontane's recollections in his
seventies:

Es gibt doch wirklich eine Art *genius loci*, und während an manchen
Orten die Langeweile ihre graue Fahne schwingt, haben andere un-
ausgesetzt ihren Tanz und ihre Musik. Diese Beobachtung habe ich
schon als Junge gemacht; wie spießbürgerlich war mein heimatliches
Ruppin, wie poetisch das aus bankrotten Kaufleuten bestehende Swinemünde, wo ich von meinem siebenten bis zu meinem zwölften Jahre
lebte und nichts lernte.[1]

(But there really is a kind of *genius loci*, and while the grey flag of bore-
dom flutters over many places, others enjoy continuous music and
dancing. I made this observation while I was still a boy; how narrowly
bourgeois was my native Ruppin, how poetic was Swinemünde, consist-
ing of bankrupt merchants, where I lived from my seventh to my twelfth
year and learned nothing.)

The Swinemünde years were certainly congenial to Fontane's innate individualism. The fascination of colourful,

swashbuckling heroism was nourished by his father's anecdotal reconstructions of Napoleonic history, by the unconstrained air of a seaport combined with local associations with the 'Likedeeler' (proto-communist Baltic pirates and rebels against authority), as well as the young Fontane's ability, through seniority and superior strength, to dominate his group of friends and thus to indulge in boyish fantasies of heroic military leadership.

A number of strands lead out from these formative experiences. So, for example, his enthusiasm for battles and things military is still alive in the 1840s, as evidenced by the ballads devoted to the Prussian heroes of the Wars of Liberation, the patriotic rebel Major Ferdinand von Schill (1847: XX, 474) and the independent-minded Junker General Ludwig Yorck von Wartenburg (1850: XX, 476), as well as the 'Preußenlieder' in praise of Prussian generals in earlier days (*Männer und Helden. Acht Preußenlieder*, 1850). The three Prussian victories that preceded German unification once more brought out all of Fontane's balladesque love of individual heroism (see 'Der Tag von Düppel', XX, 228), and even a degree of jaunty sabre-rattling which clearly recalls his boyhood love of military adventure. Contrary to Walter Müller-Seidel's suggestion,[2] such enthusiasm for war cannot entirely be explained away by Fontane's underlying liberal desire for unification. Müller-Seidel claims that all such bellicose utterances on Fontane's part are subordinate to the central idea of German unity. And yet the recurrence of military metaphors and references to the prowess of Prussian arms that we find, for example, in a quite un-military context, the theatre reviews of the early 1870s, indicates that Fontane's enthusiasm was a spontaneous and romantic, not a political one. (In later years, of course, militarism was anathema to him.)

At the same time, the cosmopolitan and worldly atmosphere of Swinemünde was a foretaste of the 'Freiheit' (freedom) and 'Welt' (wider world)[3] for which England was later to stand. These English qualities had a depth of historical

11

continuity which Prussia could not offer. Fontane was easily able to trace a line of development from Shakespeare to present-day England, a continuity as much political as cultural, which for him runs through Thomas Percy's *Reliques of Ancient English Poetry* (1765) and Walter Scott's *The Minstrelsy of the Scottish Border* (1802) down to the present, and points up the painful contrast between Prussian narrowness and repression, and the vernacular record of English independence and freedom. Here was one model of the *complementarity* of prose and poetry. For a romantically-minded nineteenth-century German liberal, the attraction of English history was that it came out right in the end. Whatever the primitive dynastic struggles and the (retrospectively) fascinating stories of treachery and derring-do, all English history converged in the modern triumph of liberalism – relative to Prussian standards of liberalism, at least. Without a similar historical depth and teleology, the short-lived moment of glory that Prussia enjoyed in the 1860s and 1870s was politically precarious and could therefore feed Fontane's heroic romanticism only during a brief period of intoxication.

It is hardly surprising that Fontane's conception of the romantic and the poetic owes very little to the native German growth of Romanticism.[4] As the essay on Willibald Alexis (1872) makes clear, he regards the Romanticism of Tieck and Hoffmann as a hectic and unhealthy growth, in contrast to the balladesque 'Altromantik' (old romanticism) of Walter Scott: robust, deeply rooted in popular culture, and, in short, 'ein Ewiges, das sich nahezu mit dem Begriff des Poetischen deckt' ('something eternal, almost synonymous with the concept of the poetic').[5] In Fontane's *Anglomanie*, political and aesthetic elements are inextricably mixed. His ideal image of England (discounting a degree of disenchantment in later years because of the country's growing mammonism) presents that intimate association of the poetic with the everyday which Fontane admired and sought throughout his creative life: a combination typified, for the sake of example, in a statement from the late

12

[handwritten margin note at top: Function of the novel is! to pleasantly move me + either raise me above everyday matters or – make everyday matters precious for me. 6]

1870s that the function of the novel is 'daß er mich wohltuend berühren und mich entweder über das Alltägliche erheben oder aber – das schön Menschliche drin mir zeigend – mir auch das Alltägliche wert und teuer machen soll' ('that it should pleasantly move me and either raise me above everyday matters or – by showing me what is fine and human in them – make the everyday precious for me').[8]

It is because of Fontane's respect for 'das Alltägliche' (the everyday) that we are obliged to modify Reuter's stark contrast of Swinemünde–Neuruppin, mother–father, or prose–poetry. As Attwood points out,[7] Reuter goes too far (Reuter's own ideological context makes this all too understandable) in asserting that Fontane's criticism of the philistinism of a small Brandenburg town, which is later broadened into a critique of Prussia as a whole, means the *total* rejection of Neuruppin and of Prussia. The love of the poetic was complemented by a strong respect for order, exemplified both in his ready acknowledgment of his mother's case against his father's fecklessness, and, in another of Fontane's reminiscences from *Meine Kinderjahre*, his ambivalent attitude to the Polish insurgents in their rebellion against the Russians in 1830 and 1831: on the one hand a poetic sympathy for the Poles, on the other a sense of commitment to the established authority and the 'law and order' for which it stood (XIV, 115). *[margin: F's criticism of a small town's philistinism ↓ Prussia as a whole ?] [margin: strong respect for law – order.]*

A sense of the poetic combined with an instinct for order; admiration for heroism, but respect for authority: this is the polarity of Fontane's world-view, if one can speak of a polarity where one of the 'poles', the attraction of the poetic, is undeniably always more powerful for Fontane than the other. At any rate, this polarization of Fontane's world is one for which Prussia constantly supplied the impetus, whether, on the one hand, as a repository of respected historical tradition, or as its modern, thrusting and bombastic self on the other. Prussia is both poetry and prose, with a gallant effort always being made to stress the poetry. As Kenneth Attwood says, he emphasized an ideal, ethical 'Altpreußentum' (old Prussian values); and *[margin: F's world view]*

13

F's vision for Prussia

his vision was of an old Prussian outlook in a modern, progressive political and social setting.[8] If this ambition failed to be realized, the reason lay in what he saw as the political and ethical failings of the Second Reich, weaknesses which manifested themselves as much to the aesthetic as to the moral sensibilities of Fontane.

Failure to observe the premium he placed upon order, as the necessary underpinning of the poetic, leads to the difficulty experienced by Müller-Seidel in interpreting the dénouement of *Frau Jenny Treibel*, according to him a 'schwer zu entziffernde Schlußszene' ('a closing scene which is difficult to decipher').[9] Müller-Seidel points to a wished-for, but unachieved, 'Verbindung der getrennten Bereiche von Poesie und Prosa, von Kritik und Sentiment...' ('union of the separate spheres of poetry and prose, criticism and sentiment'), a combination in which *Poesie* would of course predominate. My contention, argued in chapter 6 below, is that Fontane *does* suggest, in the marriage of Corinna and Marcell, something very like a synthesis of prose and poetry, in a partnership where the mercurial Corinna does not have a monopoly of poetic values. Similarly, Norbert Frei, in my view, misinterprets Fontane's presentation of Armgard's and Woldemar's retreat to Schloß Stechlin at the end of *Der Stechlin*, which Frei sees as a lapse into the narrow, prosaic ways of the backward-looking *Junkertum*. What Fontane actually tells us is that Woldemar retires from the Army to his estate because 'es stand ihm längst fest, daß er nicht berufen sei, jemals eine Generalstabsgröße zu werden, während das alte märkische Junkertum, von dem frei zu sein er sich eingebildet hatte, sich allmählich in ihm zu regen begann' ('it had long been clear to him that he was not cut out for a successful career in the General Staff; and that part of him which was still the Junker from the Mark, and which he thought he had shaken off, began to reassert itself in him'; VIII, 360). Frei discerns in the relative colourlessness of the newly-weds (cf. the 'faithful Dobbin' qualities of Marcell) the beginnings of a social-critical vein to which the secondary

14

literature on Fontane has so far devoted too little attention.[10] Accordingly, the reference to the ideology of the Brandenburg *Junkertum* is also understood by Frei as ironical in intent, for Fontane had often criticized, especially during the years when he was writing *Der Stechlin*, the Junkers' limited and self-satisfied character (Frei, ibid.).

To be sure, Fontane *did* criticize the modern Prussian aristocracy; but it is also clear that he cherished the ideal of the older Prussian Junker virtues, as Attwood repeatedly confirms (e.g. p. 216, with reference to Woldemar). Woldemar, with Pastor Lorenzen's backing, is for novelty and Tolstoyan experiments, but combined with a traditional Prussian sense of order. Here too Fontane suggests the possibility of a fusion of poetry and prose.

This, however, is to anticipate later developments. There were a number of corners to be turned in Fontane's career before the synthesis became possible. Fontane's earliest inspiration to write, and the one to which his *Ordnungssinn* is after all subordinated throughout all the stages of his art, is his love of 'Rätsel und Halbdunkel' (twilight and mystery),[11] characteristics which for him epitomized the ballad-form. During the years of the conservative literary club 'Der Tunnel über der Spree', he sought to capture the indefinable spirit of the old Anglo-Scottish ballads. When he turned his back upon both the *Tunnel* and the ballad, in favour of a new commitment to 'realism' and 'truth' (see the essay 'Unsere lyrische und epische Poesie seit 1848', published 1853), it was in response to the political developments of the mid-nineteenth century. In embracing a realism inspired, in particular, by the English novel, Fontane felt obliged to relinquish poetry.[12] Although Fontane's literary theories of 1853 were to bear fruit a quarter of a century later, it was as yet far too early for him to develop in practice the combination of 'Wirklichkeit' (reality) and 'Wahrheit' (truth) which he advocated in 'Unsere lyrische und epische Poesie seit 1848'. The moratorium that followed was filled by concentration on *reportage*, on 'Wirklichkeit' rather

1853

than poetic 'Wahrheit'; by the years in England and by the *Wanderungen*.

When Fontane launched himself into his novel-writing career, it was with a misguided attempt to combine heroic and epic themes with a low-key presentation of ordinary day-to-day life, albeit in a period of crisis. The confusion of Fontane's stated intentions in writing his first novel makes the limited success of *Vor dem Sturm* all too easily understandable. He summarized the subject of the book as 'das Eintreten einer großen Idee, eines großen Moments in an und für sich sehr einfachem Lebenskreise' ('the entry of a great idea, of a great moment into an essentially very simple class and condition of men ').[13] He wished to treat the birth of a great idea, 'das große Fühlen' ('the great emotions') of a rejuvenated Prussia fighting back against Napoleon in 1813; but he wished also 'nicht zu erschüttern, kaum stark zu fesseln' ('not to be too disturbing, or even particularly gripping'; ibid.). It was only in the latter ambition that he succeeded. It can hardly be said that the novel captures the atmosphere of the period, as evoked by a social historian: 'The resistance to Napoleon . . . engendered a patriotic enthusiasm which was akin to religious feeling. A keen sense of foreboding, of being gripped in a historic conflict between the forces of godlessness and destruction on the one hand, and traditional values on the other. . . '[14] Such heroic themes as are present in the book seem to have been injected into it as part of an attempt to raise events to an epic level. There is much reference in *Vor dem Sturm* to the problem of *Treue* (loyalty), for example: a ready-made heroic theme (perhaps *the* central theme of most heroic and epic poetry) recalling such famous Fontane ballads as 'Archibald Douglas' and 'Percys Tod' ('Die Douglas waren immer treu'), but hardly a genuine fulcrum of the action in the novel, *pace* Müller-Seidel.[15]

The value which, above all, Fontane seems to have associated with the heroic is independence of thought and decision. Dubslav von Stechlin can with confidence be accepted as Fontane's spokesman in his somewhat idealizing choice of

1813 as *the* glorious and heroic moment in the history of Prussian arms:

Alles in allem, lieber Herr Graf, find ich unser Jahr dreizehn um für ein Erhebliches größer, weil alles, was geschah, weniger den Befehlscharakter trug und mehr Freiheit und Selbstentschließung hatte. (VIII, 283)

(All in all, my dear Graf, I find our year 1813 considerably greater, because everything that happened smacked less of commands from above and had more freedom and self-reliance about it.)

Fontane would like to see 'the years before the storm' as the birth of a new Prussia, free of the old Fritzian rigidity and *Kadavergehorsam* (rigid obedience), a land of free men capable of independent thought and action for the common good. Othegraven, the Lutheran Konrektor later to become a martyr of the wars of Liberation, succinctly states the superiority of self-reliance over obedience: '*sich entscheiden ist schwerer als gehorchen*' ('to take your own decisions is harder than to obey'; I, 195; Fontane's emphasis). But the leaders of the abortive attack on Frankfurt an der Oder (the necrophiliac General Bamme and the monomaniac Berndt von Vitzewitz) fall somewhat short of heroic status. As far as the lesser participants are concerned, such is the prevailing 'social' tone of the book – the Frankfurt action being, when it comes, an unmannerly breach of the good tone of society by the intrusion of history into the private sphere[16] – that the much-mooted question of loyalty hardly seems seriously to exercise the characters, whose stature and position are not significant enough to involve them deeply in a moral dilemma of the magnitude of, say, General Yorck von Wartenburg's conflict of loyalties. On the whole they join the Frankfurt insurrection without a great deal of soul-searching.

Despite the celebration of Prussian arms in the three warbooks that Fontane produced between 1864 and 1876, prior to publication of his first novel, it is clear that he is increasingly less able – as *Vor dem Sturm* demonstrates – to identify military adventuring with the independence of mind which, for the ballad-writer, had been the supreme heroic and poetic quality. At the end of his life, in a letter of 1896 to his English correspondent Dr James Morris, he writes: 'Abgesehen von dem Entsetzlichen jedes Krieges, stehe ich außerdem noch allem Heldentum sehr kritisch gegenüber' ('Apart from the frightfulness of all war, I am very critical of heroism in general').[17] Modern warfare had become an affair of the masses, and of calculated and impersonal *Realpolitik*; a prosaic business of 'Herdenmut' ('courage of the herd'; Pastor Lorenzen, VIII, 319) and not of the glorious or fateful deeds of individuals. Fontane, the romantic, can only look to the past, to the struggling days of Prussia under the *Soldatenkönig* (Friedrich Wilhelm I) or to 1813, for an ideal of military action. It is, however, not surprising that even in *Vor dem Sturm*, set in 1812/13, the only novel to deal with momentous and potentially heroic action, and apparently offering ample scope for 'Freiheit und Selbstentschließung', Fontane fails to demonstrate convincingly the values he upholds (freedom of independent decision) in terms of the fiction, and must therefore go on in later works to seek alternative ways of doing so, for example in the tragic independence ultimately achieved – though not sought – by Effi Briest.

The movement from the male-dominated world of the ballad, the war-books, the *Wanderungen* and the historical novel, to the contemporary, non-historical and largely female sphere of action in Fontane's mature work, seems, thus baldly stated, a startling one. Yet one has to recall that Fontane had always had an intense interest in the details of day-to-day life (the famous motto is 'alles Interesse steckt im Detail'; 'all interest lies in detail', from the Alexis-essay of 1872), which is rather more at home in the traditionally limited feminine sphere than that of the masculine-heroic. He was in one sense always a 'realist'; in the sense of 'that beloved – and utopian – principle of "equal poetic justice" for *all* things, the principle of Realism itself'.[18] This formulation is an apt description of Fontane's practice in the mature novels, his protean ability to

pour himself into the mould of his characters and his un-
willingness to pass moral judgments; what Erich Heller calls
'the rout of moral righteousness at the hands of the affectionate
imagination' (ibid.). It is clear that this all-encompassing
realism and objectivity was well-suited, indeed perhaps inevitably drawn, to the contemporary fate of females, whose
dependent status and position in the cross-fire between tradition
and social change rendered moral judgments particularly at
odds with the affectionate imagination. (So much was this the
obvious case that, as Erich Heller reminds us, Tolstoy for
example – in an acute distress of spirit – was compelled by his
imagination and affection to 'leave to God the judgment that
he himself, in his novel, had intended to pass on Anna
Karenina's sin', ibid.). The fate of Fontane's heroines was a
natural vehicle both for his romantic tendencies, and for his
mundane scepticism, his knowledge of the dubious and fragile
condition of received codes and assumptions. Despite appearances, this is essentially a historical view of contemporary life,
and it is in Fontane's preference for the private rather than the
public face of history that Müller-Seidel sees the continuity
from the 'historical' Fontane to the novelist of contemporary
life. Despite his contributions to military history (which he
hoped would be taken as seriously as those of the professionals),
Fontane had never identified his historical interests, after all,
with the official and historicist view of history[19] – a matter of
battles, embassies and *Staatsaktionen*. In *Vor dem Sturm* he
had tried, none too successfully, to relate stirring public events
to private individuals; and with this interest in those affected
by history rather than those who make it, Fontane is already
half way towards his *Frauenromane*, with their fascinating
problems of conflict between the 'historical' and the 'human'.[20]
Women, Müller-Seidel suggests, become a paradigm for 'the
governed' in general (p. 165). Womankind comes to represent,
in the words of Norbert Frei's title, the 'Paradigma des
Humanen' ('paradigm of the humane'), the vehicle for Fontane's humane preoccupation with the individual above all,

19

with the 'Alltagspoesie' ('poetry of everyday') of limited circumstances, rather than the great deeds and momentous historical events which had become suspect to him. To quote Fontane in the *Wanderungen*, 'der lokale Vorfall ist immer siegreich über das historische Ereignis, das Allgemeine verblaßt, das Besondere gewinnt an Kraft' ('local incidents always take precedence over historical events: generalities pale, while the particular grows more powerful').[21]

For all his romantic leanings, Fontane's frank assessment of his own age compels him ultimately to a rejection of heroic themes which was not uncommon in the nineteenth century. Whatever their reaction to this recognition, most writers had to admit that their century was a prosaic, bourgeois one which consorted ill with the heroic tradition in general. Thackeray, George Eliot and Tolstoy were eager to repudiate the heroic, as were Grillparzer and Stifter; whereas the French novelists, Stendhal, Balzac and Flaubert, were more resentful at the demise of the age of heroism, and more anti-bourgeois in their tendency. Fontane's own predilection for the poetic was combined with a *bon sens* (one of his favourite expressions) which gave him a healthy suspicion of all false pathos and false *Romantik*. His drama reviews contain a number of complaints about the pseudo-poetry of the contemporary theatre. To give only two examples: in 1886 he wrote of a new play (Philippi's *Daniela*): 'Das Stück krankt an dem, woran von zehn modernen Stücken immer neun kranken: es ergeht sich in falschen Gefühlen und beschwört von Pathos und Leidenschaft begleitete Konflikte herauf, über die der gesunde Menschenverstand einfach die Achseln zuckt' ('The play suffers from the same disease as nine out of ten other modern plays: it indulges in false emotions and conjures up conflicts accompanied by pathos and passion, conflicts which common sense simply dismisses with a shrug').[22] Two years later, in a review of Dóczi's *Letzte Liebe*, Fontane adopts a deliberately prosaic posture in deploring money ill spent on the production of a bad, pseudo-poetic play, completely out of keeping with the spirit of the age, 'denn die Zeit dürstet nach Wahrheit und ist des Redensartlichen, selbst wenn es sich nicht bloß Poesie nennt, sondern bis auf einen gewissen Grad auch wirklich als Poesie gelten kann, herzlich müde' ('for the age thirsts after truth and is heartily sick of rhetoric, even when it not only calls itself poetry, but even up to a point can fairly claim to be poetry').[23]

In particular, Fontane attacks the poetasters who have had the temerity to adopt his own erstwhile romantic material, the balladesque and medieval themes for which he never lost his appetite. Now, however, this material gives rise only to 'die tiefe Prosa der sogenannten Romantiker' ('the profound prosiness of the so-called romantics').[24] It is worth noting that this remark falls within the period during which Fontane was working on *Unwiederbringlich*, with its references to a pseudo-medieval atmosphere and to a false-poetic solution to prosaic conditions (see chapter 5 below).

We are reminded, too, of the prosaic Innstetten's attraction to Wagner, with his medievalizing vein. One escape from the nineteenth-century dilemma of the decline of the hero – a state of affairs only too apparent in the notorious *Halbheit* (half-heartedness) of Fontane's 'heroes', including Innstetten – lay in the compensatory Titanism of Carlyle (*On Heroes*, 1841), Nietzsche and Wagner. There are many indications that Fontane himself regretted the passing of the heroic age, and that in several ways he stood closer to the French novelists' rejection of the *épicier* mentality than (despite his admiration for the English writer) to Thackeray, who 'thanks heaven that grocers rule the world nowadays instead of barons'.[25] Like Stendhal,[26] Fontane often implies that his heroes (or heroines) are 'displaced', and that they might have been capable of genuine heroism – of the individual, self-reliant kind that Fontane clearly admires, though examples are in short supply – if they had been born in a different time or place. Leo Poggenpuhl, frittering away his talents as a junior officer in a remote garrison town in peacetime, is one obvious example.

But it would have been out of character for Fontane to seize upon any 'false-romantic' or pseudo-heroic solutions to this apparent victory of prose over poetry: just as it would be out of character (as we are told often enough) for his heroes to throw over the code and the values by which they have lived and depart for a life on the Mississippi steamboats or the Californian gold-fields – a solution of the kind which Fontane himself toyed with from time to time.[27] A false-romantic view of heroism was even less likely in the light of the new Germany developing after the unification of 1871.

The Prussia of the Second Reich, in which Fontane was constrained to live, was in his view an increasingly prosaic milieu, no longer what it had been for him, 'der Staat der Zukunft' (the State of the future). As early as 1872 he complains that 'nirgends in der Welt der Sinn für die Form und im Zusammenhang damit jegliche feinere Geschmacksbildung so völlig fehlt wie hier' ('nowhere in the world is a sense of form and, along with it, any kind of cultivated taste so completely lacking as here').[28] There is a wealth of reference to the *Geldsackgesinnung* (money-bag philosophy) of his bourgeois contemporaries (e.g. XV, 14), to worship of the Golden Calf (ibid.) and to his hatred of 'das Bourgeoishafte' (bourgeois ways).[29] Fontane fulminates variously against the specifically Prussian lack of *Poesie*,[30] against the Prussian obsession with examinations and paper qualifications,[31] against the stress on external appearances ('alles dient dem Äußerlichen', 'everything is for the sake of appearances'),[32] and against the petty-minded outlook of a capital city which is in every material sense expanding and prospering: 'die Stadt wächst und wächst, die Millionäre verzehnfachen sich, aber eine gewisse Schusterhaftigkeit bleibt...' ('the city grows and grows, millionaires multiply, but there remains a certain limited mentality').[33] Müller-Seidel's chapter on 'Besitz und Bildung' covers the whole nexus of Prussian 'cultural imperialism' and parvenu materialism (see especially pp. 298–9). Like Nietzsche, Fontane warns of the danger to Germany in the hubristic assumption

F. criticises military arrogance in Prussia, alongside his criticism of false romanticism in art.

that victory over France is identifiable with German cultural superiority (Müller-Seidel, p. 298). Above all, especially after 1888, Fontane deplores the 'monumentalism' of a Prussia dominated by military arrogance and brash display. His criticism of Wilhelm II's grandiose military posturing is reminiscent of his similar dismissal of false romanticism in art. The attempt to create an aura of Prussian 'greatness' is mere bombast and vainglory: *vanity!*

Er [Wilhelm] glaubt das Neue mit ganz Altem besorgen zu können, er will Modernes aufrichten mit Rumpelkammerwaffen; er sorgt für neuen Most und weil er selber den alten Schläuchen nicht mehr traut, umwickelt er eben diese Schläuche mit immer dickerem Bindfaden und denkt: 'nun wird es halten'. Es wird aber *nicht* halten.[34]

(He [William] thinks he can procure the new by means of what is completely antiquated, and seeks to bring about modernity with the aid of weapons out of the attic; he takes care to produce new wine, but because he himself no longer trusts the old leathern bottles, he wraps ever thicker twine around these very bottles and thinks 'now it will hold'. But it will *not* hold.)

With uncanny precision, Fontane here anticipates the more laughable (and yet at the same time sinister) characteristics of the 'Great Dictators' era ushered in by Mussolini. It is quite easy to imagine the Duce uttering a typical remark attributed to the Kaiser, fatally eager to defend his 'greatness' against any attack, however trivial: 'Als der Leibarzt ihn über seinen "kleinen Schnupfen" trösten will, richtet sich der Kaiser plötzlich auf, sieht ihn ernst an und sagt: "Ein großer Schnupfen! Bei mir ist alles groß"' ('When his personal physician sympathized with the Kaiser over his "little cold", the Kaiser drew himself up, looked at him gravely and said: "A great cold! Everything about me is great"').[35] Pastor Lorenzen in *Der Stechlin* aims a controlled and telling blow at the swaggering, fancy-dress heroics of the Wilhelmine Reich:

Das Heldische hat nicht direkt abgewirtschaftet und wird noch lange nicht abgewirtschaftet haben, aber sein Kurs hat nun mal seine besondere

Höhe verloren, und anstatt sich in diese Tatsache zu finden, versucht es unser Regime, dem Niedersteigenden eine künstliche Hausse zu geben.

(VIII, 253)

(Heroism is not finished, and won't be finished for a long time yet, but it has passed its peak, and instead of resigning itself to that fact, our regime is trying to create an artificial boom in something that is in decline.)

A combination of pettiness, materialism and militarism parading as 'greatness' forms a sad picture of decline when measured against the real, ascetic greatness of the Prussian past: 'Das eigentlich Erquickliche, Glückliche, auch *Große*, [Fontane's emphasis] liegt aber doch wo anders. Unsre großen Dichter, Philosophen, Feldherrn und Staatsmänner waren arme Leute. Was bleibt vom alten Zieten, von Kant und Schiller übrig, wenn man sie mit der Geld-Elle mißt?' ('But real inspiration, felicity, even *greatness*, must be looked for elsewhere. Our great writers, philosophers, commanders and statesmen were poor men. What would be left of old Zieten, of Kant and Schiller, if you measured them by the yardstick of money?').[36]

Fontane's objections to the Second Reich extended to its official art, architecture and literature as well as its politics. The political climate inevitably degrades public taste, he implies in a theatre review of 1881: 'Unter der Wissensnudelung, unter Drill und Examennot geht aller *bon sens* verloren, und das Endresultat ist, daß der Wirrwarr angebetet und ein Stück wie "Narziß" [by Brachvogel] unter die halbklassischen Tragödien eingereiht wird' ('With all this cramming, all this drilling and examination-fever, *bon sens* is lost completely, and the outcome is that confusion is admired and a play like *Narziß* is rated as a semi-classical tragedy').[37] In this climate, Fontane could not maintain intact the original balladesque terms of his thinking about *Poesie* and *Romantik*. Müller-Seidel quotes a description of the art of ballad-writing in the nineteenth century which is strikingly appropriate, *mutatis mutandis*, to the Kaiser's Germany:

Die deutsche Balladendichtung des 19. Jahrhunderts, zeitweise mit erstaunlicher Virtuosität betrieben, bedeutet zum großen Teil das Anlegen einer Maske, die Annahme einer falschen Naivität, eines heroischen Kostüms ohne heroische Grundanschauung, zu einem andern Teil das Überwiegen stofflichen Interesses, historischen Wissens und Geschmackes, das Hantieren mit Gebärden, die weder dem Zeitcharakter noch der Persönlichkeit des Verfassers entsprechen, oder mit denen Autor und Leser sich über ihre wahre Natur, Lage und Betätigungsmöglichkeit hinwegtäuschen.[38]

(German nineteenth-century ballad-writing, some of it carried out with astonishing virtuosity, largely involves the assumption of a mask, of a false naïveté, a heroic costume without the basis of a heroic outlook; and partly it involves also a predominant interest in content, a preoccupation with historical knowledge and taste, a flourish of gestures which are unrelated to contemporary life and to the personality of the writer alike, or which serve author's and reader's delusion about their own real nature, situation and scope for action.)

After this, to return to Fontane's reservations about Wilhelm II produces a startling sense of *déja vu*. Not only does life appear to be imitating art (Wilhelmine attitudes imitating the ballad) but life has positively overtaken art. Compare the above quotation with the following remarks of Fontane in 1897:

...die Rüstung muß fort und ganz andre Kräfte müssen an die Stelle treten. Geld, Klugheit, Begeisterung. Kann sich der Kaiser dieser Dreiheit versichern, so kann er mit seinen 50 Millionen Deutschen jeden Kampf aufnehmen; durch Grenadierblechmützen, Medaillen, Fahnenbänder und armen Landadel, der seinem 'Markgrafen durch Dick und Dünn folgt', wird er es aber *nicht* erreichen.[39]

(...armaments must go and other forces take their place. Money, good sense, enthusiasm. If the Kaiser can count upon this trinity, he and his 50 million Germans can take on any challenge; but it will *not* be done with gleaming grenadier caps, medals, banners and a needy rural aristocracy ready to 'follow their Margrave through thick and thin'.)

It is no wonder that Fontane wrote to James Morris, just over a year earlier, that the kind of heroism he now admired was a *quiet* one: 'Es gibt ein ganz stilles Heldentum, das mir imponiert. Was aber meist für Heldentum gerechnet wird, ist

fable convenu, Renommisterei, Grogresultat' ('There is a completely private kind of heroism by which I am impressed.
What is usually regarded as heroism, however, is *fable convenu*,
bragging, pot-valour').[40]

In sum, increasingly under the Second Reich it was apparent
that masculine virtues were being traduced and taken in vain
by a kind of forced cult of masculinity, which had as little to do
with the real thing as, for example, the 'sense of history' cultivated by the members of the literary circle 'Der Tunnel über
der Spree' had to do with the past – or the present – as it really
was (see Müller-Seidel, p. 31). Hence Fontane's novels increasingly display a corrective to this cult of the masculine and the
man of action. One can say of him, as Müller-Seidel says of
Thackeray, that 'die Entheroisierung wird zum Stilprinzip'
('de-heroicizing becomes a stylistic principle'; p. 100), in the
sense of Thackeray's famous assertion in *The History of Henry
Esmond* (1852) 'I would have History familiar rather than
heroic.'

It is not, however, that Fontane's values had really changed,
as Attwood points out (pp. 283–4), but that he is now obliged
to attach different examples to them, to create counter-examples,
as it were, against the examples of the prevailing standard.
Dubslav von Stechlin is one of these counter-examples and,
as a male, an exception to the rule: an aristocrat who presents a total contrast to the vainglory of the Second Reich
and the parvenu aristocracy.[41] The survival of the masculine,
military code of honour (for instance), appropriate to an earlier
Prussia militarized through and through by the sheer needs of
survival, is now anachronistic. Innstetten will not therefore
serve as an example of honour heroically upheld. It is Effi
whose quiet acceptance of her fate has Fontane's support, while
Innstetten, through his decision to make public the news of his
wife's long-past adultery, displaces his own indecision by
electing for the pseudo-decisiveness of a duel, and enters upon
a fatal charade. The duel as Fontane presents it in *Effi Briest*
has all the signs of a Wilhelmine institution: an anachronistic

26

The duel = unheroic.

and absurd parody of heroic action which is actually an evasion
of responsibility for independent decision and therefore, in
Fontane's terms, thoroughly *un*heroic. The sequel is an even
more explicit 'Entheroisierung' (de-heroicizing), for as we take
our leave of him in the novel, Innstetten has been reduced to
living by a petty and ultra-prosaic definition of happiness, finding satisfaction in the fact 'that one has slept well and that one's
new boots don't pinch' (VII, 418). Nothing could be more
anti-heroic than the debased Epicurean position that the only
achievable pleasure lies in the absence of mere discomfort, let
alone pain. It is an outlook that is in stark contrast to Effi's
truly Stoic and, I suggest, poetic acceptance of death (VII, 425).
Fontane's words in the review of Ibsen's *The Wild Duck*
spring to mind: 'Liegt nicht auch in der Unterwerfung eine
Erhebung? Ist nicht auch Resignation ein Sieg?' ('Is there not
something uplifting about submission, too? Is not resignation
another kind of victory?').[42] In the same review, he makes a
statement central to his conception of his own art in the best
years: 'Es ist das Schwierigste, was es gibt (und vielleicht auch
das Höchste), das Alltagsdasein in eine Beleuchtung zu rücken,
daß das, was eben noch Gleichgültigkeit und Prosa war, uns
plötzlich mit dem bestrickendsten Zauber der Poesie berührt'
('It is the hardest thing in the world (and perhaps also the
highest achievement) to present everyday existence in such a
light that what just a moment ago was indifferent and prosaic
suddenly moves us with the most captivating magic of poetry').
This object – to invest the apparently insignificant with poetic
power – might be achievable by other means than exploration
of the condition of women in late nineteenth-century Prussia,
but such are the means that the reader will recognize as most
typical of Fontane. It is through his treatment of female characters that Fontane is able to resolve the contradictions of his own
sense that, on the one hand, prose has conquered, 'die Romantik
ist hin' ('romance is dead'),[43] but on the other hand that 'der
Sieg des Realismus schafft die Romantik nicht aus der Welt'
('the victory of realism will not expel romance from the

27

world').[44] The latter comment was made in the context of an attack on the abuse by Fontane's contemporaries of the 'romantic' material he loved above all, i.e. medieval themes. But it is not only the 'Söller und Kemenate'-syndrome which arouses Fontane's intense need to reassure himself of the continued existence of *Poesie* in the world, as witness the remark quoted above about poetry in Ibsen's *The Wild Duck*. An even more striking and, for its day, astute observation is that Hauptmann's *Vor Sonnenaufgang* 'viel von der Ballade hat' ('has a good deal of the ballad about it'),[45] an indication of Fontane's flexibility, and of his increasing capacity to carry over his original concept of *Romantik* into a literary era vastly different from that of his origins in 'Der Tunnel über der Spree'. The 'will to poetry' is indicated equally by a letter of 1895, in which Fontane attempts – as some of his characters do – to 'square the circle' of *Poesie* and *Prosa*. That frequent object of his scorn, the German *Bürgertum* of the *Gründerzeit*, momentarily becomes a vehicle for optimism. Could they not perform the miracle of turning quantity (money, power) into quality ('aristocracy', culture, *Poesie*)? Perhaps they will become 'ein neuer Adel,...von dem die Welt wirklich was hat, neuzeitliche *Vorbilder* [Fontane's emphasis] (denn dies ist die eigentliche Adelsaufgabe), die moralisch und intellektuell die Welt fördern und ihre Lebensaufgabe nicht in egoistischer Einpöklung abgestorbener Dinge suchen' ('a new aristocracy...which really has something to give the world, *models* for the new age (for that is the real duty of the aristocrat), who morally and intellectually serve the world's advancement and who do not confine their life's ambition to the selfish preservation of lifeless things')?[46]

Fontane never attempted to portray this metamorphosis in his fiction, however. The proper fictional vehicles for his reaction to *Prosa* are women and the declining minor aristocracy. On the whole women, of course, represent a more typical 'case' than the Junkers. (In *Die Poggenpuhls*, the two interests are combined, in the figure of Sophie particularly.) This is not to suggest that Fontane sentimentalized women, but only that they offer a chance of realistically presenting the survival of *Poesie*, often in synthesis with *Prosa*. Frei has pointed out, for example, the fact that as early as 1847 there was a striking correspondence between Fontane's aesthetic concepts and the qualities that fascinated him in his wife (or fiancée, as she then was) Emilie: 'Die Verbindung von Poesie und Prosa ist es weiterhin, was Fontane an Emilie fasziniert.'[47] As Fontane wrote to his close friend Wilhelm Wolfsohn:

Das Hervorstechende ihres Wesens ist, körperlich und geistig, das *Interessante*, sie wird mich auch da zu fesseln wissen, wo mir größere Schönheit, umfassenderes Wissen und selbst tieferes Gefühl auf meinem Lebenswege begegnen sollten. Mit einem Wort, sie ist 'liebenswürdig', sie hat jenes unerklärbare Etwas, was allem einen Reiz verleiht; die Schwächen selbst werden so zu Tugenden gestempelt; Unkenntnis gibt sich als herzgewinnende Natürlichkeit, launenhafte Wünsche kleiden sich in das Gewand des Eigentümlichen.[48]

(The salient thing about her physically and mentally is that she is *interesting*; she will keep her fascination for me even if I should encounter greater beauty, wider knowledge and, even, deeper emotions on my life's path. In a word, she is 'charming', she has that inexplicable quality that gives everything an attraction; even weaknesses become virtues; ignorance appears as a winning naturalness, capricious desires assume the guise of singularity.)

'Die Frau als Modell der Welt ["das Interessante"] und damit auch und nicht zuletzt der Kunst' ('woman as model of the world, and, not least, of art'), is Frei's summary of these remarks. There is indeed a remarkable parallel to them in an aesthetic statement, of the kind that could have been made at almost any time in Fontane's career, about the London Crystal Palace as a refutation of classical canons; in other words, a synthesis of the prosaic and the poetic. As an example of a typical nineteenth-century phenomenon, the raising of every-day matter to the poetic level, the Crystal Palace was cited in my introduction, and here we discover Fontane putting forward the same example:

29

...das Schönheitsgesetz...ist doch nicht alleinberechtigt, und es hat zu allen Zeiten Schöpfungen in Dichtung, Plastik, Architektur gegeben, die das Höchste und Tiefste im Menschenherzen berührt haben, ohne eigentlich schön zu sein. Ich las noch vor wenigen Tagen in einem Reisebericht, es sei nichts Ungewöhnliches, daß unbefangene, in den Krystallpalast zu Sydenham eintretende Personen zu Tränen gerührt würden.[49]

(...the aesthetic law...is not always paramount, and at all times there have been achievements in poetry, sculpture and architecture which have touched the highest and the most profound chords in the human heart without actually being beautiful. A few days ago I read in a travel report that it was not unusual for impartial visitors entering the Crystal Palace at Sydenham to be moved to tears.)

The appeal of women as Fontane's representatives of the poetic, like the Crystal Palace, has more to do with imperfections than with any idealization. Their failings do not rule out the possession (indeed, they contribute to it) of 'jenes unerklärbare Etwas' ('that inexplicable quality'), the last mystery of *Romantik* in a largely prosaicized world. 'Als zentrales dichterisches Symbol dessen, was Wirklichkeit ist oder sein könnte' ('as a central poetic symbol of what reality is or could be'),[50] females are at the heart of Fontane's social criticism. They are natural standard-bearers of the poetic, if for no other reason than that they are excluded from the world of independent action, heroic or otherwise, and dependent upon the man-made rules and masculine rulers of their age. This very dependence adds to their charm, even if it results in ignorance (the normal condition of women, even in good society, relative to their male counterparts)[51] or childishness. An example of the latter quality is Effi Briest, whose adultery is conducted in a style which is clearly a continuation of the *Versteckspiel* (game of hide-and-seek) in progress in the second chapter of the book, and represents a childish retaliation upon a neglectful, male-dominated world which she is otherwise powerless to combat.

The masculine principle of 'action' is exposed by the simple antithesis of male crudeness and feminine finesse, in the case of

30

Herr von Gordon-Leslie in *Cécile*, for example, who, as an explorer and an 'Enthusiast voll Effronterie' ('enthusiast full of effrontery'; IV, 177) tries to storm and conquer the mystery of Cécile as he would a mountain peak. Similarly, in *Der Stechlin* it is implied that Melusine's ex-husband, Graf Ghiberti, forfeited her love and faith in him by an unpardonable crassness of approach, typifying the possessive and hurtful characteristics of men's dealings with women, their attempt to seize and have the poetic by main force. Innstetten's attitude to Effi, despite a veneer of civilized courtesy, is no exception. As outsiders – and it is, as Frei says, a 'soziale Ungeheuerlichkeit' (social monstrosity) that half the human race are potentially outsiders (p. 74) – women possess an irresponsibility related to the irregular position of the writer himself, in opposition to bourgeois gravity and calculation, essentially the male preserve. 'Der Mann ist in der patriarchalischen Gesellschaft auf die kulturellen Normen stärker verpflichtet als die Frau.' ('In a patriarchal society, men are more subject to cultural norms than women.')[52] 'Deshalb [Frei summarizes Hohendahl's further argument] ist ihm die heroische Dimension versagt und er kann auch kaum ein ästhetisches Interesse beanspruchen' ('That is why they are denied a heroic dimension, and they barely exert any aesthetic attraction'; Frei, p. 110). Hohendahl goes too far when he suggests that Fontane's most important heroines 'wirken als die Agenten des Elementaren zerstörerisch' ('have a destructive role, as agents of the elemental').[53] But they do possess an elemental quality, and, by force of circumstance, they develop an independence of thought and decision which is the poetic equivalent of Lorenzen's 'eigener Entschluß' (personal decision) in the sphere of heroic action. Without necessarily wishing to assert any conscious opposition to society, their very existence as *Naturkinder* (children of nature) argues the supremacy of natural justice against the distortions of the man-made variety.

The quality of freedom that makes Effi Briest superior to Innstetten and Crampas alike is demonstrated in the argument over principles down at the jetty in Kessin. In this central scene of *Effi Briest* (VII, 278–9) the men display their *un*freedom. Crampas, a self-styled adventurer, reduced to giving his wife the slip and calling it liberty, acts not out of free will but in reaction to the restrictions of society. With him, defiance passes for independence, 'alle Gesetzlichkeiten sind langweilig' ('all legality is boring'). Innstetten, the representative of principles, is if anything even *less* free, for he is conditioned into a set of reflexes, and is 'not his own man', certainly not to the extent that the old Junker, von Briest, can claim to be. In the scene at the jetty, Effi moves away from the two arguing men, and with Rollo the dog looks out to sea, in case the 'mermaid' (a seal) should appear again. The episode is a vignette of the relationship of the poetic to two prosaic forms of conditioning. Effi, both as a woman and a minor (and there-fore doubly a minor, for women in the nineteenth century, particularly in Germany,[54] enjoyed a status hardly better than that of minors) is no more available to arbitrate in matters of principle than is Fontane's narrator himself.

The role assigned to Effi here is symptomatic of the situation of women. Fontane is not suggesting that they stand in oppo-sition, that they occupy a position outside society from which it is possible for them to subject it to thoroughgoing analysis and critique. They are as fully implicated in social convention as men, and equally conditioned. Neither is Fontane so unsubtle or so undifferentiated in his sense of society's prosaic defor-mation of poetic human substance as to suggest that men are not also victims. The difference is that women are *not* equal partners in action. So that, with all due allowance made, and when Fontane has observed (as it was in his nature to do) all the niceties of a balanced distribution of sympathy, women are so clearly disadvantaged, so much consigned to the role of passive onlooker or victims, either of men's self-willed actions or their mere prosaic limitations, that there is an extra margin of affectionate imagination available for them, affording a latitude in which Fontane's undiminished desire for the poetic/

romantic can still find an outlet. Fontane can almost be imagined holding up for inspection an attitude well known to him,[55] Schopenhauer's misogynist verdict on female *Leichtsinn* (frivolity), and inverting it. Fontane's heroines, as representative females, are dispossessed, either literally or figuratively (and in one sense they are always *literally* dispossessed, because of their legal status as minors). They are without effective responsibility, since, in a capitalist society, not to have the disposal of assets leaves one by definition with nothing but *Leichtsinn*. But by the same token, they also have more chance to develop individuality, in total contrast to Schopenhauer's assertion that they are condemned by their biological function to be merely 'gattungshaft' (generic), 'weil im Grunde die Weiber ganz allein zur Propagation des Geschlechts dasind und ihre Bestimmung hierin aufgeht; so leben sie durchweg mehr in der Gattung, als in den Individuen' ('because basically women exist solely to propagate the species, and that is the whole of their destiny; so they live altogether more through the generic type than through the individual').[56]

In his earlier fiction, Fontane tended to give his females a decided but somewhat over-romantic individuality, an alien, daemonic quality (Grete Minde is 'eine Fremde' and has 'das fremde Blut', a stranger with strange blood) which belongs to the world of the ballad. Frei argues that as Fontane's novels become more truly social in their concerns, the daemonic qualities (he lists 'das Infernalische, Dämonische, Languissante, Elementare', the infernal, the daemonic, the languid, the elemental) become assimilated into that of 'das Aparte' (the distinctive, the original), which he understands as 'den sehr reellen Adel der Humanität; dies nicht als abstrakte Programmatik, sondern in poetischer Sinnbildlichkeit, den konkreten Fall bezeichnend und trotzdem verallgemeinbar' ('the very real nobility of humanity; not as an abstract programme, but as a poetic metaphor which describes the individual case and yet lends itself to generalization'; Frei, p. 114). There is a shift in the relationship of the heroine to society. Whereas in *Grete*

33

Minde or *Ellernklipp* she represents a threat to society, in the mature novels the degree to which the female is now under threat *from* society is indicative of the strength of the forces threatening to reduce humanity itself to the level of the prosaic, banal and merely 'typical'. With reservations about Frei's desire to 'de-romanticize' the treatment of females and make it serve purely humanist ends (and similarly, Fontane's heroines must surely be exempted from Müller-Seidel's statement that 'über eine gewisse "Romantik" ist Fontane längst hinaus', Fontane has long since moved beyond a certain 'Romanticism'),[57] I would endorse Frei's analysis: women incorporate the poetry of *Romantik* as against the prose of the banal male figures; or, in other terms, females represent the interesting individual, in contrast to the contemporary levelling down of individuality reflected in Fontane's less than colourful males (Frei, p. 145).

Precisely such an unpromising subject as Mathilde Möhring drives home this point, Fontane's association of *Humanität* and *Poesie* with the potential of his female figures. The petty-bourgeoise Mathilde emerges from the most limited of prosaic worlds, and the poetic is eventually given its due. By the application of intelligence and innate aesthetic sense, Mathilde coaches her socially superior but all too poetically-minded fiancé, Hugo Grossman, towards a solid career as an administrator. The fact that he does not long survive to enjoy the fruits of their joint efforts is not Mathilde's fault, and neither does it diminish the import of the change that has come over the initially dry and calculating heroine. Mathilde now recognizes that prosaic 'ewiges Nachrechnen' (eternal calculating), far from being clever, is, on the contrary, a stupid self-curtailment (VI, 304). Under the posthumous influence of Hugo she hopes in future to spread her wings and live more for poetic values than she has before.

The thematic material of the novel makes it, although fragmentary, a central work in relation to the topos of the poetic and the prosaic. Indeed, the book's somewhat schematic, skeletal structure reduces the issues to stark outlines. Upon the reader's view of the treatment of the question of *Poesie* and *Prosa* depends his interpretation of the novel and its place among Fontane's works. Norbert Frei's conclusion is fully consonant with my own when he claims that Mathilde's combination of hard common sense and aesthetic finesse in her training of Hugo is 'die exemplarisch vorgelebte Synthese von Realismus und Romantik, von Prosa und Poesie' ('the living example of a synthesis of realism and romanticism, prose and poetry'; Frei, p. 147). She becomes what her milieu had never previously allowed her to be: 'was Apartes' (a distinctive individual). By contrast, another recent interpretation asserts that Fontane was exposing in the novel the delusory nature of bourgeois values such as 'das Höhere' (higher things) and *Bildung* (education), and that Mathilde's promise to herself at the end of the novel that she will from now on respect the claims of the poetic is a major weakness of the book. For it means that Mathilde has fallen prey to the very delusion which the novel's events have exposed: 'ein Festhalten an Idealen des Bürgertums, deren verkümmerte Form ansonsten im Roman deutlich beschrieben wird' ('a clinging to bourgeois ideals whose atrophied form is plainly described in the rest of the novel').[58] This view reduces the novel to an unambiguous social-critical statement quite out of keeping with Fontane's usual tone, and is obliged to regard the ending as an aberration, an *Inkonsequenz*. It distorts the significance allocated by Fontane to the poetic, which finally gains a hold on even the most prosaic of natures; and it ignores the fact that the novel is thematically fully congruent with Fontane's other work, even if rather more abrupt and elliptical in its treatment of his favourite themes. Far from representing 'ein anderer Fontane' (a different Fontane), *Mathilde Möhring* is a demonstration of the unity of Fontane's artistic interests.

In the heroines of his best novels, Fontane's earliest loyalties can be seen to emerge in a curiously transformed manifestation. The independence either innately possessed by, or forced upon, his female characters is reminiscent of Fontane's admiration for *Quitzowtum*, the independence of mind of the old Prussian Junker class (for example, in the 'Oderland' volume of the *Wanderungen*, X, 20, Fontane quotes the 'disgrace before dishonour' epitaph of Johann Friedrich Adolf von der Marwitz, who refused to obey what he considered to be a dishonourable command of Friedrich II's: 'Wählte Ungnade, wo Gehorsam nicht Ehre brachte', 'chose disfavour where obedience brought no honour'). When Effi Briest is rejected by society, she does not choose *Ungnade*. But, none the less, she becomes a representative of the independence required to face adversity: she is 'auf sich selbt gestellt' ('thrown back upon herself'; VII, 391) and in her final aloneness – in stark contrast to Innstetten – she achieves a stature equivalent to that of the self-validating heroic model who loomed so large in Fontane's romantic imagination.

If Effi retains many of the characteristics of the romantic heroine, as the next chapter will argue, Lene Nimptsch in *Irrungen, Wirrungen* combines poetry with *Ordnung*, the sense of order that was a basic need for Fontane and was epitomized historically by the era of the *Soldatenkönig*. In Lene's case, one can discern a surprisingly clear link with Fontane's enduring belief in the value of *Altpreußentum* and its loyal, stalwart *Gesinnung* (mentality). As Attwood has pointed out, the vocabulary used to describe Lene is identical to the terms Fontane was in the habit of employing in praise of the old Prussia.[59] She possesses 'eine Einfachheit, Wahrheit, Natürlichkeit' ('simplicity, truth, naturalness'; III, 170), and she has 'das Herz auf dem rechten Fleck und ein starkes Gefühl für Pflicht und Recht und Ordnung' ('has her heart in the right place and a strong feeling for duty, justice and order'; III, 205). She has not been ruined by education, the modern Prussian disease, and so, in Botho's words, she has 'Charakter und Tiefe des Gemüts. Arme Bildung, wie weit bleibst du dahinter zurück' ('Character and depth of soul. As for "education", what a poor thing it is in comparison'; III, 215). Corinna

Schmidt and her father together similarly represent the old Prussian virtues in *Frau Jenny Treibel* (Attwood, p. 221; VII, 156). 'Corinna hat nun wohl für immer mit der Modernität und dem krankhaften Gewichtlegen aufs Äußerliche gebrochen, und hat statt dessen die von ihr verspotteten Lebensformen wieder anerkennen gelernt, in denen sie groß geworden ist.' ('Corinna has now finished for good with modernity and the morbid stress on externals, and instead has learned to appreciate again the mode of life in which she was brought up, and which she used to mock.') The word *Gesinnung* (VII, 156) is the key to Fontane's manifest association of his modern heroine's sterling qualities with those of the past.

It is true that Dubslav von Stechlin, too, 'bleibt in der altpreußischen Tradition' ('stays within the old Prussian tradition'), for his 'schönster Zug war eine tiefe, so recht aus dem Herzen kommende Humanität...' ('his finest trait was a deep humanity coming truly from the heart'; VII, 7). The object here has not been to suggest that males – least of all the best and last surviving male of the old Prussian *Landadel* (landed aristocracy/gentry) – cannot represent the triumph of *Humanität*, and therefore *Poesie*, as can the females; but that in Fontane's works it is the heroines who emerge as the clearest example of the possibility that poetry may not be defeated by prose. They do so because they have a greater depth than the males, even Dubslav, and because *Humanität* does not entirely exhaust their attraction. Effi's elemental, *märchenhaft* (fairy-tale), 'creature of air' quality, Lene's mysterious origins and wisdom beyond her schooling and station, Melusine's affinity for rockets and fireworks – all are part of the evidence for the romantic aura with which Fontane continues to surround his heroines. It is the continuity, and yet the maturing, of Fontane's conception of *Poesie* as measured by his presentation of female characters, that is the concern of the chapter that follows.

3 · ELLERNKLIPP AND EFFI BRIEST

Between *Ellernklipp* (1881) and *Effi Briest* (1895) there is a similarity of inspiration, notwithstanding the considerable distance between the two works, both in time and mood. Beneath the society-novel surface of *Effi Briest* there are, as in the *Schloon* (the 'slough'), mysterious underground forces at work, whose ambivalent nature can only be encompassed by poetic means. Fontane's mature achievement is measurable in the extent to which these forces and this poetry are presented in and through, and not at the expense of, concrete social realism.

Clearly it must be said, before any elaboration of this comparison, that, in one sense, it is a distortion to compare works as different as these; for in *Ellernklipp* Fontane employed deliberately rough-hewn, simple effects, epitomized by his own tongue-in-cheek reflections on the style of the Novelle, and its reliance on the conjunction 'und':

Je schlichter, je mehr *sancta simplicitas*, desto mehr 'Und'. 'Und' ist biblisch-patriarchalisch und überall da, wo nach dieser Seite hinliegende Wirkungen erzielt werden sollen, gar nicht zu entbehren...In 'Grete Minde' und 'Ellernklipp' herrscht eine absolute Simplizitätssprache, aus der ich, meines Wissens, auch nicht einmal herausgefallen bin; in 'L'Adultera' und 'Schach von Wuthenow' liegt es umgekehrt.[1]

(The plainer, the more *sancta simplicitas*, the more 'and'. 'And' is biblically patriarchal and indispensable wherever that kind of effect is desired....In *Grete Minde* and *Ellernklipp* a language of absolute simplicity prevails, from which, as far as I know, I never deviated even once; in *L'Adultera* and *Schach von Wuthenow* the opposite is the case.)

The development I want to trace moves away from the spareness and concentration of the Novelle, to the more complex texture of the social novel, employing the incidentals of social life as the metre and rhythm which make the poetry possible.

Above all it is the abandonment of specifically *historical* settings that marks the novelist's emergence to his great period. For reasons which will be explored towards the end of this chapter, there is always a discernible sense of contrivance when Fontane is writing historically: for all the imaginative effort to create 'poetic' costume, his imagination is confined.

A few superficial similarities between the two works present themselves immediately, among them features which have been identified as linking Fontane's novels with their fore-runners, his ballads. Here I take issue with Wandrey's negative views on the balladesque period of Fontane's novel-writing career. It is not only more productive, but more likely to be true, to see Fontane's early balladesque efforts not as an aber-ration but as a stage in the development of his refined novel of society, and a recent study plausibly suggests that not only the balladesque novels but also the *Gesellschaftsromane* (novels of society) benefit from the lessons learned in Fontane's long apprenticeship to the ballad-form.[2] Leckey isolates such ele- ~style~ ments as the refrain or repetition (the 'Effi komm' motif which forms the balladesque heart of *Effi Briest*); the tendency of the story to return to its beginnings; *Sprunghaftigkeit* or narrative leaps, connected with the art of leaving much unsaid, the art of suggestion that actively engages the reader's imagination; presentiment or prefiguration; exposition and plot-advance-ment through conversation; the evolution of a *Volkston* or colloquial manner; and, on the thematic level, the motifs of infidelity and adultery together with the themes of guilt and retribution. Above all, the novels display a 'rounding-off', a neat and self-contained balance of construction evocative of the ballad's conscious and formal presentation of itself as art with the *appearance* of art.[3]

A closer comparison of the specific features of *Ellernklipp* and *Effi Briest* (as against the balladesque features found to some extent throughout the novels) reveals, on the surface level, that both heroines, Hilde and Effi, take husbands not of their own choice who are old enough to be their fathers; and both men do indeed see themselves in the triple role of husband, father and educator to their girl-brides. Both heroines are torn suddenly out of the security of an innocent and ignorant state of nature, though in the case of the orphaned Hilde the illusory character of this early *Geborgenheit* (safeness) is a good deal more explicit than in Effi's. Both females find themselves involved in a triangular situation with tragic or fatal consequences for the men involved. Each gives birth to one child, and each is deprived of this child – Hilde by death, Effi by social disgrace. Effi and Hilde undergo a similar process of *Verklärung* (transfiguration) at the end of their stories, and, after a period of hectically heightened awareness of life, both die with dignity, resignation, even heroism; in the words of a phrase from *Der Stechlin*, 'mit dem Ergebnis eines betont unauffälligen, stillen Heldentums' ('with the effect of a markedly unobtrusive, quiet heroism').

The similarity does not end there, for the characters of the two heroines recognizably place them in a line of development spanned by a familiar topos, the 'Melusine-motif', named after a figure in an early fragment (who later became 'Oceane von Parceval')[4] as well as a character in Fontane's last novel. The line runs via Marie in *Vor dem Sturm*, Hilde in *Ellernklipp*, Melanie in *L'Adultera*, Franziska in *Graf Petöfy*, Cécile in the novel of that name, Lene in *Irrungen, Wirrungen*, Corinna in *Frau Jenny Treibel*, to Effi Briest and the last Melusine in *Der Stechlin*. There are other female characters who share some or many of the characteristics of the Melusine-type, though usually with a preponderance of one particular quality – often a negative one – which disqualifies them as full representatives of the type. There is, for example, Grete Minde, or Gräfin Ebba in *Unwiederbringlich*; even Mathilde Möhring has a good deal of the *Naturkind* (child of nature) in her make-up. Fontane's own description of his heroine in *Ellernklipp* covers most of the traits of the Melusine-type, but stresses the melancholy that, while latent in others of her type, is particularly marked in Hilde:

Hauptfigur: ein angenommenes Kind, *schön, liebenswürdig, poetisch-*
apathisch, an dem ich beflissen gewesen bin, die *dämonisch-unwider-*
stehliche Macht des Illegitimen und Languissanten zu zeigen. Sie tut
nichts, *am wenigsten etwas Böses*, und doch *verwirrt regelrechte*
Verhältnisse. Sie selbst, *ohne den Grundton ihres Wesens zu ändern,*
verklärt sich und überlebt das Wirrsal, das sie gestiftet.[5]

(The main character: an adopted child, lovely, charming, poetically
apathetic, in whom I have striven to show the daemonically irresistible
force of the illegitimate and the languid. She does nothing, least of all
anything evil, and yet she throws into confusion the established order of
things. She herself, without altering the basic tenor of her character, is
transfigured and survives the confusion she has caused.)

I have italicized the qualities in this description which seem
most consistent in the Melusine-type: another very important
trait which ought to be added to the list is the inability of these
characters, in their natural state, to lie or deceive (see *Ellern-*
klipp, II, 205; *Effi Briest*, VII, 359). Representatives of the
type range between the poles of the passive and the relatively
active heroine; Hilde, and the Melusine of *Der Stechlin*,
stand at the two extremes, with Effi at an intermediate point
between them. At the heart of this character-type there is often
a potential for aloneness, for isolation, which is developed to
the full when circumstances are right. In Hilde's case this
solitariness is part of the fictional *donnée* from the beginning,
in her situation as the only child of an impoverished young
widow, isolated in two senses: physically, by their dwelling on
the edge of the forest, well away from the village of Emmerode;
and morally, by her birth, the result of her mother's affair with
the young Graf Emmerode, heir to the local estates and to
semi-feudal dominance in the strict village hierarchy. The Graf
has fallen in battle long before the story opens, and his love-
child Hilde grows up accustomed to solitude as a condition of
life. Effi, on the other hand, develops her talent for solitude
only under the pressure of circumstances, along with that
'grand talent pour le silence' which was once said to be the
mark of the true hero.[6] With Effi we have, on the face of
it, a Naturalist case of 'Anlage potenziert durch Milieu'

41

('predisposition intensified by milieu'; an implication supported by some remarks of Frau von Briest: VII, 355, 356). But more than that, it is an indicator of Fontane's poetic development that he can set out, in *Effi Briest*, with fairly unexceptional human material, and create a paradigm of the solitary state *per se*, almost an absolute, a metaphysical fact of human existence. Here already is the contrast between romantic, sensational and abrupt effects in the balladesque novel – Hilde's highly unusual upbringing and conditioning to solitude – and a similar motif in a later work, developing analytically through the course of the action, maintaining realistic cause-and-effect links with the norms of a society in which such events take place, revealing the hidden nature of these 'norms' and substituting for the balladesque a more lyrical poetic effect. Parallel to her increasing solitude, the quality of the *Sehnsucht* (longing) Effi experiences undergoes a refinement, from mere home-sickness for Hohen-Cremmen to a *Sehnsucht* liberated from any immediate object (VII, 423), as powerful in its lyric effect as, say, the Romantic Eichendorff's poem 'Sehnsucht'.

Similar purifications take place on other levels. One such purification is the relative distancing of the central issues in *Effi Briest* from the sphere of Old Testament morality which is prominent in *Ellernklipp*. It is in this respect that *Effi Briest* most clearly resembles a *gesteigert* (heightened, intensified) version of *Ellernklipp*, for both books deal with breaches of the same traditional moral laws, and both are set in a background of oppressive Lutheranism, though in *Effi Briest* this background is confined almost entirely to Kessin[7] and is an obviously archaic feature of a somewhat backward-looking area of Prussia.

The Commandments are frequently referred to in *Ellernklipp*, the relevant items in the Lutheran Decalogue being the fourth ('Du sollst Vater und Mutter ehren', 'Honour thy father and thy mother'), the fifth ('Du sollst nicht töten', 'Thou shalt not kill'), and the sixth commandment ('Du sollst nicht

42

immanent ?

ehebrechen', 'Thou shalt not commit adultery'). Both heroines run into trouble because of the breaking of the sixth Commandment, both are the cause of the breaking of the fifth, and, owing to circumstances, both find the fourth almost impossible to observe (though it can be argued that Effi's excessive and typically nineteenth-century respect for the spirit of this Commandment at the *beginning* of the story is what leads to her downfall). Ironically, in *Ellernklipp*, it is the fourth Commandment which the enlightened Lutheran Pastor Sörgel particularly recommends to Hilde (II, 196). Her illegitimacy makes for difficulties in this respect; as does the fact that she marries her adoptive father, a man for whom she has no love, but only fear.

Although, by all humane criteria of justice, Hilde is almost completely free of personal guilt, compared to Effi, in her 'Old Testament' world a harsh, unremitting morality is immanent (like the cruel, elemental justice associated with the folk-ballad[8]) and retribution is visited upon her for her *parents'* breaking of the Commandment 'Du sollst nicht ehebrechen', in accordance with the severe doctrine of inherited guilt proclaimed in Exodus, 20.v. ('for I the Lord thy God am a jealous God, visiting the iniquity of the fathers upon the children unto the third and fourth generation...') and quoted with approval by Luther in the commentary to the Fourth Commandment in his *Kleiner Katechismus*.[9] (In the same novel, the most powerful statement of the retribution theme arises from Baltzer Bocholt's murder of his son Martin, which is visited with grim and appropriate vengeance, Bocholt killing himself, *Judenbuche*-style, on the very spot where he committed murder. Compare the same retribution motif in a ballad, 'Lord Athol', XX, 292.)

The characters in *Ellernklipp* live in an uneducated world, and their belief that 'evil will out' ensures that it does so. Effi, though herself undereducated, lives in an educated world. And yet the notion of retribution is not lost in *Effi Briest*, but, like other 'undomesticated', balladesque[10] or *Märchen* aspects of

43

education

the earlier works, is subtly commuted by Fontane, in this case
into an unobtrusive poetic justice – an aesthetic as much as a
moral kind of justice. Order and natural justice are almost
inevitably in conflict, and the awareness of two irreconcilable
qualities epitomizes the complexity of *Effi Briest* as against the
simplicity of *Ellernklipp*. It is poetic justice that Innstetten,
the man of principle, should be put in a position to be forgiven
at the end of the novel by the 'transgressor', Effi, and that she
by contrast should soar as far above the petty concerns of the
everyday as he is dragged down *into* them. 'Was man emp-
fängt, das hat man auch verdient.' ('What you receive is what
you deserve.') These are Innstetten's words (VII, 296), but they
apply to the story in more senses than the 'man of principle'
might wish. Public justice is seen to be done, but, by way of
compensation, poetic justice operates also. (There are forward-
looking moments even in the ballads where justice is not a
simple matter of primitive Mosaic ethics: in 'Jung-Musgrave
und Lady Barnard', for example, the husband who has violently
avenged his wife's adultery utters what might be an epitaph
for Innstetten – 'Die Ehre ist genesen,/Mein Herze ist es
nicht', 'Honour has been restored, but my heart never will be';
XX, 286.)

Fontane approaches artistic mastery only when, in the
society novels, he makes this complex of problems felt through
concrete social circumstances. 'Erst das Individuelle bedingt
unsere Teilnahme, das Typische ist langweilig'[11]; or, 'An
etwas bestimmt Gegebenes muß man doch immer anknüpfen'
('Only individual matters command our interest; the typical
is boring...You must always start from something specific';
letter to Paul Lindau, 15 February 1885) – these remarks
typify Fontane's somewhat un-German predilection for the
presentation of his characters in all the specific aspects of their
actual social conditions. And it is precisely these actual conditions which allow him to develop the general and universal,
in fact the *poetic* qualities of his work.

The process can be seen on the stylistic level in *Effi Briest* in

44

the quite realistic, apparently purely descriptive, metonymic[12] rather than metaphorical use of light and shade motifs. Working backwards, it is possible to trace this development as a process in Effi towards a subtler knowledge of good-and-evil, and the irreconcilability of social order with natural justice. On the occasion when Effi approaches the Minister's wife (chapter 32) to ask her to arrange a meeting for her with Annie, she is dressed in 'ein dezentes Schwarz' (a respectable black outfit) – i.e. as a penitent. And yet this self-imposed, sombre sign of acceptance of guilt is counter-balanced by the symbolic message of the pictures on the wall in the *Ministerin*'s ante-chamber: 'Da war zunächst Guido Renis Aurora, gegenüber aber hingen englische Kupferstiche, Stiche nach Benjamin West, in der bekannten Aquatintamanier von viel Licht und Schatten. Eines der Bilder war König Lear im Unwetter auf der Heide' ('First there was Guido Reni's "Aurora"; but on the other side were English prints, engravings after Benjamin West, in the familiar aquatint manner with much light and shade. One of the pictures was King Lear in the storm on the heath'; VII, 404). Dawn on the one hand, King Lear on the other, and a chiaroscuro style involving the interplay of light and shadow, add up to a résumé of Effi's fate: the promise of youth, knowledge of life ('viel Licht und Schatten', much light and shade[13]); guilt and innocence inextricably involved; betrayal by those who have loved her. By this point, Effi has learned nearly all that she is going to learn, and has experienced all the major events that life holds in store for her.

At an earlier moment in the story, in chapter 20, Effi is at a crisis point between innocence and knowledge, as light and shade fight for dominance in the room. Since the seduction scene, Effi has found that she cannot put a stop to the affair with Crampas, even if she wants to, for 'Das Verbotene, das Geheimnisvolle hatte seine Macht über sie' ('The forbidden, the clandestine had gained a hold on her'). In this mood, she examines herself in the mirror:

45

Einmal trat sie abends vor den Spiegel in ihrer Schlafstube; die Lichter und Schatten flogen hin und her, und Rollo schlug draußen an, und im selben Augenblicke war es ihr, als sähe ihr wer über die Schulter. Aber sie besann sich rasch. 'Ich weiß schon, was es ist; es war nicht *der*,' und sie wies mit dem Finger nach dem Spukzimmer oben. 'Es war was anderes... mein Gewissen... Effi, du bist verloren.' Es ging aber doch weiter so... (VII, 315).

(One evening she stepped in front of the mirror in her bedroom; light and shade came and went, and Rollo gave voice outside, and at the same moment she felt as though someone were looking over her shoulder. But she quickly collected her thoughts. 'I know what it is, it wasn't *him*'; she pointed to the haunted room above. 'It was something else... my conscience... Effi, you are lost.' But so it continued...)

The repeated use of 'und' to introduce a series of paratactic main clauses heightens our expectation of some revelation, but when it comes it is not the *Spuk* (ghost) her childish mind is half wishing for, but the first intimations of adult conscience. Never before has Effi had to come to terms with the world's view of her actions and assume responsibility for them. Although previously she has conformed to and obeyed her parents' wishes and the demands of society, she has always had an inner freedom which is now destroyed by knowledge: there can never again be an easy relationship between her natural self and her social existence, which, in that Garden of Eden at Hohen-Cremmen, were virtually synonymous.[14] Good and evil, in her Hohen-Cremmen paradise, were self-evident quantities as distinct as day and night, light and shade, like the bright sunshine and the broad shadow that lie peacefully across the garden on the book's first page. The picture of peace is elegiacally recalled, but translated from summer to autumn, and from midday to the hours before midnight, on Effi's return with Annie to Hohen-Cremmen from Berlin (chapter 24, VII, 358); an eloquent unspoken comment on her loss:

Alles schimmerte silbern, und neben den Schattenstreifen lagen weiße Lichtstreifen, so weiß, als läge Leinwand auf der Bleiche. Weiterhin aber standen die hohen Rhabarberstauden wieder, die Blätter herbstlich gelb, und sie mußte des Tages gedenken, nun erst wenig über zwei

Jahre, wo sie hier mit Hulda und den Jahnkeschen Mädchen gespielt hatte. Und dann war sie, als der Besuch kam, die kleine Steintreppe neben der Bank hinaufgestiegen, und eine Stunde später war sie Braut.

(Everything had a silvery shimmer, and next to the bands of shadow lay white bands of light, as white as linen laid out on a bleaching-green. But further on stood once more the tall clumps of rhubarb, their leaves an autumn yellow, and she could not help thinking of that day, now a little over two years ago, when she had played here with Hulda and the Jahnke girls. And then, when the visitor came, she had climbed the little flight of stone steps by the bench, and an hour later she was engaged.)

The peace of light and shade here is the peace after the battle, the colourless peace of death (the ominous associations of *Leinwand, Bleiche* reinforce the suggestion). From the vantage point that Effi now holds, from which she is already composing her mind to accept that a part of her old self is dead (presaging the discovery of the adultery and her actual death in due course thereafter), Innstetten is seen, rather touchingly, once again as 'der Besuch' (the visitor, 'company'), the stranger he has essentially remained despite his enormous and conclusive impact on Effi's life.

I am not suggesting that it was only in his later masterpieces that Fontane developed his grasp of this kind of duality; but simply that he needed to develop the fusion of the social and the poetic in the late novels before his knowledge of the subtle interactions of 'light and shade' could find artistic expression.

Such sophistication can be observed, for example, spilling over into his politics, even in earlier years – which is why his politics have always been so difficult for the critics to pin down. In his 1860 series of lectures on English politics, entitled 'Whigs und Tories', he refers to 'Den unablässigen und fruchtbaren Kampf zwischen Bewahrung und Erneuerung, zwischen Ruhe und Bewegung', and urges 'Sei jeder von uns ein Whig auf dem Wege zu fortschreitender Erkenntnis, aber in des Herzens Liebe und Treue ein Tory' ('The unceasing and productive struggle between conservation and renewal, between rest and movement...Let each of us be a Whig on the road to progressive awareness, but in the love and loyalty of our hearts let us be Tories').[15] Progress towards self-expression and justice must be allowed always to be in fruitful conflict with the conservatism of the prevailing order. This is easily said, but was a profound political recognition for a German in Fontane's day. (Bismarck's Reich, when it came a decade later, was not conceived in the light of the two-party system.)[16] It is rare, indeed, for a German writer to be able to present a duality which is not a clash of extremes, and present it with sympathetic understanding of a range of characters in contemporary society. Ernst Robert Curtius's verdict on Fontane's fellow-countrymen serves to bring out, *per contra*, Fontane's qualities: of the Germans, Curtius says 'viel Weltgefühl, abcr wenig Welt; viel Weltanschauung, aber wenig Weltkenntnis' ('much "world-soul", but little world; much world-view, but little worldliness').[17] Such was Fontane's fond familiarity with the world's ways, by contrast, that nothing in the external world was too insignificant for his notice. 'Alles hat sein Gewicht und seine Bedeutung, auch das Kleinste, das "Äußerlichste".' ('Everything has its own substance and significance, even the least thing, the most "superficial".')[18] For Fontane, as for Thomas Mann, detail is poetic; and no detail of his late novels is too insignificant to bear poetic import.

The importance of 'insignificant' detail lies in the art of suggestion, one of the lessons, it was said earlier, which Fontane learnt during his ballad-making apprenticeship. This art attains such heights in the later novels that it presupposes a very acute reader. Leckey points out, for example, that a reader need not be particularly casual to miss altogether, in *Der Stechlin*, 'that strange moment which constitutes Woldemar's and Armgard's engagement':[19] almost everything of importance is left unsaid (VIII, 226–7). Similarly, it is a mark of increasing refinement, from the balladesque Novelle to the poetic novel, that a pattern of relationships that was writ large in *Ellernklipp* becomes merely a subtle and easily overlooked suggestion in *Effi Briest*. The pattern is that of the interloping, naive young bride displacing the well-established housekeeper in a bachelor household. In *Ellernklipp*, Hilde displaces the formidable Grissel in the literal sense that the latter is forced to surrender her room to Hilde (long before Bocholt marries her) and takes up far inferior quarters. The consequences are predictably dire: Grissel blackens Hilde's name and fans the flames of Bocholt's suspicions of an affair between his son Martin and Hilde (II, 226). Thus Grissel contributes to the outcome, the uncontrollable outburst of jealous rage which leads to Bocholt's murder of Martin. In *Effi Briest*, Effi similarly displaces Johanna in Innstetten's household. But the consequences are no longer so brutally direct as in *Ellernklipp*: Johanna never openly informs Innstetten of Effi's affair with Crampas, nor are we told in so many words that she was even aware that it existed. But we do know that she (like Innstetten) has a very sharp eye, and it seems unlikely that the Crampas liaison can have entirely escaped her attention, any more than that Innstetten can have been entirely unaware of it. It is not surprising, then, that it is Johanna who, on the pretext of finding a bandage to bind Annie's wounded forehead, forces open the drawer of Effi's work-table which contains the fatal correspondence with Crampas (but does not contain the bandage; VII, 368). We have no evidence that she knew the letters were there – but she *is* in a position to be intimate with most of the details of Effi's private life. These insinuations must of course rest on speculation, just the sort of speculation which Fontane frequently encourages. (Compare also the Johanna–Roswitha conversation on pp. 383-4.) We are on firmer ground however when we observe that it is the strong position of Johanna in Innstetten's household (she is, so to speak, his *alter ego* on the servant level, as Roswitha is Effi's)[20] that from the beginning undermines Effi's position in it. Upon her arrival in Kessin (VII, 230), Effi in her youthful innocence and insecurity gives far too much away to Johanna, and in leaning heavily on the servant ruins her chances of establishing herself securely as mistress of the house. Innstetten contributes to the undermining process in what is surely an unforgivable betrayal of Effi to a servant, when, on his return from a visit to Varzin, he cross-questions Johanna about Effi's behaviour during his absence (VII, 233). He shows visible annoyance at Effi's childish fears of ghosts and Chinamen (although he has previously done his best to foster these fears) and thereby betrays his young wife just as surely as if he had chosen some other, more conventionally immoral intimacy with Johanna. The incident parallels Effi's own later verbal betrayal of Innstetten to Crampas, which begins when she shows herself prepared to listen to Crampas's criticisms of Innstetten's intimidation technique (VII, 282). Language events, at this stage of Fontane's art, are real events in the action. Every conversation between the central characters is an irrevocable act by which their relationships change. Thus the actual adultery is almost irrelevant: it is merely the outcome of smaller betrayals, on both sides of the marriage, but occurring first on Innstetten's side. (Poetic justice operates here, too, for Innstetten later has to pay for his earlier intimacy with Johanna by being thrown back upon her ministrations after his separation from Effi, and forced to put up with her claims on *his* intimacy and her ridiculous airs: 'Dieses Sich-in-Szene setzen, diese halb komische Büstenplastik, die wie mit einem Spezialanspruch auftritt...', 'This demand for attention, this semi-comical posture of the bust which seems to assert a special claim'; VII, 419.)

Poetry, Edwin Muir once said, arises where intellect and emotion fuse on equal terms. Whatever the status of this remark from a rigorously academic point of view, it offers a working assumption which serves well to demonstrate the essential difference between *Ellernklipp* and *Effi Briest*. *Ellernklipp* is a residual crime-story with the beginnings of a novel of marriage. Emotional advantage is derived from the *genius loci* (note that the novel's title derives from a place-name, not that of the heroine) and local colour, the sense of mystery and of warring spiritual forces (the enlightened Pastor Sörgel and the mystic seer Melcher Harms), the melodrama of sudden death (there are three violent killings in the course of the story), and the use of superstition, fate-motifs and the supernatural. Intellect and emotion do not yet fuse on equal terms. In *Ellernklipp*, all the main characters act out of the promptings of a deeply felt but rarely expressed inner life: the presence of ghosts in their world, the sense of unseen powers all around express by projection the intensity of their emotions and imaginings, in a state still relatively close to nature and open to magic beliefs. Pastor Sörgel's enlightenment falls far short of covering all the exigencies and contingencies of felt life – it is notable that, generally speaking, Lutheran pastors in Fontane's works are not spiritually impressive – and serves only to point up the intensity of that life. Hence Hilde's mysterious inability (II, 195) to learn the third article of the Credo (concerning the role of the Church in salvation)[21] or the 'was ist das' commentary on the creed, the official Lutheran explanation of first and last things, which raises far more questions than it can answer.

In *Ellernklipp* the supernatural and *Spuk*-motifs must, for the modern reader, be a matter of 'local colour' also, which therefore distances, rather than involves him, and it is only through the use of suspense and sensation that these motifs remain credible, able to carry the reader along, albeit with reservations about that 'enormous condescension of posterity'[22] which is inevitably involved in the attempt to recreate the states of mind of an earlier generation. There are also grounds for suspicion that mystification and obscurity are created for their own sake, to thicken the atmosphere.

In *Effi Briest*, the use of *Spuk*-motifs remains acceptable on the intellectual plane while still retaining considerable emotional force. Here, too, the alleged haunting of the Kessin house, the Chinaman and other necromantic effects, such as Frau Kruse and her sinister black hen, externalize the intensity of Effi's inner life.[23] The contrast here is not, any longer, as in *Ellernklipp*, simply that between the superstitious mind of the countryman and the cheerful enlightenment of a Pastor. Effi is contending with Innstetten, an apparently rational being, but one who maintains his equilibrium by resolutely suppressing any inner life he has: his famous *Grundsätze* (principles) can be seen, as Crampas shrewdly suggests (VII, 279), as compensation for a basic weakness. His true quality becomes apparent when, in a crisis, he avoids making the internal adjustment to the fact of Effi's six-year-old adultery, which would involve a review of his entire *Weltanschauung* (such as it is) and raise immense questions of a 'was ist das?' variety. Retrospectively he acknowledges his failure: 'ich hätte...alles im eigenen Herzen auskämpfen sollen' ('I should have fought the matter out in my own heart'; VII, 374). At the time, however, he turns the personal decision into an external, bureaucratic affair, to be settled according to regulations governing conduct. The language of his discussion with Wüllersdorf in chapter 27 is extraordinarily cool. It might as well be a chat with a colleague about any of the 'cases' he deals with as a civil servant, one that has surfaced to the top of the pile and can no longer be denied urgent attention: 'Es gibt eine Verjährungstheorie, *natürlich*, aber ich weiß doch nicht, ob *wir* hier einen *Fall* haben, diese Theorie gelten zu lassen' ('There is a theory of limitation by time, of course, but I don't know if we have a case here to which this theory might be applied'; VII, 372; my italics). 'Nun, Geert ist ja auch Landrat' ('Well, Geert *is* a provincial governor, after all'), says Effi in their courting days (VII, 193), and a small-calibre *Landrat* he essentially remains.

By contrast, Effi's longings and fears are recognizable to both heart and mind as the very stuff that the sympathetic life of the imagination is made of. Recourse to the irrational appears an understandable response, while the over-rational (as represented by Innstetten) becomes irrational and neurotic, a tendency implicit in Innstetten's complaint that his nerves let him down at the crucial moment (VII, 374); in his putative anti-semitic leanings and his associated attraction to Wagner (VII, 256); and in certain remarks that indicate psychological problems belied by his controlled exterior (e.g. VII, 251).

The part played by the life of the imagination is central to

Effi Briest, as it is to Fontane's work as a whole. In its positive manifestation it is the mediating power between rationalized order presented by Innstetten, and the chaos of libertinism represented by Crampas. Fontane goes out of his way to dispel any notion that the values he himself endorses predicate some kind of Byronesque diametrical opposite of Innstetten. Crampas's way is as inauthentic as Innstetten's: it too throws the emphasis on to society's repression, as a way of avoiding self-analysis; the only difference being that Crampas, on the receiving end of the law-giving process, rejects the rules as automatically as Innstetten enforces them. Innstetten and Crampas are incomplete by themselves, like two complementary aspects of one character, comparable to other dual-character manifestations in literature, such as Don Quixote and Sancho Panza, or Don Juan and Leporello. While Innstetten can be seen as the inhibited, overcontrolled superego, Crampas is a Don Juan figure (the last of his line?), or, to use the same Freudian terminology, the uninhibited libido. To pursue the Freudian analogy a little further: the superego, that 'higher' part of ourselves which monitors morality, inner criticism and conscience, is a representation of inner demands or claims which have already assimilated the external demands of society. The essential link between superego and libido is the mediating power of the imagination. Without it, or when it is ignored or repressed, the demands of the superego for conformity to the acknowledged rules can lead to a drastic loss of humanity.

Fontane's subject-matter offers a perfect example of this process. Simply because the custom of duelling is not *quite* extinct, the correct and outwardly well-adjusted Innstetten forces himself into the atavistic and uncivilized act of fighting a duel and killing a man (an action better suited to the libidinous Crampas, who has indeed previously slain an opponent in a duel). The reduction of action (the duel) to a meaningless though lethal charade well illustrates Fontane's mature attitude to action in general. He suspects it as a displacement outwards of problems that can only be mastered inwardly. Thus he can be seen, in *Effi Briest*, gravitating towards the position of the twentieth-century 'livre sur rien';[24] what has in fact been called the poetic novel, the uneventful novel of pure circumstance, at the opposite pole from the balladesque and 'unerhörte Begebenheit' (unprecedented event) domain of *Ellernklipp*. Two actions are very important in *Effi Briest* – the act of adultery and the duel – and yet the importance of both is thoroughly relativized by the power of an imagination that amply comprehends them, in which we are invited to share. (The benign old Dr Rummschüttel, approaching Fontane's age when he wrote the novel, comes as close as any character in the book to embodying Fontane's own attitudes; see VII, 342.) Adultery and duel are two acts of desperation taking the form of a passionless travesty of passion, a symmetrical pair, as is apparent in their very stage-setting. In both cases the mise-en-scène is chosen by Crampas, and his choice of venue for the duel appears to be the precise spot in the dunes near Kessin where he and Effi had their picnic, and their first intimate conversation without Innstetten (compare VII, 287 and 377). The site is reached in each case by subterfuge, and the duel is as furtively conducted as the adultery.[25]

There are people who can only act in situations which have in some way been formalized for them, and Innstetten is one of these. In his anxiety to comply with the social code, he seeks out the formalized role where one is available, even (or perhaps especially) where this role is under review as archaic and increasingly inappropriate to an age of transition. The farcical nature both of an absolutist view of adultery as an automatic affront to 'honour' and of duelling as its inevitable consequence is placed in perspective by this remark from Otto Rank's famous early twentieth-century book on the Don Juan theme (and Crampas is clearly a late representative of the Don Juan type):

Don Juan can only exist in a country where the women must be protected by the barred windows of the harem from the inordinate desires of men, and in a country where blood-revenge holds sway over the consciousness of law.[26]

The duel, ideally, presupposes the harem: the further the one is removed from the other, the more the element of travesty predominates. The duel is as much of a *Komödie* (play-acting) as the adultery ('ein verstecktes Komödienspiel', 'covert role-playing'; VII, 315), and Innstetten suffers the additional chagrin of being aware of the danger of his exposure to ridicule in some degree, whether or not he chooses to fight Crampas. Such is the weakness of his character that he (like Schach von Wuthenow) fears ridicule more than almost anything else.

In *Effi Briest*, Fontane is on his way to discarding action – as he quite consciously did in *Der Stechlin* and *Die Poggenpuhls*.[27] At this stage in the process of refinement that takes him from the balladesque Novelle to the novel of pure circumstance, action still occurs, in amounts dictated by poetic economy. But, crude, decisive and final as it is, it serves only to heighten the significance of the true events of the novel, which are inner events, the subtle record of states of mind and of atmosphere.

While purifying his writing of superstition, sensational action and 'local colour' magic, Fontane does not purge the imagination. He presents a world which is only apparently 'entzaubert' (emptied of magic), and in *Effi Briest* he retains the pre-scientific power of magic to which we are all still subject, however rational we like to think ourselves. It is in this sense that Fontane employs references to the Catholic religion throughout his novels (it is represented in *Effi Briest*, of course, by the servant Roswitha). He attributes to Catholicism the capacity to respond to innate spiritual demands, the desire for the irrational to be given form. In other words, Catholicism is a more poetic form of religion than Protestantism, more satisfying in its answers to the quest for eschatological certainty, and better able than Protestantism to stand for the phenomenon of faith in general. This does not mean, of course, that Fontane had personal leanings towards Catholicism. In fact, he shows at times considerable antipathy towards it.[28] The difference between his private feelings and the recurrence of Catholicism in his works (particularly the recurrence of death-bed conversions) indicates the essentially aesthetic usefulness of the theme to him.

The irrational has been defined as 'the senseless substratum that lies outside the reach of reason, the amorphous content that resists all imposition of form, the being that is the ineluctable "other" of consciousness'.[29] Form can only suggest the irrational, never impose itself upon it. In *Effi Briest* the irrational never finally submits to a bourgeois *Problematik*, and this is not, in the end, a novel about an interesting problem in polite society. Fontane's manner is social, but his matter implies something different, something which in the early *Novellen* took melodramatic, overtly irrational, daemonic forms. Protestantism, being the typical religion of an 'entzaubert', prosaic world, cannot supply psychological needs. (This is why the Protestant Effi feels the need of Roswitha's more elemental religion as a talisman against the 'bad magic' of the Chinaman; VII, 266–7.) Protestantism represents order and an acceptable, enlightened mode of thought, capable of producing, at best, only the kind of secularized work-ethic by which such men of principle as Innstetten live, straddling an abyss. (Thomas Mann was soon to make this abyss all too painfully visible, in *Buddenbrooks* and *Der Tod in Venedig*, where he demonstrates that work does not necessarily have value in itself.)

Fontane, with his feeling for 'das romantisch Phantastische' (the romantic and the fantastic), was always attracted by the strange, the irrational and the picturesque.[30] In *Ellernklipp* these elements are ready-made, folkloristic survivals of a more primitive and perhaps more poetic age. In *Effi Briest*, survivals from the past tend to be more comic than poetic; for example, the somewhat bizarre figure of the 'old-world' apothecary, Gieshübler, in his *Spitzenjabot* (lace jabot), the institution of duelling, or the backwoodsman mentality of aristocratic Kessin society. What Fontane does in this novel is to make the familiar strange; to poeticize the prosaic world of nineteenth-century society, and to do so without depending on the picturesque and the archaic.

The making strange of the familiar is demonstrated when a comment of Müller-Seidel's on *Ellernklipp* is applied *verbatim* to *Effi Briest*: 'Daß aus so gut fundierter bürgerlicher Ordnung unversehens ein Mörder hervorgeht, ist das Unerhörte der erzählten Begebenheit' ('The uniqueness of the event narrated lies in the fact that a murderer emerges from such a solid bourgeois order'). Two deaths occur, that of Crampas and that of Effi, and neither falls far short of socially-sanctioned murder,[31] though nothing could be further from Fontane's stratagem than to make this suggestion explicit. To do so would be to plunge the novel back into the sensational world of *Ellernklipp*. Yet in both novels a similar process can be seen: what appears to be a dislocation is in fact a connexion. There is in each case a causal link between the prevailing *Ordnung* and the murder or death emerging from it; and the deaths in the two novels take place in ways characteristic of their respective societies. The connexion lies in the deep, non-rational impulses in each social climate, low motives disguised as high principles.[32] Innstetten's 'Art Angstapparat aus Kalkül' ('kind of frightening device based on calculation'; a curious phrase for Effi to have produced, though attributed to her in a passage of free indirect speech, VII, 283) is an example of this: intended ostensibly as a pedagogical instrument, Innstetten's use of intimidation by arousing fear of the supernatural 'grenzte schon fast an Grausamkeit' ('almost bordered on cruelty'; ibid.). It is difficult to see how Innstetten can escape from the suspicion of Sadism, in a quite narrow sense. The *widest* definition of Sadism is 'the pleasure felt from the observed modifications on the external world produced by the will of the observer'.[33] Innstetten's pleasure in manipulating the minds of others is apparent in Crampas's report of such activities in their army days together:

Aber hatte eine Vorliebe, uns Spukgeschichten zu erzählen. Und wenn er uns dann in große Aufregung versetzt und manchen auch wohl

57

geängstigt hatte, dann war es mit einem Male wieder, als habe er sich
über alle Leichtgläubigen bloß mokieren wollen. (VII, 281)[84]

(But he had a fondness for telling us ghost-stories. And when he had us
agitated, and even in some cases really scared, suddenly it seemed as
though he had just been making fun of his gullible listeners.)

If there is pleasure to be had in observing one's success in
modifying the external world, and especially other people's
states of mind, the easiest satisfaction is likely to be derived
from modifications which combine cruelty with sexuality.
(The mental cruelty inflicted by Innstetten can be read as
compensation for what appears to be a lack of sexual vitality,
to judge by the narrator's words in chapter 13: 'Um zehn war
Innstetten dann abgespannt und erging sich in ein paar
wohlgemeinten, aber etwas müden Zärtlichkeiten, die sich Effi
gefallen ließ, ohne sie recht zu erwidern', 'Then, at about ten,
Innstetten was weary and indulged in a few well-intended,
but rather tired caresses, which Effi tolerated without actually
responding'; VII, 256. After a pause, the narrator continues in
the next section 'So verging der Winter...', 'Thus the winter
passed...'.)[85] This line of thought takes us admittedly into deep
waters. Enough has been said to indicate, however, that Innstetten's behaviour, outwardly quite often kind and considerate,
cannot always be accounted for in rational terms (especially
when we juxtapose his indulgence in ghost-stories and the
narrator's comment early in the novel that superstition was
anathema to him: 'Er glaubte nicht an Zeichen und Ähnliches,
im Gegenteil, wies alles Abergläubische weit zurück', 'He did
not believe in portents and things of that sort: on the contrary,
he firmly rejected all superstition'; VII, 183).

The dressing up of low motives as high principles is presented transparently in *Ellernklipp* in Baltzer Bocholt's soliloquy
in chapter 12, reflecting the struggle between conscience and
instinctive drives that precedes his murder of his son. His argument that duty demands his intervention between Martin and
Hilde ('Ich habe für Recht und Ordnung einzustehen und für
Gebot und gute Sitte. *Das* ist meine Pflicht. Und so muß ich

ihr Gebaren und ihr Vorhaben stören', 'I must uphold law and order, right principles and morality. *That* is my duty. And so I must take steps against their behaviour and their plans') is contradicted in the very next breath, when Bocholt recognizes these sentiments for the self-deceiving humbug they are:

Ordnung und gute Sitte! Hab ich *sie* denn gehalten? Aus aller Zucht des Leibes und der Seele bin ich heraus, und die gute Sitte, von der ich sprech, ist Neid. Ich neid es dem Jungen. Das ist alles. Ich neid ihm das schöne müde Geschöpf, das müd ist, ich weiß nicht um was. (II, 235-6)

(Order and morality! Have I kept to *them*? I have thrown to the winds all discipline of body and soul, and the morality I talk of is jealousy. I envy the boy. That is all. I envy him that lovely, weary creature, weary I know not why.)

An abyss has opened up which Fontane does not examine further in *Ellernklipp*. Outer action distracts from inner: the murder follows abruptly as a relief from the torments of introspection.

Conflicts emerge here in embryonic form which are central to *Effi Briest*, where they appear in more acute form as society becomes outwardly more civilized, the increased claims of civilization clashing with an irrational element in human behaviour which remains constant. The exploitation of this constant is the opposite of Naturalism: it has to do with poetry (as opposed to documentation). Müller-Seidel, in his chapter on *Ellernklipp*, observes that the conflicts in the book are founded in human nature, and are, ultimately, immutable, whatever is done by human agency to try to change them.[36]

Such a conflict is inherent, for example, in the realization that to set oneself up as the representative of *Ordnung* is always dubious, a way of expressing the will to power and domination over others. In the case of Baltzer Bocholt (unlike Innstetten) this is transparent. Originally a stranger to the area, he is an ex-soldier with a crude and insensitive vitality, precisely the type to identify himself wholeheartedly with the interests of the governing class, to congratulate himself on the power it delegates to him, and to exploit this power to the very considerable limits allowed. To say he is a Fascist type is anachronistic, if tempting. (His deferential outlook and ambitions towards self-betterment may well account for his initial interest in Hilde, for in marrying her he acquires a wife related by blood to his liege-lords, notwithstanding the bend sinister.) The tragedy of Hilde begins with a perfectly understandable assumption on the part of Pastor Sörgel that such an outstanding representative of *Ordnung* is just the right person to take over the raising and educating of the orphaned child. The Pastor's equation of support for order with innate morality is not justified by subsequent events.

But is the case much better in *Effi Briest*? If Bocholt is crude, he is also wholehearted, lusty, loves life and hates hypocrisy, even in himself. When Effi is delivered up to Innstetten, it is like the transposition of a simple folksong into another mode altogether. As retribution is transmuted to poetic justice, so domineering and violence give way to the psychological cruelty of over-refinement. Innstetten's attempts to 'reassure' Effi are blatantly insincere, and calculated to have the opposite effect (VII, 206): he throws into doubt the rational explanation for the mysterious noises in the empty room upstairs (VII, 216); he shows a reluctance amounting to refusal to make any changes in the rooms above, to fill them up or, as it were, supply the 'furniture' which Effi's mind needs (VII, 219); and when Effi finally tries to pin him down on the question of the Chinaman, he refuses to deny the existence of such apparitions, sliding out of the trap by suggesting that Effi, the daughter of an old aristocratic family, should be used to hauntings: 'Spuk ist ein Vorzug, wie Stammbaum und dergleichen...' ('Ghosts are a privilege, like a family tree and so on...'; VII, 236). At least twice in the novel the point is implicitly made that psychological torment is worse than physical cruelty: in chapter 10 Effi remarks 'Die Wirklichkeit kann mich nicht so quälen wie meine Phantasie' ('Reality cannot torment me as much as my imagination'; VII, 239), and in chapter 14, 'Aber Einbildungen sind das schlimmste, mitunter schlimmer als alles' ('But imaginings are the worst, sometimes worse than anything else'; VII, 266).

Psychological torment is particularly unbearable when it derives from the application of a refined intelligence to the undermining of the mental stability of others ('Angstapparat aus Kalkül'), and the aspect of cold calculation and deliberate intent is worse than any spontaneous outburst of rage or physical threat. The refinements of mental cruelty call to mind Henry James's over-refined characters, like Osmond in *The Portrait of a Lady* (the theme of art-gallery visiting, of Innstetten as a *Kunstfex*, which dominates the honeymoon, reinforces the association with Henry James's cultured villains; but Dorothea Brooke in George Eliot's *Middlemarch* (1871), endures a very similar honeymoon). Effi reminds us of some of James's natural and ebullient heroines, like the eponymous Daisy Miller (1878) who is destroyed by her own overreaction to a solid front of self-righteous social disapproval.

As the crime in *Ellernklipp* is 'ein Geschehen in der Gesellschaft' (an occurrence in society),[37] so are Effi's adultery and death. 'Wie stehst du zur Ressource?' asks Innstetten in the early days of their married life in Kessin, and continues: 'Daran hängt doch am Ende Leben und Sterben' ('How do you feel about the social club?...after all, life and death depend upon it'; VII, 225). His words are prophetic. Effi's dependence on Kessin society really is a life-and-death matter, and her relationship to the *Ressource* (which is for her nothing but a vacuum) seals her fate. Effi can say, along with Roswitha when she talks about her long-past sin, 'ich war es nicht, das waren ja die anderen' ('it wasn't my fault, it was the others'; VII, 364). The collective share in Effi's downfall is analogous to the part played, in recent thinking about neurosis, by the interaction of the subject and his family and social environment. It is only now being recognized in modern medical practice (but has always been known in 'primitive' societies) that mental illness is an 'event in society', not an isolated misfortune of the individual. There are always social implications in the factors which contribute to the manifestations of neurotic illness.[38] Similarly (*mutatis mutandis*) in *Effi Briest*: if it is true of Innstetten, as Effi says of him at various points in the novel, that he is 'ohne rechte Liebe' ('lacking proper love'; VII, 425; see also 255), this is also true of Kessin society as a whole, with very few exceptions, usually outsiders like Gieshübler and Roswitha. Effi seems to have a presentiment of this coldness when she asks to be supplied with a fur coat for her move to Kessin (VII, 189), a request symbolic of her perception of the aura of frigidity and icy correctness which Innstetten radiates ('frostig wie ein Schneemann', 'frosty as a snowman', in Effi's later simile; VII, 224) and which is to characterize Kessin in general. It is not that Kessin society on the whole is actively hostile, with some exceptions like the poisonous Sidonie von Grasenabb, the embittered Frau Crampas (see VII, 294) and (in Effi's imagination at least) the unbalanced Frau Kruse (VII, 259). Most of Kessin is simply cold, like Innstetten (see VII, 255) although some inhabitants are overtly envious and critical (VII, 222). Effi's offers of friendship are not returned except in the most formal and stilted fashion (VII, 315). Her view of Kessin society hardens in the course of her stay: she declares that 'manches, was wie Teilnahme aussieht, ist doch bloß Neugier' ('a good deal of what looks like sympathy is just curiosity'), and once again expresses her feelings about the people in the area indirectly, through a contrast between the climates of Kessin and Hohen-Cremmen – 'hier ist es fast immer rauh und kalt' ('it's nearly always raw and cold here'; VII, 252). As time goes on, Effi begins to despise the Kessiners rather than fear them (VII, 356: 'die einen zu fromm, die anderen zu platt', 'some too godly, the others too dull and vulgar') or in other words comes to share Geert's attitude ('halb sind es Philister und halb Pfiffici, nicht sehr nach meinem Geschmack', 'they're half philistines and half crafty devils, not much to my taste'; VII, 378), which is all very well for Geert, but not helpful for Effi, who is dependent on outside society. With suitable adjustment, Effi's retrospective words about the Innstetten of the Kessin period could be applied more or less to Kessin as a whole: 'Innstetten war immer ein vortrefflicher Mann,...aber ich konnte nicht recht an ihn heran, er hatte so was Fremdes. Und fremd war er auch in seiner Zärtlichkeit. Ja, dann am meisten; es hat Zeiten gegeben, wo ich mich davor fürchtete' ('Innstetten was always a splendid man,...but I could not really get close to him, there was always something of the stranger about him. And he was a stranger even in his tender moments. Yes, then most of all; there were times when I was really frightened of them'; VII, 356).

In a sense, Kessin is a social vacuum for Effi. It demands that she play an onerous social role for which she is badly prepared by nature and nurture, but offers her no support in this role. *De facto*, and by default, the social vacuum allows the censorious views of Sidonie von Grasenabb to prevail, while Effi suffers from an overwhelming sense of isolation. The love to which she is accustomed, even addicted (cf. VII, 183–4 and 298) is abruptly withdrawn. But to fail to love Effi, whom it is not too far-fetched to equate with the very principle of youth and innocence itself (and this is surely the point of Fontane's contrast of Effi with a parallel figure, Oberförster Ring's daughter Cora, arch and coquettish at fourteen in a way that the genuine *Naturkind* Effi never was: 'ich habe mich nie geziert', 'I was never affected'; VII, 298) – to fail to love Effi is tantamount to rejecting all that is positive in life; and, for reasons to be sought in the collective unconscious of Kessin society, it does appear that life is negated there. It is this realization that saps Effi's initial strength and vitality. Worse still is the realization, at a later stage, that Kessin is not entirely *sui generis*, for with the treatment that Innstetten metes out to Effi after their separation, with regard to her child, it becomes clear that a blatant act of cruelty is supported by society in general. Sick with this knowledge, Effi finally 'turns her face to the wall', in almost balladesque style, and by implication determines to die:

'Mich ekelt, was ich getan; aber was mich noch mehr ekelt, das ist eure Tugend. Weg mit euch. Ich muß leben, aber ewig wird es ja wohl nicht dauern.'

Als Roswitha wiederkam, lag Effi am Boden, das Gesicht abgewandt, wie leblos. (VII, 409)

('I am sickened by what I have done; but what sickens me more is your virtuousness. Away with you all. I must go on living, but it cannot last forever.'

When Roswitha came back Effi lay on the floor, her face turned away, as though lifeless.)

Effi's fate has something of the appearance of the triumph of age over youth, beginning with Frau von Briest's argument that by marrying Innstetten Effi will achieve at twenty what many have achieved by forty (VII, 180), a dubious proposition if properly examined. The first cause of Effi's downfall is not, of course, her adultery,[39] which is merely the result of a misdirected quest for the love and interest that Kessin denies her. Primitive peoples with an intact magico-religious view of the universe tend to look outside of themselves for the first causes of personal difficulties, disappointments and illness. Fontane's heroines tend, as *Naturkinder*, to live in such a universe and to feel strongly the 'evil eye' influence of those hostile to them. Both Hilde, in *Ellernklipp*, and Effi suffer from this tendency, which is focussed on that powerful force prominent in Fontane's works, 'das Gerede der Leute' (people's talk). Hilde might be speaking for Effi, too, when she expresses her vulnerability to the feelings of others about herself and the withdrawal of their love, which 'zehrt' (preys upon you) and is fatal: 'Und wenn ich gar einen sehe, der mich beneidet, dann ist's mir immer wie ein Stich und als fiele mir ein Tropfen Blut aus dem Herzen. Und ist ganz heiß hier und tut ordentlich weh' ('And when I see someone who envies me, it gives me a stab and makes me feel as though a drop of blood were falling from my heart. And it burns inside and really hurts'; II, 197). The combination of envy and indifference in Kessin seems to express the will of society that Effi should fall. *How* she falls is unimportant, disgrace following upon the discovery of adultery being merely a fall typical for women in nineteenth-century society. It is noticeable that in *Ellernklipp* we are introduced to a very narrow range of characters, and are not actually offered many chances to encounter 'das Gerede der Leute' at first hand. To have introduced us to a larger cast would have brought *Ellernklipp* closer to a novel of society and diminished its Novelle qualities. It is after all a traditional feature of the Novelle to concentrate on a few events and a very few main characters. This poetic economy stresses the unexplained *Märchen* aspect of the Novelle's events.

In *Effi Briest*, however, Fontane reconciles the novel of society with the underlying poetic structure of the Novelle. Society is both an abstract force (as in *Ellernklipp*) and a concrete reality, represented by a wealth of characters. In both cases, *Ellernklipp* and *Effi Briest*, there is a sense in which the heroine can be seen in the light of a sacrificial victim who symbolically dies for the sins of her particular society, so that Frau Briest's words of reproach to her husband at her daughter's wedding breakfast acquire prophetic overtones – 'Wir haben eben eine Hochzeit und nicht eine Jagdpartie' ('This is a wedding, not a shooting party'; VII, 196: Briest replies that 'er sähe darin keinen so großen Unterschied', 'he could not see any great difference between the two'). The recurrence of sacrifice-motifs in *Effi Briest* has been little commented upon. (But see the references to Peter-Klaus Schuster's book in my foreword, p. xvii above.) In the first chapter Effi seems unconsciously to court martyrdom with her flippant remark that 'eine Geschichte mit Entsagung ist nie schlimm' ('a story with renunciation is never bad'; VII, 174), and her innocent re-enactment of the execution by drowning of unfaithful women in Constantinople (VII, 177), an exact parallel to Effi's treatment by society after her adultery, though she says explicitly 'Hier kommt so was nicht vor' ('That doesn't happen here'). The underlying barbarity of the social code is already linked with the dangerous self-confidence of Effi's uncontrollable, imaginative spirit. Later in the novel the symbolic association of the dangers of water with adultery (echoing that most famous German novel of adultery before *Effi*, *Die Wahlverwandtschaften*, and also a scene from Fontane's own *Graf Petöfy*) recurs in a group of references in chapter 20, including the rescue of the shipwrecked foreign mariners, which gives Effi (also a 'foreigner' in these parts) a surrogate sense of rescue from her own 'drowning' in the depths of deception. 'Alle wurden gerettet, und Effi hätte sich...in die Dünen werfen und sich ausweinen mögen' ('All were saved, and Effi would have liked to throw herself down between the dunes and cry her heart out'; VII, 313). Adultery is for her almost as much punishment as crime.

Other sacrifice-motifs include Frau von Padden's reference to Effi as 'ein junges Lämmchen weiß wie Schnee' ('a young lamb, white as snow'; VII, 346), the sacrificial stones Effi comes across on Rügen Island, not far from the village of Crampas (VII, 352), and Crampas's account of Heine's ballad of Vitzliputzli, the Mexican god to whom human sacrifices are made (VII, 287). The latter example recalls Wüllersdorf's invocation of the *Götzendienst* (idol-worship) to which Innstetten is urged to submit, though in point of fact it is Effi who is sacrificed (VII, 375). The suggestion of collective social guilt is brought home to the reader in a resumption of the *Opferstein* (sacrificial stone) motif at the end of the novel. Effi describes the sacrificial altars on Rügen, for the benefit of Kantor Jahnke in Hohen-Cremmen, adding that ever since seeing them she has had an antipathy to the Wends. Jahnke corrects her:

Ach, gnäd'ge Frau verzeihen. Aber das waren ja keine Wenden. Das mit den Opfersteinen und mit dem Herthasee, das war ja schon wieder viel, viel früher, ganz vor Christum natum; reine Germanen, von denen wir alle abstammen...(VII, 414)

(Ah, excuse me, my dear lady, but that was not the Wends. The sacrificial stones and Lake Herta and so on, all that goes back much,

much further, to before the birth of Christ; pure Teutons, from whom we are all descended...)

We cannot help recalling Effi's words in chapter 1 about the harsh customs of Constantinople, 'hier kommt so was nicht 'vor' (VII, 177).

The *Opferstein*-motif occurs in *Ellernklipp*, too, but in a cryptic, undeveloped form compared to *Effi Briest* (see II, 211, 216), part of the high novellistic colour, and offering yet another prefiguration of the story's outcome. Martin and Hilde have 'lain on the sacrificial stone' and must therefore be sacrificed to the dark powers ('Es ist ein Opferstein. Und sie sagen: wer darauf schläft, den opfern die finsteren Mächte', 'It is a sacrificial stone. And they say that anyone who sleeps on it is sacrificed by the dark powers'; II, 216). The 'dark powers' in *Effi Briest* are no longer mere superstition. They are partly subjective, the fears and the *horror vacui* that dominate Effi's mind in Kessin, and they are partly objective, the self-righteousness and hypocrisy of the collective closed mind of official Prussian society. But they are not much less mysterious for being more 'real'. The scapegoat still performs a ritual function.

Another Novelle feature carried over into *Effi Briest* is the frequent mention of graves and graveyards. In both *Ellernklipp* and *Effi* a churchyard is mentioned on the first page, and in each case the reference takes a form characteristic of the respective concerns of the two works. In *Ellernklipp* the churchyard is part of an order in which secular and ecclesiastical interests are thoroughly integrated in an ascending scale:

Die Frau...ruhte jetzt...an der Berglehne drüben, die, dreifach abgestuft, auf ihrer untersten Stufe den von Mauer und Stechpalmen umfaßten Kirchhof, auf ihrer mittleren die kleine Kapellenkirche zum Heiligen Geist und auf ihrer höchsten das zacken- und giebelreiche Schloß der alten Grafen von Emmerode trug. (II, 171)

(The woman now lay at rest on the hillside over there, with its three terraced levels: the lowest level bearing the churchyard, surrounded by a wall and by holly bushes; the middle terrace the small Chapel of the Holy Ghost; and the highest, the castle of the Counts of Emmerode with its many-gabled, jagged outline.)

Here in this remote Harz village at the end of the eighteenth century, death is still part of an official order which takes care of the large metaphysical questions, from cradle to grave. Churchyards are symbolic of a spiritual home, and the prospect of coming finally to rest in the allotted place alongside one's ancestors can offer a solace for the sense of not belonging in *this* life, as it does for Hilde. Vaults and last resting places figure largely in Fontane's works as part of a preoccupation with the continuity of generations. Aristocrats in particular can look forward to 'a better death after life'. Waldemar von Haldern's suicide in *Stine* is no bar to a fine burial in the ancestral vault, to the accompaniment of martial music and military honours. If family graves are symbolic of being at home in this world by right of dynastic succession, churchyards can, by the same token, be a poignant reminder of their state for those who are 'homeless', disconnected from the chain of generations (as Effi temporarily is in her Berlin flat, opposite a churchyard, during the period of exile from society: see VII, 400).

The churchyard on the first page of *Effi Briest* features not in a positive sense (family resting place) but in the ominous one of a prefiguration of her death (the only way out from the garden of her childhood is through a gate into the churchyard). Neither is she buried in the churchyard, but in her parents' garden. In Kessin, the ultimate expression of homelessness and alienation is the grave of the Chinaman, *outside* the church-yard, among the dunes where Effi buries her childhood innocence and optimism. But this is only one extreme mani-festation of the general spirit of Kessin, a town without ancestors, for 'die ganze Stadt besteht aus solchen Fremden, aus Menschen, deren Eltern oder Großeltern noch ganz wo anders saßen' ('the whole town consists of such strangers, people whose parents or grandparents were natives of very different parts'; VII, 205). As an 'objective correlative' of Effi's overwhelming sense of estrangement, this state of affairs is bound to weigh heavily upon her psyche. To the daughter of a house as solid as the 'schon seit Kurfürst Georg Wilhelm von der Familie von Briest bewohntes Herrenhaus zu Hohen-Cremmen' ('the manor house at Hohen-Cremmen inhabited by the von Briests since Elector Georg Wilhelm's time'; VII, 171) it must be only too apparent that, as Geert von Innstetten tells her, 'hier ist alles unsicher' ('everything is precarious here'; VII, 204).

It is significant that in the later Fontane, churches are rarely entered (in contrast to sight-seeing episodes in, for example, *Vor dem Sturm* and *Schach von Wuthenow*) though church-yards and cemeteries frequently are. It is as though official religion is a spent force (Effi finds no comfort in the Berlin church during her years of social ostracism, the sermons being too Old Testament and 'alles bloß, wie wenn ich ein Buch lese', 'as though I'm just reading a book'; VII, 401). The residue is a half-pagan cult of the dead which has to supply the apparently limited spiritual needs of contemporary Prussia. (A glimpse of a Victorian necropolis tells the same tale, however.) Whereas there is a part of Effi that 'knows death' – a knowledge conveyed in the symbolic motifs associated with her: the trains which come and go, from nowhere, to nowhere; the mysterious rustling of plane-trees in the garden; *Nachtluft*; *Sehnsucht* – for Innstetten death, like everything else, is conventionally known only in the terms of the Prussian code. Wüllersdorf tells him: 'Oder auch wohl nach Potsdam fahren und in die Friedenskirche gehen, wo Kaiser Friedrich liegt, und wo sie jetzt anfangen, ihm ein Grabhaus zu bauen. Und wenn Sie da stehen, dann überlegen Sie sich das Leben von *dem*, und wenn Sie dann nicht beruhigt sind, dann ist Ihnen freilich nicht zu helfen' ('Or go to Potsdam and go to the Friedenskirche, where Kaiser Friedrich is buried, and where they are just beginning to build him a vault. And as you stand there, just consider *his* life, and if you don't find any comfort then, then I must say you are beyond help'; VII, 421). Innstetten is confined to help such as this, the closest the corpus of beliefs offered by the Prussian code can get to the question of man's beginnings and his end. With this corpus of beliefs, a limit is firmly set for ever upon Innstetten's spiritual horizons, and herein lies a contrast to both Hilde and Effi.

Over both of them hangs, finally, the enigma of unrealized potential. *Could* they have loved, or are both condemned to the fate of the Melusine-prototype, Oceane von Parceval, to the basically tragic situation of someone who, instead of feeling, merely longs to feel, as Müller-Seidel (p. 447) suggests of Effi? If limitation is prosaic, unrealized potential is poetic. Effi's gravestone just outside the churchyard (like the Chinaman's) counter-balances the rusty Blücher–Wellington monument in the garden at Hohen-Cremmen and suggests Effi's position as the pioneer who, unlike Hilde, buried safely in the Emmerode churchyard, has been forced to occupy a frontier position in unknown territory that anticipates the twentieth century, and to rely entirely on personal resources to create her own salvation. Effi emerges as a modern heroine in a story of transition. This is a world in which there are no *Instanzen*, no authorities left, only 'ein Götzendienst' (idolatry) and something vaguely called 'jenes uns tyrannisierendes Gesell-schafts-Etwas' ('that certain social entity which tyrannizes us'; VII, 374). At a moment of intense emotional crisis, Effi kneels before a Bible and a hymn-book, because she must have *something* to support her: 'sie griff danach, weil sie was haben mußte, vor dem sie knien und beten konnte' ('She reached out for them because she had to have something before which to kneel and pray'; VII, 408). But these are only relics, all the same. And the notion of *Gesellschaft* (society) as a possible replacement for religion and traditional morality is succinctly dismissed by Effi's father in a little exchange with his wife just before the story draws to its close. He implies that a new morality would invert the Fourth Commandment and give pride of place to the love of parents for their children: his wife replies:

'Dann ist es vorbei mit Katechismus und Moral und mit dem Anspruch der Gesellschaft.'

'Ach, Luise, komme mir mit Katechismus so viel du willst; aber komme mir nicht mit "Gesellschaft".' (VII, 411)

('Then it's all over with the catechism and morality and the claims of society.'
'Now, Luise, the catechism's all well and good; but don't give me "society".')

Throughout her troubles, Effi harbours an imprecise conviction that the prevailing morality leaves out of account some vital aspects of her case. Yet she is by nature a conformist: for her, as for most of Fontane's characters, there is no salvation outside society. Hence her disapproval of any suggestion that the Chinaman should have been buried in the Kessin churchyard, and her strictures against loose morals on the part of servants. It is natural to her to conform, but to conform to an inhumane society brings inevitable conflict and destruction. The point will bear repeating (see chapter 2, p. 32) that Fontane's *Naturkind* heroines are as fully conditioned, as fully implicated in social convention as are his male characters. But the latent contradiction between the concepts of *Naturkind* and 'conformist' is only an apparent one. To the extent that the society around her nourishes her, Effi is implicated in its norms and values. Her conformism does not follow upon a discriminating choice of codes of behaviour, but is a naive inclination towards the source of affection and approval.

She is in a direct line of descent from other Fontane heroines, including Hilde in *Ellernklipp*, in being essentially receptive or passive. Even the most spirited representative of the type, Melusine in *Der Stechlin*, whose advanced views are largely consonant with those of the Christian reformer, Lorenzen, shrinks from an active role. In a symbolic – and critically vexed – episode in chapter 28 (VIII, 247), Melusine is disappointed with the placid winter appearance of the 'revolutionary' Lake Stechlin, motionless beneath its thick layer of ice. But when Dubslav teases her by offering to have the ice breached so that the legendary red cockerel may emerge if it so wishes, Melusine hastily rejects the suggestion: 'Die Natur hat jetzt den See überdeckt; da werd ich mich also hüten, irgend was ändern zu wollen' ('Nature has covered the lake, and far be it from me to try and change anything'). She is attracted in theory by the romantic notion of the cockerel's revolutionary clarion call, but in practice she is not inclined to disturb the *status quo.*

The *frisson* Effi derives from Crampas's swaggering lawlessness (VII, 278) is a variation on the same theme, in this case reflecting the sexual attraction of the illicit for a young woman who enjoys the privilege of comfortable social circumstances. As Innstetten puts it (with Crampas's concurrence), 'die Weiber schreien sofort nach einem Schutzmann, aber von Gesetz wollen sie nichts wissen' ('females are the first to shout for a policeman, but they don't want to hear about the law itself'; VII, 279). Although she may flirt with danger, as 'midshipman' Effi loves to do, the *Naturkind* is not by her own volition in conflict with society. She lands in a conflict nonetheless between her naturalness (innocence, naïveté) and social propriety, because both her conformism and her responsiveness to romantic attractions are products of her innocence.

Females are not the active principle in society, and they therefore fall more readily into the role of victim. There is a margin of affectionate imagination allowed to them because they have even less room to manoeuvre than the males, so that the limitations under which females suffer are less clearly self-imposed. Whereas in the case of Fontane's males unrealized potential is usually presented in a manner which is critical of them, in the case of his heroines it is seen both as a criticism of society, and the product of a particular historical moment which tragically curtails their development. At the end of her life, Effi remarks: 'Es ist komisch, aber ich kann eigentlich von vielem in meinem Leben sagen "beinah"' ('it's funny, but there is a lot in my life about which I can say "almost"'; VII, 413). This 'beinah' of unrealized potential is turned to good account as a poetic vehicle.

Effi is the last person we would expect to see evolving any

kind of new morality. And yet at the end of her life she does transcend the conscious values by which she has lived, and in her very nobility point the way to a more humane society. In this society an important place would be granted to that one quality above all which Innstetten conspicuously lacks – 'das Kreatürliche' (a natural, animal quality). The dog Rollo and Herr von Briest, who both incorporate this quality, are privileged, significantly, to share the last word (so to speak) in the book. Thus Fontane foreshadows twentieth-century insights into the importance of the life of instinct, and even its underlying role in the formation of ethics.

It is in this suggestion of transition that the greatest single contrast to *Ellernklipp* lies, and it is an important one. Society in *Ellernklipp* is static, not under strain as it is in *Effi Briest*. Though basically stable, in a way that the West no longer is, society in *Effi Briest* is nevertheless in a state of disequilibrium.[40] Part of the problem of *historical* fiction is that it sometimes represents the society of the past as static: this tends to be the case in the ballad or the balladesque Novelle. The lack of any social conflict reduces the work to one plane only, what might be called 'universal human relationships' in an antique framework. *Ellernklipp*, in this sense, omits all but the structure of interesting dramatic events. The historically-conditioned social conflict that usually lies behind dramatic events is missing, as in the fairy-tale.

Fontane is interested in universals, but experience of the range of his fiction suggests that these can best be established within the particular. The alternative to presenting a static society is to try to recreate the pattern of social dynamics prevailing in the chosen period. This Fontane attempts to do in *Vor dem Sturm* by depicting, as he puts it, 'das Eintreten einer großen Idee, eines großen Moments in an und für sich sehr einfache Lebenskreise' ('the entry of a great idea, of a great moment into an essentially very simple class and condition of men'; letter to Wilhelm Hertz, 17 June 1866). Most critics agree that the attempt is less than successful, and the relative decline in the fortunes of the historical novel today among serious students of literature[41] suggests that *Vor dem Sturm* is one example of a general problem. Of course, historical fiction must always be a comment on the author's own time. But then the historical costume might merely obscure the comment, and it would seem unnecessarily oblique to dress up analysis of the contemporary world in historical guise, unless forced to do so to evade censorship or for the limited purposes of satire.

The problem of historical fiction is similar to the problem of history, the question of the validity of an attempt to extract a scheme of interpretation from events long past. Claude Lévi-Strauss has forcibly argued that this is an impossibility. 'It suffices...for history to move away from us in time or for us to move away from it in thought, for it to cease to be internaliz-able (*intériorisable*) and to lose its intelligibility, a spurious intelligibility attaching to a temporary internality (*intériorité*).'[42] (By this last expression, he means a contemporary's internal picture or grasp of his own world.) Historical fiction puts the past at three removes from the reader. The author's attempt to 'internalize' the period is at one remove from history, which itself, as a product of the 'internalization' performed either by contemporaries or by later commentators who supply the historical novelist's material, is at one remove from the actual events of the day; and our view of the fiction from our own even later vantage point puts us at a further remove. At least when the author writes about his own period the number of removes is reduced to two. Despite the provisional character of all 'internalizations' of events, even by a contemporary, there is no doubt about the validity of what the author writes on contemporary subjects, in the sense that he *is* a contemporary and that what he chooses to present to us could only be pre-sented by a contemporary. Through an author's writings on contemporary society we can have access to a valid internaliza-tion of his period – valid for one person at one time. It is not in a man's power to sever himself from this internality, as Lévi-

Strauss says (ibid.). 'Wisdom consists', he goes on, 'in seeing himself live it, while at the same time knowing (but in a different register) that what he lives so completely and intensely is a myth – which will appear as such to men of a future century, and perhaps to himself a few years hence. . . .'

This is precisely the wisdom of *Effi Briest*, with its tantalizing central preoccupation with *Verjährung* (limitation by time). It is the wisdom of old age, for age is mere *Verjährung*. Respectable age begins at seventy, the point which Dr Rummschüttel has almost reached: Fontane was in his seventies when he wrote *Effi Briest*. Another point in the novel where this magic age is mentioned is chapter 29, where Innstetten is plagued by the concept of *Verjährung* and the difference in perspective on human affairs that the passing of a few years can make. Does it affect the issue of his duel with Crampas that six years have passed since the affair? Or would he still be justified in demanding satisfaction if he had found the letters twenty-five years later – by which time he would have been seventy? From the vantage point of three score years and ten, with a view of the entire span of life, many things are excusable: the urge to condemn or to judge or to exact vengeance is laughable. But if it is laughable then, it is in a sense always laughable, 'eine Komödie' (play-acting), as Innstetten realizes (VII, 380–1). However, the knowledge that this is so cannot save him from having to play out his part in the tragi-comedy. The novel is permeated with the septuagenarian spirit. Fontane almost plays with Innstetten in giving him a glimpse of his own perspective, from above the battle. Innstetten's uncomfortable relationship to the *Verjährung*-question, with its incipient comic overtones, is rendered even more precarious by being taken up on a parodistic level by the servant Johanna, who mimics what she conceives to be her master's attitudes: 'Was heißt lange her? Sechs Jahre ist nicht lange her' ('What do you mean, long ago? Six years isn't long'). She even hypothetically adds ten years to Effi's age, and finds that it makes no difference to the verdict (VII, 384). Roswitha, in her direct, *kreatürlich* way, puts the whole issue in its proper perspective with her simple description of the appearance of the fatal letters – 'die Briefe, die mir gleich so sonderbar aussahen, weil sie die rote Strippe hatten und drei-oder viermal umwickelt und dann eingeknotet und keine Schleife – *die sahen ja schon ganz gelb aus,* so lang ist es her' ('the letters, which looked so strange to me because they had the red twine round them, wrapped round three or four times and no bow – they looked quite yellow, because it's so long ago'; VII, 383; my italics).

The wisdom of old age which speaks in *Effi Briest* produces a statement about social transition as such, a statement that cannot be made with the same validity about any *historical* period. The poetic substratum is similar in *Ellernklipp* and *Effi Briest,* but because we have in *Effi* a more valid internalization (of the society Fontane knew) the substratum is more plausible and better integrated than it is in *Ellernklipp,* where, paradoxically, it is a world closer to 'magic' that Fontane is trying to create. One might say that in *Ellernklipp* the 'myth' element ('myth' being diachronic magic, the accumulation of irrational beliefs across time) is too apparent, because too colourful, and undermines the 'magic' element, i.e. the understanding of the subterranean forces which make particular events happen in society.

This is another way of saying that where Fontane tries to be most poetic, with the aid of the enchantment lent by distance in time, he is less convincingly so than when he presents a world ostensibly prosaic and familiar to him. The contemporary novel is timeless: it can grasp the world as both a synchronic and a diachronic totality. But try as it will, historical fiction can only grasp the past diachronically, and then with dubious validity. I mean by this that historical fiction is by definition analytical, that the author analyses and selects the parts of the historical world he cares to present (thereby putting a limit on our understanding of the past) in terms of before and after, cause and effect, according to a scheme he has already established. History, to give it its due, was the midwife at the birth of many a nineteenth-century talent. But contemporary fiction, on the other hand, offers material for the reader's own imagination to establish a scheme of poetic interpretation of contemporary life.

4 · IRRUNGEN, WIRRUNGEN

Irrungen, Wirrungen goes further than any other novel of Fontane's in laying before the reader those confusing and enigmatic aspects of life which Herr von Briest understandably shrugs off with an evasive 'es ist ein zu weites Feld'. The title of the book could be translated 'Confusions and Entanglements',[1] and this theme is pursued on a number of different levels. Confusions arise where categories are mixed or unclear, and in the novel such hybrids and ambiguities range from the peripheral, such as the mingling of country with town in the case of the Dörrs' Berlin market-garden, to the central, exemplified by the oxymoron of *süßer Schmerz* (sweet sorrow) which denotes the essence of Botho von Rienäcker's reaction to his affair with Lene Nimptsch. Out of the not particularly original story of a fleeting summer affair between an aristocratic officer and a lower-class girl, Fontane creates a delicately interwoven texture pervaded throughout by the questions implicit in Victoire's words at the end of *Schach von Wuthenow*: 'Ein Rest von Dunklem und Unaufgeklärtem bleibt' ('There remains a residue of the obscure and the inexplicable'; II, 385). This enigmatic quality engenders a poetry transcending the prose of a mundane Berlin setting of the 1870s. Thus it illustrates the theme with which this book is concerned, the rearguard action fought by poetry against prose in Fontane's novels.

But I do not mean that it does so only as German Poetic Realism in general can be said to do. That aspect of the novel has already been explored, in an illuminating study which showed that '*Irrungen, Wirrungen* exemplifies the Realist method of transfiguring reality'.[2] This kind of transcendence is a matter of the sophisticated and subtle handling of simple subject-matter, average characters and everyday situations, to yield 'the intensity of feeling which is the transfiguring power of art'.[3] But above and beyond that transfiguring power, the novel is imbued with a sense that life is a strange business,

78

tempting us always to drift with its fantasy, as Hugo Gross-mann does in *Mathilde Möhring*. There is among some of Fontane's key characters a fugitive tendency (to be seen, for example, in the dénouement of *Frau Jenny Treibel*), to disengage from the normal obligation to discriminate or make distinctions, and assert an almost enervatingly impartial view of the larger questions of life. Corinna in *Frau Jenny Treibel*, for example, asks 'wer ist glücklich? Kennst du wen?' ('Who is happy? Do you know anyone?'; VII, 160). She is very Fontane-esque in rejecting such an absolute as the notion of *Glück* (happiness). Effi's remark at the beginning of *Effi Briest*, 'jeder ist der Richtige' ('everyone is the right one'; VII, 182), is not only the careless conceit of a young girl sure of her attractiveness, but also incorporates a Fontane-esque sense of the lottery that decides almost all the chief issues of our lives, and the ability of human beings on the whole to accommodate pretty well whatever fate allots them. (Compare *Cécile*, chapter 14: 'Der Himmel legt einem nicht mehr auf, als man tragen kann', 'Heaven does not make our burden heavier than we can bear'; IV, 200). Twice in *Irrungen, Wirrungen* it is remarked by females that 'one man is much like another': 'zuletzt ist einer wie der andere' (Lene to Botho, III, 137); 'einer ist wie der andere' ('Königin Isabeau' to Lene at Hankels Ablage, III, 162). Although these are very different statements within their all-important contexts, Lene is reduced to silence by the echo of her own words from the lips of the demi-mondaine: 'Lene sah vor sich hin und schwieg', 'Lene sagte kein Wort' ('Lene looked ahead and was silent', 'Lene said not a word'). Fontane's art of suggestion leaves the reader to presume that Lene is, surely, silenced by the futility of attempting to maintain the very real distinctions which mark her off from the average officer's mistress: an attempt rendered more hopeless by an overall awareness of the relativity and uncertainty of such assumptions as predestined unions or ideal partnerships ('zuletzt ist einer wie der andere', 'one man is much like another').

79

Life is conditioned by chance encounters and the accidents
of birth, a point made symbolically yet forcefully in the motif
of Botho's windfall, a painting by Andreas Achenbach which
he won in a raffle. This chance acquisition has, in a modest
way, conditioned his life, as the accident of patrimony determines his acquisition of another prize, Käthe von Sellenthin,
and his rejection of Lene. The painting, like Käthe, stands to
cost him dear. He himself is fond of remarking ' "daß ihm
sein Lotterieglück, weil es ihn zu beständig neuen Ankäufen
verführt habe, teuer zu stehen gekommen sei", hinzusetzend,
"daß es vielleicht mit jedem Glück dasselbe sei" ' ("that,
because it had tempted him into constant new purchases, his
good fortune in the lottery had come to cost him dear", adding "that it was perhaps the same with all good fortune" ';
III, 119). Käthe is expensive for her husband, both in a financial sense (viz. the expensive outfit she requires for the
Schlangenbad journey, including 'ein Riesenkoffer mit
Messingbeschlag, den Botho nicht ganz mit Unrecht den
"Sarg seines Vermögens" nannte', 'a huge brass-bound trunk,
which Botho, not without justification, called "the coffin of
his fortune" ') and also, of course, in the limitations she imposes
on him in return for the salvation of his patrimony. In reality,
however, the limitation she brings into his life is nothing new,
but a reintroduction; for, as the painting he acquires actually
begins to modify his personality – he no longer has a free choice
of specialization as a collector of works of art, and neither can
he freely express his true discrimination, for fear of depressing
the market for the paintings he happens to hold (III, 123)[4] – so
also has the accidental fact of his birthright conditioned and
limited his personality well before he settles for the marriage to
his cousin. His self-awareness is highly enough developed by
the end of the story for him to recognize this limitation in
himself, and to give expression to it in the course of his advice
to the young officer Rexin: ' ...ein Bild, daß uns in die Seele
gegraben wurde, verblaßt nie ganz wieder, schwindet nie ganz
wieder dahin. Erinnerungen bleiben und Vergleiche kommen'

('...a picture which is engraved on our minds can never fade completely, never quite disappears. Memories remain and comparisons arise'; III, 222).

It is this early limitation of horizons by upbringing and expectations that compels him *and* Effi to say 'jeder ist der Richtige' or 'jede ist die Richtige' – as long as he or she is of aristocratic birth, is materially well placed, and looks good. (Cf. Effi: 'Natürlich muß er von Adel sein und eine Stellung haben und gut aussehen', VII, 182.)

Lene, by contrast and symbolically, has no patrimony and no birthright whatsoever; in fact her origins, like those of Marie in *Vor dem Sturm*, are obscure. In itself this makes her a native of the realm of possibilities. There is no proof, after all, that she is *not* a princess, as Frau Dörr remarks to Frau Nimptsch in the early pages of the book: 'Sie haben sie ja bloß angenommen un is nicht Ihr eigen Fleisch und Blut, un vielleicht is es eine Prinzessin oder so was' ('You only adopted her and she's not your own flesh and blood, and maybe she's a princess or something'; III, 95).[5] This, the fact that she is not conditioned by birth, is one of the aspects of her character which makes her a representative of the poetic, in the 'conflict between the poetry of the heart and the opposing prose of circumstances'.[6] Along with her honesty, naturalness and purity, the poetic quality allows her to come to terms (as does Professor Schmidt: see chapter 6) with the ineluctable facts of life as conditional, confused and transient. In their parting scene, Lene tells Botho: 'Du...hast mich nicht auf Irrwege geführt' ('You...did not lead me astray'; III, 174). The 'Irrungen, Wirrungen' which their affair presents to the onlooker are for her, however painful, the most natural thing in the world, the realm in which she lives and breathes; just as only the *poetic* can fully comprehend, state and contain the ambiguities and contradictions of life.

So it is that she is able to wander, charmed and unscathed, across what was, for the nineteenth century, a moral quagmire,[7] symbolized by the swamp, the weeds and the fallen angels of the walk to Wilmersdorf in chapter 9,[8] whose motifs are taken up metaphorically by Gideon Franke in the homily that ends his interview with Botho in chapter 20, with its references to *Unkraut, Morast, Sumpf* and *Irrlicht* (weeds, swamp, will-o'-the-wisp; III, 205–6). His point, essentially, is that her purity has allowed Lene's passage intact through this morass, in accordance, incidentally (but surely not merely *coincidentally*), with the words of young Wedell to Baron Osten in chapter 7, 'nur der Reine darf alles', 'to the pure all things are permitted' (III, 127).

Lene is another representative of the heroic, for as an earlier chapter suggested (p. 36 above), she is capable of an independence of thought and decision which is the poetic equivalent of a former, masculine standard of heroic action. 'Alles war mein freier Entschluß. Ich habe dich von Herzen liebgehabt, das war mein Schicksal, und wenn es eine Schuld war, so war es *meine* Schuld' ('It was all my own free decision. I loved you with all my heart, that was my fate, and if there was any guilt, then it was *my* guilt'; III, 174). Her self-generated, 'old Prussian' moral force and her toughness (Botho thinks of her as 'herb und entschlossen' – a prefiguration of Mathilde Möhring: III, 144) are the armour needed by the new heroine on the metaphysical and spiritual battlefield which, for Fontane, has replaced the crude trials of action that tested heroic mettle before the onset of a prosaic, unheroic, modern age.

The multiplicity of levels in *Irrungen, Wirrungen*, which in itself contributes to the theme of entanglements implied by the title, ensures that there is nothing ponderous in the treatment of the book's serious subject-matter. The opening descriptions of the Dörrs' market-garden admirably illustrate the ability of the narrative to suggest more than one level of interpretation. The first paragraph playfully allows us only a tantalizing glimpse into the curious premises of the *Gärtnerei*, with a technique close to parody of the nineteenth-century convention of narratorial control:

Überhaupt schien sich nichts mit Absicht verbergen zu wollen, und doch mußte jeder, der zu Beginn unserer Erzählung des Weges kam, sich an dem Anblick des dreifenstrigen Häuschens und einiger im Vorgarten stehenden Obstbäume genügen lassen. (III, 95)

(Altogether, nothing seemed to be deliberately trying to hide, and yet everyone who passed this way at the beginning of our story was obliged to be content with a view of the little three-windowed cottage and a few fruit trees standing in the front garden.)

We are reminded of Fontane's rather self-conscious and conventional handling of the narrator's perspective in *Vor dem Sturm*, especially the trick of viewing the scene through the eyes of an imagined onlooker. Compare, for example, the Christmas scene in *Vor dem Sturm*:

Wer von der Dorfstraße aus diesem Herabsteigen zusah, dem erschloß sich ein anmutiges Bild: der Schnee, die wendischen Trachten und die funkelnde Sonne darüber. (I, 37)

(An attractive picture presented itself to anyone on the village street who was watching this procession downhill: the snow, the Wendish costumes and the brilliant sun above.)

In the *Irrungen, Wirrungen* example, the onlooker's eyes are allowed to penetrate so far and no further. We move in, to a certain extent, and then, baulked of a closer view, we move away again from the house, to take in the irrelevant fact of fruit trees in the front garden. Like the imagined observer, 'wir müssen uns genügen lassen' ('we must be satisfied'), and this is an apt summary of a serious poetic principle of the novel, a combination of limitation to mere facts, and reliance on the art of suggestion; particularly evident in the treatment of Lene, who, in contrast to the treatment of Botho which renders him all but transparent, is never fully revealed. The mere curiosity aroused by the introduction to the house – Lene's home – is paralleled by the genuine preservation of mystery around the person of Lene.

A comic parallel to the serious comment on the class system in the novel is provided by the juxtaposition of the so-called 'Schloß' and the Nimptsch cottage. Seen in the 'ruthless' light of day ('in unerbittlich heller Beleuchtung daliegend', III, 98) the castle is no more substantial than a stage set, and the cottage by contrast is shown to be solid and real: it is here that the fire burns, day after day, literally the focus of life, implying warmth, sincerity and solidity in the lower-class milieu. The sham 'poetry' of the castle (significantly, a Gothic mock-up, suggesting all that is pseudo-romantic and pseudo-heroic in the late nineteenth century) is put to shame by the prose of the cottage, which, when graced by the presence of a Lene, represents not only prose, but also genuine poetry. By extension, the exposure of the theatrical castle (a mere *Kulisse*, a piece of scenery; III, 95) is an *exposé* of the theatrical aristocratic role Botho is finally obliged to adopt, that of his wife's escort at the trivial gatherings of polite society, whose tone he himself wittily caricatured, with great theatrical skill, for Lene's benefit in chapter 4 (III, 110–12).

By contrast, we are only granted an occasional glimpse or delicate suggestion of Lene's true thoughts; enough to suggest the depth of her feelings, which lie too deep for expression in tears or words. The pain of the final separation from Botho is conveyed most vividly by the streak of white hair which grows in from her left temple (cf. Botho's remark in chapter 4 – 'die Linke [Hand], die kommt von Herzen', 'the left hand comes from the heart'; III, 109) and 'replaces' the single hair with which she bound the little posy of wild flowers for Botho at Hankels Ablage (chapter 11, III, 148). Lene is sparing with words, but what she says is never for effect ('Du bist doch nicht so, daß du so was sagst, bloß um etwas zu sagen', 'You're not the one to say something like that simply for the sake of talking', says Botho, III, 173) and never trivial, so that there is a powerful charge in her simple statement, on parting from Botho, that death would be welcome to her (III, 173); or in her unaffected words after she has caught a glimpse of Käthe and Botho together and perhaps (but this only by a typical Fontane implication) has overcome the temptation of suicide:

Lene war inzwischen...bis an den Kanal gekommen...und erst als jenseits des Zoologischen die Häuser am Kanal hin aufhörten und die große Schleuse mit ihrem drüberwegschäumenden Wasser sichtbar wurde, blieb sie stehen und rang nach Luft. 'Ach, wer weinen könnte.'

(III, 181)

(Meanwhile Lene...had reached the canal...and it was not until, beyond the zoo, there were no more houses along the canal-bank and the great lock came into view with the foaming water pouring over it, that she stopped and fought for breath. 'Oh, to be able to cry.')

The turbulent water expresses both the turmoil of Lene's heart and the temptation to indulge in capitulation to the full power of her emotions. Her words, 'Ach, wer weinen könnte', remind us of those of the heroine at the end of *Stine*: 'Ach, wer fliegen könnte' ('Oh, to be able to fly'). And yet at the same time the echo points to a significant difference between the two novels. Unlike Stine's, Lene's *cri de coeur* is not the last word; the story continues with her heroic adjustment to the deprivation of her love, which has been interrupted by a chance glimpse of Botho in his new marital status.

What makes her adjustment possible is, on a prosaic level, the continuing responsibility for her ailing mother, which is clearly part of her reason for marrying Gideon Franke; and, on the other hand, on a poetic or metaphysical level, it is the healthy ability, despite suffering, to grasp life's *Irrungen* and *Wirrungen* and to assimilate them, in an almost Goethean fashion, as part of an indivisible whole, that enables her to say 'yes' to continuing life. The two motives, the prosaic and the poetic, are neatly woven together in the moments before her sighting of Botho and Käthe. Lene stands lost in fascination at the confusing busy-ness of an everyday scene of *Wirrungen*:

Die Sonne tat ihr wohl, und das Treiben auf dem Magdeburger Platz, wo gerade Wochenmarkt war und alles eben wieder zum Aufbruch rüstete, vergnügte sie so, daß sie stehen blieb und sich das bunte Durcheinander mit ansah. Sie war wie benommen davon und wurde erst aufgerüttelt, als die Feuerwehr mit ungeheurem Lärm an ihr vorbeirasselte. (III, 179)

(The sun made her feel good, and the activity on the Magdeburger Platz, where it happened to be market-day and everyone was just beginning to pack up, was such a pleasure to her that she stopped and gazed at the colourful confusion. She was as though bemused by it, and was only shaken out of her reverie when the Fire Brigade clattered past with a terrible din.)

The urgent sound of the fire engine brings her sharply back to an awareness of the legitimate demands of the outside world, and it is then that she remembers her obligations to her mother, who will be impatiently awaiting her return (III, 180).

Fontane rarely brings to the surface any explicit formulation of Lene's thoughts but, once again, makes use of his highly developed art of suggestion. In Botho's case, however, there is voluble evidence of his emotional life; and the very fact that this is so indicates a value-judgment on Fontane's part – not, it must be added, an absolute one in the sense of a negative verdict on Botho, but only an implication of his lesser status relative to Lene. Botho is, above all, free to indulge in his reactions to the end of the love affair, and has the necessary leisure and lack of distraction to do so. Such freedom for self-indulgence inevitably incurs the risk of producing an impression of shallowness. And yet it is Botho's overt and almost self-cultivated turmoil that most obviously justifies the title of the novel. His version of Lene's affirmation of the contradictions of life is the unresolved paradox of 'Viel Freud, viel Leid. Irrungen, Wirrungen. Das alte Lied' ('Much joy, much sorrow. Confusions, entanglements. The old story'; III, 215). The theme is apparent in references to 'süßer Schmerz' (sweet sorrow; III, 215), in remarks like 'wie wenig und wie viel' ('how much, and yet how little'; III, 216), in Botho's indulgence in bitterness on receipt of the ultimatum from his mother ('er...gefiel sich darin, sich bittere Dinge zu sagen', 'he enjoyed saying bitter things to himself'; III, 169), or in the cynically platitudinous consolation, after burning Lene's letters and thus closing a chapter of his life, that he finds in the society columns of the *Kreuzzeitung*:

Und wahrhaftig, so zu sehn, wie sich's weiter lebt und liebt in der Welt, ist eigentlich das Beste. Hochzeit und Kindtaufe! Und ein paar Todesfälle dazwischen. Nun, die braucht man ja nicht zu lesen...(III, 217)

(And truly, to watch how the world goes on its way living and loving, that is really the best. Marriages and christenings! And a few deaths here and there. Well, you don't have to read about them...)

Above all, the key to his emotional life, and also to the novel's central theme, is found in the lingering pleasure he takes in the pain of destroying the letters from Lene:

Und siehe da, langsam, als ob er sich das Gefühl eines süßen Schmerzes verlängern wolle, ließ er jetzt Blatt auf Blatt auf die Herdstelle fallen und in Feuer aufgehen. (III, 215)

(And behold, slowly, as though he wanted to prolong the feeling of sweet pain, he now let page after page fall into the grate to be consumed by flames.)

Botho is, after all, by his own confession, a 'Durchschnittsmensch aus der sogenannten Obersphäre der Gesellschaft' ('an average person from the so-called top level of society'), and we can expect from him nothing more nor less than the feelings of the average man in his position. 'Unser Herz hat Platz für allerlei Widersprüche' ('Our hearts have room for many contradictions'): his thought (III, 217) could serve as a motto for the book. It can include Lene's heart, too, while illuminating a qualitative difference between Lene and Botho, of which he is well aware:

Ach, sie hatte die glücklichste Mischung und war vernünftig und leidenschaftlich zugleich. Alles was sie sagte, hatte Charakter und Tiefe des Gemüts. Arme Bildung, wie weit bleibst du dahinter zurück.

(III, 215)[9]

(Ah, she was a most fortunate mixture, both sensible and passionate. Everything she said showed character and depth of soul. As for 'education', it's a poor thing in comparison.)

Like most of us, Botho is temperamentally unsuited to tragedy; he represents a norm for Fontane, who sees his age as neither tragic nor heroic. In chapter 21, Botho is not at all disappointed that the flower-seller from whom he buys Frau Nimptsch's wreath cannot offer him camellias, the sentimental and operatic Victorian symbol of tragic *mésalliance* (III, 209).[10] He is content with white roses. But, in true nineteenth-century fashion, there is no flower without a meaning; in literature roses, with their thorns, generally represent the bitter-sweet, and this is indeed the cliché area of sensibility to which Botho naturally belongs, quite powerful enough for his 'armes bißchen Leben' ('poor little bit of life', in Lene's phrase; III, 118). The theme of pleasure mixed with pain reaches a crescendo in the juxtaposition of the fairground booths standing next to the advertisements for the wares of monumental masons that Botho passes on his way to the cemetery (III, 210).

In accordance with Fontane's usual procedure of working by comparisons, and of creating characters who display gradations of the qualities possessed by the protagonists, whatever has been said about Botho von Rienäcker must be seen in relative terms. 'Relativity', both for the reader and, to a certain extent, for Botho himself, is a method of establishing his identity. Among the officer circle, for example, and by the side of his flighty young wife, Botho appears over-serious, whereas at the Nimptsch cottage he is ebullient and amusing. (In a similar way, Graf Holk in *Unwiederbringlich* is frivolous at home, but in Copenhagen court circles is regarded as staid and rustic.)

Käthe is an extension almost *ad absurdum* of qualities that are undeniably present in Botho: a certain shallowness of feeling, for instance, a certain resilience and insouciance (see his Panglossian reflexion at the end of chapter 6, a chapter whose developments have not augured well for him: 'Es ist doch wohl eine der besten Welten', 'It is one of the best possible worlds, after all'). Käthe exhibits these qualities to such a degree that she is in danger of dehumanization, like Vogelsang in *Frau Jenny Treibel* (see p. 146 below) – and in both cases the point is driven home by a more or less explicit comparison of these characters with a pet bird: in Käthe's case, with a canary. She must inevitably be in the reader's mind, if not in Botho's, when this creature's antics are described:

Das Tierchen...piepte so lange und eigensinnig, bis ihm der Wille getan war. 'Alle Lieblinge sind gleich', sagte Baron Rienäcker, 'und fordern Gehorsam und Unterwerfung.' (III, 119)

(The little creature... cheeped long and stubbornly until he got what he wanted. 'All pets are the same', said Baron Rienäcker, 'they demand obedience and submission.')

But something similar can be seen at work in the juxtaposition of Lene with Gideon Franke. Like the Viennese lady, 'Madame Salinger geb. [née] Saling', Botho and Lene each 'marry their comparative' ('Joa, schaun's, i hoab halt mei Komp'rativ g'heirat't'; III, 199). Franke's earnest and enthusiastic talk about gasworks and sewage systems is as extreme and comic in its way as Käthe's chatter about hats and Guards uniforms. This is a parallel which draws together extremes, and therefore confuses categories in a manner characteristic of the novel. If Käthe is almost a caricature version of Botho's gregariousness and love of comfort, Franke is a caricature of Lene's seriousness, her love of order, her hatred of clever talk and artificiality, and above all her moral independence. Franke is so independent that no established religion suits him, and he has had to found his own sect (Fontane always represents *Sektierertum* as somewhat comical). These distorting mirrors of the two chief figures serve to take the tragic edge off the story, and they also emphasize, by contrast, the protagonists' respective balance and humanity.

In much the same way, the keen awareness of the two lovers that their affair is conditioned by time is moderated by the fact that the consciousness of transience which pervades the novel is not immune to comic treatment. Even the figure of Death itself is exposed to comic reduction, in the shape of the saleslady in the flower-shop: 'Das schwarzgekleidete Fräulein, das, vielleicht mit Rücksicht auf den Umstand, daß hier meist Grabkränze verkauft wurden, in seiner Gesamthaltung (selbst die Schere fehlte nicht) etwas ridikül Parzenhaftes hatte...' ('The salesgirl dressed in black who, perhaps out of respect for the fact that it was mostly funeral wreaths that were on sale, had in her general bearing something ridiculously reminiscent of the Fates (even the scissors were not lacking)'; III, 209): a touch of macabre humour worthy of that Fontane-admirer and satirist of Death, Thomas Mann. The humour of the book prevents the theme from becoming either banal or sentimental. Fontane forestalls the charge of banality by making the theme of transience *utterly* banal in the mouth of Frau Dörr when she remarks, with the air of one who has made a discovery, 'so jung kommen wir nicht wieder zusammen' ('we'll never be so young again'), a remark construed by the narrator as 'die von niemandem bestrittene Tatsache des täglichen Älterwerdens' ('the fact, disputed by nobody, that we grow older daily'; III, 138). The novelty of what is essentially a banal tale is closely related, after all, to the plot of *Irrungen, Wirrungen*, which makes new a banal truth. 'No new thing under the sun' (Ecclesiastes 1:8); and yet to themselves and to the reader, Lene's and Botho's affair *is* novel, however clear its parallels to the traditional wild-oats affairs indulged in by Botho's fellow-officers.

To return to the theme of transience and its humorous treatment: Frau Nimptsch is continually harping on the subject of dying, her unselfconscious sentimentality keeping the potentially morbid atmosphere of the novel within the bounds of everyday realism. Fontane has introduced a good deal of 'graveyardism' into the book on a comic level, again with the effect of warding off any real morbidity. In chapter 13, Johanna, one of the three officers' mistresses at Hankels Ablage, wishes to make a cemetery the goal of their walk, and remarks lugubriously ' . . . es ist immer gut, sich zu erinnern, daß man sterben muß' ('. . . it's always good to remember that you must die'; III, 161–2). She is undoubtedly aping her betters, morbid obsessions with death and disease being a part of the fashionable neurosis of Victorian ladies.[11] Käthe, the very mirror of 'good' society, announces that her first outing after her return to Berlin from Schlangenbad (where she has been 'taking the cure' for infertility) must be to the Mausoleum in the Stadtpark: 'Das stimme dann andächtig und zu frommer Betrachtung' ('It created a mood of devoutness and pious contemplation'; III, 228). By attributing these sentiments to the more frivolous characters, those 'far too freely moved to tears', Fontane induces in the reader the idea that to *dwell* on death and the ravages of time is frivolous and silly, rather than evidence of a serious mind. Lene does not dwell on the past, but finds consolation in the precise opposite, 'das bunte Durcheinander', the colourful and confusing life of the Berlin market-place.

The confusion of categories is pursued throughout the novel with great skill, reducing the inflated effect of extremes and reproducing the tone of life itself, which rarely presents clearcut issues. Especially useful is the narrative technique of allowing characters to speak for themselves, revealing themselves and the situation of other characters, in conversation, in letters, or occasionally in interior monologue, so that issues are personalized and made relative by a human and deliberately 'confused' pattern of presentation. Frau Dörr, whose every thought emerges 'man bloß halb und so konfus', is only the most extreme example of this process.

The theme of 'Irrungen, Wirrungen' is conveyed in a multitude of other ways in the novel. Most of them can be subsumed under three aspects of the theme, those of class, moral or metaphysical import. These categories overlap to a great extent, and they do so functionally as part of the subtle working-out of the pattern of confusion of categories. Some examples of the three categories might illustrate the point. Within the category of class-distinctions, we can take the account of the Scotsman, Armstrong, as delivered to Käthe and her companions at Schlangenbad, of the way in which his ancient family acquired its wealth and dignity – by cattle-stealing on the border. He cheerfully confuses the categories of *Viehraub* (cattle-stealing) and *Länderraub*, seizure of land (the latter deemed by aristocrats and Prussians to be a more noble one) and thus undermines the sanctity of aristocratic status, often acquired by ignoble means in the distant past (III, 226–7). Here of course, a moral point is also implied. Directly within our second category (the moral one), it is made very clear that Lene is not by any means innocent before the affair with Botho. But morality, too, is a relative thing which can be seen from different perspectives, such as the respectively pagan and Christian views of love expressed in the doggerel verses in chapter 4 (III, 110). The 'Himmel und Hölle' (Heaven and Hell) motif of the 'pagan' verse is taken up again by Botho in chapter 22: 'Ja, es gibt solche rätselhaften Kräfte, solche Sympathien aus Himmel oder Hölle...' ('Yes, there are such mysterious powers, such affinities made in Heaven or Hell'; III, 214). Whether Lene is innocent or not, in terms of conventional sexual morality – and it is a question Fontane is not at all concerned about[12] – her integrity contrasts very favourably with a society which would be happy to see an aristocrat like the officer Rexin 'living in sin' with his lower-class mistress, as he himself proposes to do, rather than see them married. Moral ambiguity is preferable to class ambiguity.

The third category, the metaphysical level, includes references to one of Fontane's favourite themes, that of *Sein* and *Schein*, or in other words the deceptive nature of appearances and of the differences that control life, including class differences. There is a sly allusion to this theme in Lene's ironic remark about Käthe, whom she has seen in the *Korso* (fashionable parade):

So was Schönes hab ich all mein Lebtag nicht gesehn. Als Kind hätt ich gedacht, es müss' eine Prinzessin sein; aber jetzt weiß ich, daß Prinzessinnen nicht immer die schönsten sind. (III, 121)

(I've never seen anything so lovely in my whole life. As a child I would have thought it must be a princess; but now I know that princesses aren't always the fairest.)

(The irony is perhaps more than slight, if we remember her revealing, democrat's remark in chapter 17, '...trotzdem ich die feinen Herren nicht leiden kann', 'although I can't stand the gentry'; III, 185.) The play on 'cottage and castle' in the opening pages serves similar ends.

A related but more far-reaching theme is that of *Vorstellung*

and *Wirklichkeit* (imagination and reality), which is introduced by Frau Dörr with her quite unfounded fear that Lene
will confuse 'das Einbilden' (imaginings) with reality, and
summed up by the officer in the Club when he says:

Alle Genüsse sind schließlich Einbildung, und wer die beste Phantasie
hat, hat den größten Genuß. Nur das Unwirkliche macht den Wert und
ist eigentlich das einzig Reale. (III, 131)

(In the final analysis all pleasures are in the mind, and the better your
fancy, the greater your pleasure. Only what is illusory has value and
is actually the only reality.)

This is not mere word-play, but relevant to the individual perception of reality. Things *are* what we perceive them to be, and
by seeing them in a different light we can change their nature.
So, to give a straightforward example, for Botho the meadow
at Hankels Ablage is bare of flowers, 'die reine Wiese, nichts
als Gras und keine Blume' ('pure meadowland, nothing but
grass, and no flowers'), whereas for Lene there are flowers in
plenty: 'Doch. Die Hülle und Fülle. Du siehst nur keine, weil
du so anspruchsvoll bist' ('Yes there are: masses of them. But
you can't see them because you're so demanding'; III, 146).
Even Käthe knows that 'Vorstellungen sind überhaupt so
mächtig' ('the imagination is so powerful'; III, 223). Dörr is a
happy man because he fondly imagines his wife a sought-after
beauty: but then the question of the desirable female shape is
itself entirely a matter of fashion (cf. III, 164).

A more important example is the episode in chapter 14
where Botho's horse leads him to the grave of the Chief of
Police, Hinckeldey, killed twenty years earlier in a duel. Like
other animals in Fontane, the horse is an expression of its
master's personality. A present from his uncle, Baron Osten,
and his most admired status-symbol among his brother officers,
the beast represents quite directly Botho's privileged life, for
the maintenance of which he depends on his links with society
and family. This creature, then, representing all that Botho
stands to lose, is given its head ('seit einer Viertelstunde kaum

noch im Zügel'). Botho fails to control the horse because his thoughts are on the 'Lene' part of his inner life; and significantly, this very lack of control (another version of *Irrung*: wandering) takes him towards a symbol of class-obligation and duty, Hinckeldey's isolated grave (III, 170). We are told that Botho is strongly possessed of a sense of the natural ('Rienäcker, der sich den Sinn für das Natürliche *mit nur zu gutem Recht* zugeschrieben', 'Rienäcker, who was only too right in crediting himself with a sense of the natural'; III, 171; my emphasis), but for him the natural, *das Kreatürliche*, leads to duty, not away from it, for 'das Herkommen bestimmt unser Tun' ('our origins condition our actions'; ibid.). Hinckeldey's Quixotic act of aristocratic duty, overriding his prosaic, essentially bourgeois professional and civic obligations, can be seen as an example of the mystery of *noblesse oblige*, somewhat romantic and above all irrational. *Why* did Hinckeldey go to his death? asks Botho, and his reply to himself is:

Einer Adelsvorstellung, einer Standesmarotte zuliebe, die mächtiger war als alle Vernunft, auch mächtiger als das Gesetz, dessen Hüter und Schützer zu sein er recht eigentlich die Pflicht hatte. (III, 171)

(For the sake of a notion of aristocracy, a vagary of class which was stronger than all reason, stronger too than the law whose protector and guardian it was his real duty to be.)

Botho can site within this same *Adelsvorstellung* (notion of aristocracy) his own very unromantic, quintessentially prosaic act of concluding a marriage of convenience with his cousin. He finds in Hinckeldey's example the face-saving device he is looking for, a counterweight to *love* which resembles love in being stronger than reason, and is the very opposite of the act of calculation his convenient marriage must otherwise appear to be. It is a question of *Vorstellung* (imagination), or how one chooses to view reality. What is most prosaic *can* be poetic, seen in the right light. Botho squares the circle of poetic and prosaic in the well-known passage, immediately following the Hinckeldey episode, where he rides towards a large factory and sees the workers in the middle of a rather idealized lunch-break. As Demetz long ago pointed out, the lives of the proletarian workers are reassuringly translated into a rustic idyll.[13] And yet one cannot overlook the fictional context. This is Botho's idealization, not Fontane's: he has just decided that he must relinquish Lene, and is trying to reassure himself that Lene is better off – even enviable – in her lower-class milieu, enjoying the *Ordnung* to which she will be able to return once he has released her from the 'Irrungen, Wirrungen' of their affair.[14] Beyond this, however, the orderly scene of the workers lunching in the open air reminds him of his origins in the Mark of Brandenburg, and the poeticized version of *Ordnung* just glimpsed lends an air of plausibility to the circle-squaring exercise which enables him to see marriage to Käthe as not entirely devoid of a poetic quality, after all:

Wenn unsre märkischen Leute sich verheiraten, so reden sie nicht von Leidenschaft und Liebe, sie sagen nur: 'Ich muß doch meine Ordnung haben.' Und das ist ein schöner Zug im Leben unsres Volks *und nicht einmal prosaisch*. Denn Ordnung ist viel und mitunter alles. (III, 171, my italics)

(When our people in the Mark get married, they don't talk about love and passion, they simply say: 'I must have order.' And that is a fine thing in the life of our people, and not even prosaic. For order means a great deal, sometimes everything.)

Lene, by contrast, can keep *Traum* and *Wirklichkeit* (dream and reality) firmly in perspective: she tells Botho only a few pages later: 'Wenn man schön geträumt hat, so muß man Gott dafür danken und darf nicht klagen, daß der Traum aufhört und die Wirklichkeit wieder anfängt' ('When you've had a lovely dream, you should thank God for it and not complain that the dream is over and reality has begun again'; III, 174). She does not seek the poetic – as Botho does in his attempt to reconcile *Vernunft* with *Poesie* – because she is poetic in herself. Her love affair was, like Melanie's in *L'Adultera*, but unlike Botho's, an 'Einsetzen ihrer Existenz' (a commitment of her whole existence), and she is not capable of any *Vorstellung* (act of imagination) that might obscure her sober perception of the shock to her very being that is caused by its demise.

A further, related difference between Lene and Botho is that for him, 'the natural' is a pastoral antidote to the artificial *mores* of his own society; whereas Lene simply is natural. The very manner of her speech places her in a pre-industrialized world: she displays in particular the 'Und-Stil' employed in Fontane's earlier balladesque Novellen (see chapter 3, p. 38 above):

Wenn ich einen liebe, dann lieb ich ihn. Und das ist mir genug. Und will weiter gar nichts von ihm, nichts, gar nichts; und daß mir mein Herze so schlägt und ich die Stunden zähle, bis er kommt, und nicht abwarten kann, bis er wieder da ist, das macht mich glücklich, das ist mir genug. (III, 106)[15]

(If I love somebody, then I love him. And that is enough for me. And I don't want anything else from him, anything at all; just to feel my heart pounding and count the hours till he comes and not be able to wait till he's here again – that makes me happy; it's enough for me.)

Their love affair is a microcosm of the tension between individual and society, nature and man-made constraint, signified in the sense of elapsing time in the novel, and the moments when time seems to stand still. Timelessness is equated with harmony, so that there is, for example, a marked contrast between the stifling summer atmosphere of crowded Berlin (the gesture of throwing open windows is recurrent) and the quiet spots where Lene and Botho meet. The opening scenes point to this theme. The stillness of the Dörr's market-garden is reminiscent (like Hohen-Cremmen at the beginning of *Effi Briest*) of some latter-day Garden of Eden, with the doves of peace fluttering around its tower. The tower has a clock-face, though it has no clock, so that the suggestion of idyllic timelessness is already bound up with the idea of illusion or even self-deception.

This paradise, like Hankels Ablage, is firmly fixed in nineteenth-century reality, a market-garden being an economic unit associated with the rise of large cities and dependent upon the

city, despite its appearance of enviable independence. The
Dörrs are urbanized peasants, rather than inhabitants of the
'total city', and their lives present the most complete contrast
to life in, say, nineteenth-century London, where 'the individual
was submerged in the mass of anonymous toilers, whose whole
world was circumscribed by the bricks and mortar of whatever
nook or cranny they had been shoved into by circumstances'.[16]
But the inevitable process of urbanization is bound to be
completed and to overwhelm the Dörrs, too. Their state of
suspended animation parallels the deceptive timelessness which
is a precondition of Botho's and Lene's affair. Evidence of this
creeping urbanization is to be seen, for example, in the question
'ob die Panke zugeschüttet werden soll' ('whether the Panke
is going to be filled in'; III, 112: curiously enough, the question
was also posed in *Frau Jenny Treibel*, VII, 39). The editor's
note at this point in the Nymphenburg edition of Fontane's
works explains: '–die Panke: ein meist übelriechender kleiner
Fluß, der sich durch das nördliche Berlin zog' ('–the Panke, a
little river, mostly evil-smelling, that wound through northern
Berlin'; III, 419). In opposition to this survival, a natural water-
way whose abolition the city's growth now seems to make
inevitable, is the man-made, state-financed canal (the canals,
like the railways, were a nationalized industry in Prussia)[17] to
which frequent symbolic reference is made throughout the
book.

After their abortive outing to Hankels Ablage, where the
meandering river (note that 'meander' is one possible translation of the *Irrung* of the novel's title!) represented for the
lovers the unconstrained state of nature which is their unattain-
able ideal, there follows in Berlin a depressing journey along
the deadly-straight banks of the canal: 'so hatten sie denn in
einer klapperigen alten Droschke die lange, lange Fahrt am
Kanal hin gemeinschaftlich gemacht' ('So they had shared, in
a ramshackle old cab, the long, long journey along the canal';
III, 165) – 'gemeinschaftlich' being a word which denotes that
sensation of being together yet apart, which characterizes all

too well the state of lovers whose relationship has lost its first freshness. Symbolic references to the river–canal dichotomy are finally made explicit in chapter 23, where Rexin explains what stands between him and marriage to his lower-class girl-friend:

Ritten wir hier statt an diesem langweiligen Kanal, so langweilig und strippengerade wie die Formen und Formeln unserer Gesellschaft, ich sage, ritten wir hier statt an diesem elenden Graben am Sacramento hin und hätten wir statt der Tegeler Schießstände die Diggings vor uns, so würd ich die Jette freiweg heiraten.... (III, 220)

(If we weren't riding along this tedious canal, as tedious and undeviating as the forms and formalities of our society, if we weren't riding along by this miserable ditch but by the Sacramento River, and if instead of the Tegel shooting-range we had the Californian goldfields in front of us, I'd marry Jette without another thought...)

It is ironic, and surely no coincidence, that when Lene finally throws in her lot with another man, Gideon Franke, he should be professionally interested in *Kanalisation* (drains) and the installation of the gas-supply, prosaic services which are the basic necessities of the creeping growth of the metropolis. The growth of Berlin represents a prosperous future for Franke, whereas for Botho it can have nothing but negative connotations. The technocrat is the coming man, and the days of the aristocrat are already numbered (the latter theme is to become the central one of *Die Poggenpuhls* and *Der Stechlin*). For Botho and Rexin, the canal with its tedious, unrelieved straight line is a reminder of the remorseless generalizations to which they are inevitably led, as Botho is led to Hinckeldey's grave by his horse.

The urbanization and canalization of greater Berlin are a symbol of an unremitting process that the individual must live through, the process by which he discovers his function and his place in society. This is a lesson for Botho, not for Lene, for the lower-class girl is, from the beginning, very well aware of her place, and sees the world already in terms of the general as well as the particular. Botho von Rienäcker, on the other hand, is used to a self-centred life of privileged consumption; he has thus far felt few constraints upon his individuality. In the course of the novel he is led gently and almost unconsciously towards an acceptance of the relevance of generalizations to his own case. Generalizations play a large part in the novel, and at all sorts of levels, from Frau Dörr's garbled folk-wisdom, to the pronouncement by one of the girls at Hankels Ablage that 'wer so dick ist, ist nie gut' ('people as fat as that are never good'; III, 163), to the grave-digger's generalization (cutting through *Irrungen* in the simplest possible vernacular way!) about what lies behind Botho's visit to Frau Nimptsch's grave – 'Da muß so was sein' ('There must be something like that going on'; III, 213), and finally to Botho's own generalization for the benefit of Rexin on the subject of the *mésalliance* the latter contemplates. It is typical of Fontane's writing that the full force of the generalization governing Botho's life emerges only when he is playing the part of confidant for another officer who faces the same problem. He convinces himself of the need for renunciation by at last formulating his own inner life in publicly recognizable terms. The episode is highly reminiscent of the similar scene in *Effi Briest* where Innstetten takes Wüllersdorf into his confidence, and in doing so seeks refuge from a private problem in a generalization. The contrasting individualism of Fontane's heroines is indicated by their social isolation and lack of an adequate confidante, and this holds true for Lene as for Effi. They must forge their own salvation.

It was said above that Lene's lower-class status from the beginning teaches her to see the world in terms of the general as well as the particular. She is therefore well aware – however often she forgets herself and represses the awareness – that the affair lives on borrowed time, expressed in the timeless moments that fleetingly interrupt the inexorable process of Botho's alignment with his own class. Such 'moments out of time' occur, for example, on the walk to Wilmersdorf ('oben auf dem Pedenhaufen, wo sie sich ausgeruht und geplaudert hätten, hätten sie die Zeit ganz vergessen', 'on top of the pile of weeds, where they had taken a rest and chatted, they had completely forgotten the time'; III, 139) and on the river at Hankels Ablage, where the passing barges are described (III, 144) as 'still' and 'wie ein Gespensterschiff' ('silent...like a ghost-ship'), drifting past in 'eine wahre Totenstille'('a veritable deathly silence'; III, 151), by way of contrast to the barges on the city canal in chapter 16, which show evidence of colourful life (III, 181). Here too, at Hankels Ablage, the stillness and the sense of suspended time are an illusion, both in particular and in general: the place is regularly invaded by whole boat-loads of noisy Berliners or hordes of rumbustious villagers, and on this weekend in particular Botho's fellow-officers deliberately see to it that the illusion of seclusion is soon destroyed. The influence of the dominating class permeates everywhere. There is no neutral territory: at best there are only places avoided by 'Menschen' (cf. 'Frau Dörr...ist unbezahlbar, aber nicht unter Menschen', 'Frau Dörr is priceless, but not among people'; Botho, III, 144), i.e. by good society, which implies that Botho and Lene can only remain together if banished to a wilderness, which, like America and the Sacramento River, is *not* a setting for lasting happiness.

Botho's instant adjustment to the imposition of the atmosphere of the *Klub* upon rural Hankels Ablage ('Botho sah, welche Parole heute galt...', 'Botho realized what was required'; III, 158) teaches Lene more about him than any answers to her earlier naïve questions. Time and the process of alignment with his comrades are both resumed at once. The leisurely programme Botho and Lene had set themselves is instantly discarded, to be replaced by one that is parcelled out according to the clock, with military precision (III, 159). The group is, furthermore, immediately divided along both class and sex lines, the women being left to their own devices while the men resume the normal officers'-club activity of card-playing. 'Königin Isabeau's' unsolicited intimacies to Lene, as well as her symbolically stained, though elegant parasol (III, 161) reveal the double standard imposed by the upper-class male in this society, and, what is worse, willingly accepted by females of her type.

If the general overwhelms the particular, if Lene is forced into a pattern of class and moral ambiguities that is ethically and even politically repugnant to her, she has a consolation in a broader and even more general view than the generalizations in which Hankels Ablage embroils the lovers. The shedding of class identity may be an illusion at Wilmersdorf or Hankels Ablage, but there is a poetic dignity in Lene which effectively renders such distinctions ephemeràl and trivial. It stems from an insight into the transience and impermanence of all things. The timelessness of the moment on the *Pedenhaufen* near Wilmersdorf is counterbalanced, after all, by an increasing atmosphere of desolation, fatalism ('Zuletzt ist einer wie der andere', 'In the end one is much like another'; Lene, III, 137) and finally death, at the end of their walk, with the quotation of a line from a popular song proclaiming 'Morgen in das kühle Grab' ('and tomorrow into the cool grave'; III, 138). A surer kind of timelessness supersedes that of the love affair, the timeless perspective of 'die Menschen waren damals so wie heute' ('people were the same then as now'; Frau Nimptsch, III, 142), and of 'time the healer', invoked by Lene in her parting words to Botho: 'Es rückt sich alles zurecht, auch das' ('Everything puts itself right, even that'; III, 174).

We return, then, to that mysterious numinous quality in Lene, quite independent of breeding or culture, which seems to make her at home with the modality and relativity of life. She has an innate balance which places her above the petty motives of others. Thus, for example, she welcomes the hurtful barb of the anonymous 'well-wisher' (embodying a gratuitous hostility similar to that shown to both Hilde and Effi; see chapter 3, p. 64 above) who sends her a newspaper cutting containing the news of Botho's marriage to Käthe:

Aber gerade dieser Extraschabernack, der den schmerzhaften Stich verdoppeln sollte, kam Lenen zustatten und verminderte das bittere Gefühl, das ihr diese Nachricht sonst wohl verursacht hätte. (III, 176)

(But precisely this gratuitous trick, which was supposed to turn the knife in the wound, came in useful for Lene by diminishing the bitterness of the feeling this news would probably have caused in her otherwise.)

No doubt it reminds her that the idyll was never the reality, and reinforces a fine sense of the vanity of human wishes.

In the 'conflict between the poetry of the heart and the opposing prose of circumstances', it is undeniably true that 'the victory of circumstances is registered quietly and without fuss'.[18] Botho gains the instant, prosaic reward of a fine apartment furnished by his mother-in-law, and swift promotion to *Rittmeister* (captain of horse; III, 216) from the First Lieutenant he was when the story began. And the love affair? 'Alles Asche': 'Und *doch* gebunden' ('All ashes. And yet I'm bound'; Botho, III, 215). Botho is forever bound by an irreparable sense of loss. The last word is, and will always be, Lene's. 'Gideon ist besser als Botho' ('Gideon is better than Botho'; Botho, III, 232), for Gideon enjoys the dignity of a free choice of his bride, a freedom enjoyed even by the humble Dörrs, whose marriage was a *Neigungsheirat* (marriage of inclination; III, 99). Freedom, represented at its highest, most poetic level by Lene, is after all superior to a winning ticket in the lottery of life.

5 · *UNWIEDERBRINGLICH*

It is a cliché of human experience that established married life tends to a prosaic condition, whatever the poetry of its preludes in courtship and honeymoon. Perhaps that is why the serious treatment of an established married couple is a rare event in Fontane. Marriages in his novels are often excessively mundane and generally humorously presented: prime examples are the Briests and the Treibels. *Unwiederbringlich*, Fontane's major novel of marriage, is the exception. While other novels describe marriages and deal with the theme of adultery, what might be called the 'average' marriage is nowhere as fully explored as here. Some critics put *Effi Briest* in the same category, but the differences between the two serve to clarify the central role of matrimony in *Unwiederbringlich*. Effi's marriage is an unequal affair which never develops into a three-dimensional relationship, let alone a partnership. In *Unwiederbringlich*, on the other hand, the marriage of Graf Holk and Christine is a long-standing and mature one: they have known love, lived through the years of childbirth and child-rearing, and shared the experience of the death of a son.

As though to offset the prose of the Holks' marriage, Fontane sets *Unwiederbringlich* in one of his favourite romantic settings, the nordic landscape which supplies so much sonorous name-poetry in ballads like 'Hakon Borkenbart', 'Gorm Grymme', 'Admiral Herluf Trolles Begräbnis', 'Gulbrandsdal' and others. This contrast between subject and setting immediately sets in motion the opposing forces of prose and poetry. The strikingly modern depiction of a deteriorating marriage is given perspective by a backdrop which is, in many respects, the same romantic world as that evoked by the enthusiast Hansen-Grell in *Vor dem Sturm*:

Sigurd Ring und König Helge, Ragnar Lodbrok und Harald Hyldetand entzückten mich durch ihren bloßen Klang, und sooft ich dieselben höre, ist es mir, als teilten sich die Nebel und als sähe ich eine wundervolle Nordlandschaft, mit klippenumstellten Buchten und vor ihnen ausgebreitet das blaue Meer und hundert weiß gebauschte Segel am Horizont. (I, 369)[1]

(Sigurd Ring and King Helge, Ragnar Lodbrok and Harald Hyldetand thrilled me by their very sound, and whenever I hear them it is as though the mists had parted and I saw before me a marvellous nordic landscape, with bays surrounded by cliffs and spread out before them the blue sea and a hundred billowing white sails on the horizon.)

If marriage is a prosaic condition, middle age is the period in life with the least poetic potential, though also the age where the absence of a sense of poetry can have a most destructive effect. There is neither youth's joyfully and painfully heightened sense of life (as in *Irrungen, Wirrungen*) nor the sublime ability of old age to reconcile conflicts (as in *Der Stechlin*).

Unwiederbringlich is the novel of established marriage, as well as a novel of middle age. When a marriage survives long enough to be an established and stable relationship, it is in middle age that the most testing crisis is likely to come. The children of the marriage are probably growing rapidly towards their independence and departure from the home. (In fact, the crisis in *Unwiederbringlich* is precipitated by the vexed question of whether the teenage children should be sent away to school.) In this phase of a marriage there is a need to reassess the relationship, perhaps a chance to re-establish it on a different basis; but the adjustment is made difficult by a hardening of attitudes, a tendency in each to become set in separate ways. As the partners to some extent reassert themselves as individuals, they subject each other to a more searching examination than has hitherto been their habit, and perhaps the 'faults of their virtues' (to quote a favourite Fontane phrase, used again in *Unwiederbringlich*, V, 30), the inevitable reverse side of the attractions that first brought the couple together, become increasingly prominent.

To the degree that middle-aged marriage is aware of and seeks an escape from its own prosaic condition, it is a microcosm of nineteenth-century life, neither tragic nor heroic. And yet these – the heroic and the tragic – are precisely the poles towards which Holk and Christine are drawn in reaction to the prose of their lives; and in these two modes their clashing self-images are formed. Lest there be any doubt about his intentions in this novel, Fontane for once is not prepared to allow the poetic suggestion to speak for itself, and in this there is an implication of anxiety about the effect of a work dealing with such untransfigured events as the breakdown and dissolution of a marriage. Fontane's own views on the sanctity of the marriage vows, as expressed in a letter to his son Theodor, were unusually uncompromising:

'Du sollst nicht ehebrechen', das ist nun bald vier Jahrtausende alt und wird auch wohl noch älter werden und in Kraft und Ansehn bleiben. Es ist ein Pakt, den ich schließe und den ich schon um deshalb, aber auch noch aus andern Gründen, ehrlich halten muß; tu ich's nicht, so tu ich ein Unrecht, wenn nicht ein 'Abkommen' die Sache anderweitig regelt.[2]

('Thou shalt not commit adultery'; that is nearly four thousand years old and will get older still and yet remain hallowed and in force. It's a pact which I conclude and which for that reason alone – but for other reasons besides – I must honestly abide by; if I don't, then I do wrong, unless an 'agreement' has ordered things otherwise.)

Unwiederbringlich, likewise, contains some of the very few overtly moralizing sentiments in Fontane's works. Generally speaking it is difficult to construe an unambiguous moral interpretation from his novels, which are close enough to life to induce puzzlement rather than certainty. But if there is a 'moral' to this tale, it is the sermon that Holk cannot help reading on the face of the old rouée Princess in chapter 28, after the fire incident which puts an end to the sojourn at Fredericksborg and Holk's 'escapade' with Ebba:

Von der freigeistigen Prinzessin, die sonst ein Herz oder doch mindestens ein Interesse für Eskapaden und Mesalliancen, für Ehescheidungen und Ehekämpfe hatte, war in der alten Dame, die da vollkommen greisenhaft unter dem feierlichen Königsbilde saß, auch nicht das

Geringste mehr wahrzunehmen, und was statt dessen aus ihrem einge-
fallenen Gesicht herauszulesen war, das predigte nur das eine, daß bei
Lebenskühnheiten und Extravaganzen in der Regel nicht viel heraus-
komme, und daß Worthalten und Gesetzerfüllen das allein Empfehlens-
werte, vor allem aber eine richtige Ehe (nicht eine gewaltsame) der
einzig sichere Hafen sei. (V, 187)

(In the old lady who sat there, undeniably looking her age, beneath the
solemn portrait of the king, there was not the least trace of the free-
thinking Princess who usually had a strong sympathy for, or at least an
interest in, escapades and *mésalliances*, divorces and marital strife:
instead, what could be read upon her sunken features preached only one
thing; that as a rule not much comes of dangerous living and extrava-
ganzas, and that keeping one's word and the law is the only advisable
way; above all, that a proper marriage (not an imposed one) is the only
safe haven.)

It is possible that Fontane, who had been rather taken aback by
the scandal surrounding the supposed 'immorality' of *Irrungen,
Wirrungen*, was trying to ward off a similar attack on this
subsequent novel. As far as he was concerned, the world was
hypocritical when it took a moralizing attitude to Lene's affair
with Botho, which had in his view 'mit der Moralfrage gar
nichts zu schaffen' ('nothing to do with the question of
morality'; letter to Theodor, 8 September 1887). But the case
was entirely different with *Unwiederbringlich*. As I noted
above, failure to keep faith is one of the chief crimes in Fontane's calendar, and it seems that on this issue he wants to
emphasize that while there is understanding and sympathy for
those too weak to maintain the standard, there is no moral
ambiguity. His private views concur with those that emerge in
the novel. It is surely no coincidence that the words on adultery
penned by Fontane in the letter to his son, quoted above, were
written at the time when Fontane was working on the first
draft of *Unwiederbringlich*, completed by Christmas 1887
(see 'An Emilie', XX, 541).[3]

The drastic, but unformulated, question that hangs over
Holk and Christine asks what reason there is for maintaining
their marriage. It is an important question, in the same category

as the one implicitly raised by Corinna in *Frau Jenny Treibel*: why should she *not* adopt the prevailing standards of the *nouveaux riches?* And the answer to both questions is not a single article of wisdom, but one of textures and tone; not content, but atmosphere and nuance: 'Der Ton macht das Gedicht' ('The tone makes the poem'; as Holk says of the 'Herluf Trolle' ballad, V, 141). It would require great sensitivity, heroic restraint and some very fine tuning to maintain the Holks' relationship; qualities which, Fontane suggests, bring their own reward. Christine and Holk are not incapable of finding such a *modus vivendi*, as Christine reveals to her confidante in her description of some of their intimate moments together (V, 57). But, true to the complexities of a real-life relationship, at the crucial point the right tone eludes them, and all is lost because of a fault of Christine's virtues, the martyr-complex which makes her provoke Holk to the confession that he wants to divorce her. In fact this issue is by no means closed for him, despite his earlier impulse (chapter 29, V, 192). Holk's letter from Copenhagen to his brother-in-law Arne indicates that the difficulty of maintaining the right tone is that of maintaining the will to do so, and he all too readily attributes this loss of will on his part to 'false' suspicions in Christine. The adultery has not yet taken place, but in a sense it does not need to. Already at this point – in chapter 24 – Holk is making a confession of guilt, not of adultery, but more importantly, of loss of will to maintain the right tone:

Ich...will...einräumen..., daß mir in meiner Korrespondenz mit Christine der richtige Ton schließlich verloren gegangen ist. Von dem Augenblick an, wo man sich beargwohnt sieht, ist es schwer, in Ton und Haltung korrekt zu bleiben...(V, 162)

(I...must...admit..., that the right tone now eludes me in my correspondence with Christine. From the moment when you know yourself to be under suspicion, it is difficult to remain correct in tone and behaviour...)

Another part of the answer to the question 'why *not* divorce?' (or to Corinna's question) lies in understanding what would be forfeited, rather than gained by such a step. This realization of loss does finally come to Holk, but far too late: 'auf Augenblicke stand nur all das vor ihm, was er verloren hatte, nicht das, was er gewinnen wollte' ('at some moments he saw before him all that he had lost, and not what he hoped to gain'; chapter 30, V, 198). There is not, then, in *Unwiederbringlich* a clear victory of poetry over prose, as can be said of *Frau Jenny Treibel*. The odds against it are, after all, so much higher than they are for Corinna: to *regain* a tone or texture once lost is much harder than to attempt such a creation in the first place. Hence the book's title, *Unwiederbringlich*. Relationships are precarious: once destroyed, they are almost impossible to resurrect, as evidenced by the failure of the ostentatious rededication of the Holks' marriage. But the suggestion of value in relationships, of the average man's or woman's inestimable dependence on an order once established, is the positive and poetic tenor of *Unwiederbringlich*, not in the least diminished by the fact that it is conveyed by an elegiac vehicle.

Fontane does not believe in the concept of a *Musterehe* (model marriage), nor in ideal and predestined partnerships, but he does believe in the almost infinite flexibility of the human being and in his ability, given the will to do so, to make adjustments in relationships. Once again, it comes down to a matter of belief or *Vorstellung*, whose power was noted in, for example, *Irrungen, Wirrungen*.

The point about *Vorstellung* is made in an early chapter of *Unwiederbringlich* in one of those political discussions which, in Fontane, invariably turn out to reflect significantly on the book's central subject. Holk throws doubt on the future of Prussia, which he dismisses as a mushroom growth 'auf diesem brandenburgischen Sumpf- und Sandland' ('on this Brandenburg swamp and sand'), lacking what for him are the essentials of an enduring state, which must 'natürliche Grenzen haben und eine Nationalität repräsentieren' ('have natural borders and represent a nation'; V, 24). His brother-in-law Arne's reply is that Holk has overlooked the vital ingredient: 'eine Vorstellung, ein Glauben' ('a conception, a belief'). Whatever Fontane's opinion of the Prussian State in later years, he never lost his conviction that the acquisition of Schleswig-Holstein was an act of liberation and a new and proper assertion of Prussia's will to live. Looking back in 1897, Fontane writes in a letter to James Morris: 'So brauchten wir Schleswig-Holstein. Wir mußten es haben, und wir haben es gekriegt' ('So we needed Schleswig-Holstein. We had to have it, and we got it'; 8 February 1897: note the similarity to Arne's tone in *Unwiederbringlich* – 'In den Russen lebt die Vorstellung, daß sie Konstantinopel besitzen müssen, und sie werden es besitzen', 'The Russians are firmly convinced that they must have Constantinople, and they will have it'; V, 24).

Holk's jibes at Prussia rebound upon himself, for it is he who lacks the *Vorstellung* and the *Glauben* to sustain his marriage and hence the organic pattern of his life. Like Prussia, his new home is a mushroom growth compared to the now relegated, centuries-old ancestral seat in the nearby village of Holkeby; and the new Schloß Holkenäs, like the house in the biblical parable and like Prussia, is built on sand, 'auf der Düne'.

The union of Holk and Christine resembles the troubled 'marriage' of Denmark and Schleswig-Holstein on the eve of the German–Danish war, a conflict which arose out of the new nineteenth-century spirit of nationalism, to destroy a centuries-old, if uneasy, *modus vivendi*.[4] Whereas, however, in the relations between Denmark and the two duchies neither side was truly convinced of the *raison d'être* of the union – in other words, neither side had ever possessed the necessary *Vorstellung* or *Glauben* in respect of it – in the case of the Holks' marriage such a conviction is not completely beyond recovery until the point of no return is reached in chapter 29. Adjustments are still possible, are even, up to a point, automatic, when the couple are still physically together. But they part relatively early in the story, not to meet again until very late. It is Holk's absence, and the tenuous continuation of the relationship only through letters, which makes the rift between them apparent.[5]

An important and unmistakeable theme of the novel is the relationship between the old and the new. Here, too, the title is programmatic, for in both Christine and Holk there is a tendency to live in the past or recall past glories. The Gräfin is an eighteenth-century throwback, as her brother observes: 'Christine braucht immer jemanden, um sich auszuklagen, ganz schöne Seele, nachgeborene Jean Paulsche Figur' ('Christine always needs someone to unburden her troubles to, a real "fine spirit", a belated Jean Paul type'; V, 28). Gräfin Holk's true setting is perhaps an even earlier one, for she is the type of the great lady of heroic poetry, the solemn and aristocratic 'exemplar of womanhood'. Her taste in sepulchral decoration, the Lübeck *Totentanz* (dance of death), similarly takes her back in time, to the late Middle Ages. The Graf himself is equally attracted by the archaic style of life at the court of the Princess, who knows better than anyone that the days of the monarchy in its old form are numbered, and that princesses are a living anachronism, their very title congruent only with the world of ballads and fairy-tales:

Wir arme Prinzessinnen, wir haben schon nicht viel, und aus der Welt der Wirklichkeiten sind wir so gut wie verdrängt; nimmt man uns auch noch die Märchen- und Balladenstelle, so weiß ich nicht, was wir überhaupt noch wollen. (V, 93)

(We poor princesses, we haven't got much as it is, and we have been pretty well ousted from the world of realities; if you take away our place in the fairy-tale and the ballad as well, then I don't know what we're there for at all.)

The relationship between old and new is always delicate and difficult. One of the more foolhardy responses to this complex, Fontane suggests, is to make a radical break with the past. Such a break is symbolized by Holk's impulsive indulgence of his *Baupassion* (building craze) in building the grandiose new castle, which, as Christine rightly remarks, is 'eigentlich unnötig; ein Umbau hätte dasselbe getan' ('actually unnecessary; rebuilding would have been just as good'; V, 12). Likewise, instead of an *Umbau* (rebuilding) of their relationship, Holk disastrously chose a *Neubau* (new building). The illtimed summons to the Danish court allows him to drift into a fantasy solution to his marital problem, the likewise grandiose concept of a new union with Ebba Rosenberg, as pretentious and out of keeping with Holk's true nature and capacities as the Grecian *Schloß am Meer* (castle by the sea), or, for that matter, the coffee drunk in chapter 2 which Arne declares to be 'etwas zu gut, besonders für dich, Holk' ('rather too good, especially for you, Holk'; V, 11: we are reminded of Leo's 'unsuitable' coffee-passion in *Frau Jenny Treibel*). Holk drifts to the outermost limits of romantic self-delusion, one of the faults of his virtues, while Christine, in reply, moves to the opposite posture of a tragic martyr. They are looking for the 'large' things, a *grande passion* (like the grand new castle) or a *grande douleur* (like the magnificent family vault planned by Christine) both of them anachronisms in a fundamentally prosaic century.

Such nostalgic anachronisms are, however, only one facet of the influence exerted by the past in this novel. Denmark's romantic past was highly attractive to Fontane: for local colour in *Unwiederbringlich* he draws upon earlier writings of his own, either the account of the Danish war (*Der Schleswig-Holsteinsche Krieg im Jahre 1864*, published 1866) or his travel journalism. The novel is full of references to excavations, finds of Viking treasure-hoards, names of battle-fields, and all the balladesque glories of Danish history. Holk himself is said to be interested in antiquities, and, like other Lutheran clerics throughout Fontane's works, so is old Pastor Petersen. On the evidence of the novel, excavations would seem to have been a national passion in nineteenth-century Denmark, extending up the social scale to the King himself, to judge by a remark dropped by his aunt, the Princess, about the King's mistress, her arch-enemy Gräfin Danner:

...um die Gräfin archäologisch oder, was dasselbe sagen will, als ausgegrabenes vaterländisches Altertum anzusehen, ein Standpunkt, von dem aus mein Neffe so ziemlich alles betrachtet, dazu ist sie, trotz ihrer Vierzig, doch schließlich noch nicht alt genug. (V, 77)

(...to be seen archaeologically or, what amounts to the same thing, as national treasure trove – a point of view from which my nephew looks at practically everything – the Countess is not quite old enough yet, despite her forty years.)

The Schleswiger Holk joins the Danish courtier Pentz in a toast to 'old Denmark':

Gewiß, Pentz, Gamle Danmark. Und je 'gamler' desto mehr. Denn was uns je trennen könnte – gebe Gott, daß der Tag fern sei –, das ist das neue Dänemark. Das alte, da bin ich mit dabei, dem trink ich zu. Friedrich VII. und unsere Prinzessin...(V, 63)

(Certainly, Pentz, Gamle Danmark. And the 'gamler' the better. For the only thing that could come between us – God grant we never see the day – is the new Denmark. The old one, that's for me, I'll drink to it. Frederick VII and our Princess...)

But an alluring national heritage can offer also the temptation of a false-poetic or romanticized view of the past, inspiring a curious anomaly, the romantic fever of nationalism, arising out of the prosaic, industrialized world of the nineteenth century precisely in reaction to modern developments which threaten the old values.

A concomitant of the new strength of nationalist and pan-Scandinavian feeling was the successful attempt in 1848 of the 'Eider-Danes' or nationalist party, to detach the duchy of Schleswig from its close historical links with Holstein and incorporate it into Denmark proper.[6] Nationalism, with its attendant cult of the past, is a kind of false-poetic response to the encroaching prose of the age. Fontane suggests that an abrupt new departure in an old-established state is fraught with perils. (See his views on Wilhelm II, chapter 2, p. 23.)

Once more, the political situation is a close parallel to Holk's personal one. His move to the court at Copenhagen is at first deceptively harmless, for it springs from one of his cherished aristocratic privileges, to enjoy the status of a gentleman-in-waiting and parade in court dress. If nationalism, building as it does upon the national past, offers the illusion of continuity in the transition to an entirely new and dangerous state, so does Holk's sojourn at the anachronistic court offer him an easy transition to the complete divorce from his past resulting from his infatuation with the seductive lady-in-waiting, Gräfin Ebba.

The manner in which Fontane brings about this transition is masterly. It is as a man rather than as a courtier that Holk makes his first reacquaintance with Copenhagen. Suddenly released from a difficult phase of his relationship with his joyless wife, he reacts expansively to the air of the sea-port capital, a playground for the release of pent-up Eros and energy for life which is a perfect 'objective correlative' for Holk's psychic needs: in Christine's description, 'eine Stadt für Schiffskapitäne, die sechs Monate lang umhergeschwommen und nun beflissen sind, alles Ersparte zu vertun und alles Versäumte nachzuholen' ('a town for sea captains who've been floating around for six months and are now determined to squander their savings and make up for what they've missed'; V, 39). The libertine Hansens, mother and daughter, in whose house he lodges, epitomize the spirit of Copenhagen, as Adolar Krola, the socialite tenor, does that of Berlin in *Frau Jenny Treibel*. Their ill-defined network of connexions with the court and the city, and their ambivalent display of respectability coupled with the suggestion of illicit affairs not quite adequately concealed, excite in Holk an appetite for flirtation which carries him to the brink of dangerous entanglement with the exotic, younger Frau Hansen (chapter 15, V, 97): the scene prefigures a symbolic incident later, when Holk skates with Ebba towards the brink of the ice and the open sea (chapter 25, V, 167). Thus, before he has properly begun his association with the court, the reader is prepared for his capitulation to its immorality. In accepting the moral ambiguities of the Hansens, just as Hugo Grossmann, in *Mathilde Möhring*, accepts the ambivalent class standing of the two Möhring females, Holk reveals that he is not the man to make a stand on principles. Having failed to discern that the search for poetry must be made within the apparently prosaic confines of the marriage contract, he turns from his middle-aged marriage towards the seductions of the false-poetic, the mysterious and romantic.[7] The attractions of the younger Frau Hansen are blatant and almost lurid, although, or perhaps *because*, they reside precisely in her deliberately cultivated air of mystery, conveyed by the half-closed, langorous eyes and the clothes that seem to hide while they actually reveal. Like Doll Tearsheet in Shakespeare's *Henry IV Part II*, described by Pentz as 'ein grobes Zerrbild' ('a crude caricature') of Ebba (V, 111), Frau Hansen, too, is a coarse distortion of the lure of 'das Geheimnisvolle, Mystische'[8] which will attract Holk to the sophisticated lady-in-waiting. Frau Hansen's romantic, indeed fabulous story of the homage paid to her by the King of Siam is half-believed by the gullible Graf Holk, and thus the 'false-poetic' aspect of Ebba's attraction for him is luridly prefigured. Boyish and romantic enthusiasm for the mysterious is channelled, after the Graf meets Ebba, into an infatuation so intense as to suggest a second adolescence.[9]

Holk is a traditionalist, as well as a weak character, so that what might be disturbing, even to his easygoing mind, at home in rural Schleswig, is acceptable in the court. There he finds a long tradition of sophistication in such matters, and nothing but disdain for a morality that properly belongs to shopkeepers. The courtier Pentz is representative of these attitudes:

...und sich über Moralfragen zu erhitzen – bei deren Erörterung er regelmäßig die Griechen, Ägypter, Inder und Tscherkessen als Vertreter *jeder* Richtung in Leben und Liebe zitierte – war ihm einfach ein Beweis tiefer Nichtbildung und äußerster Unvertrautheit mit den 'wechselnden Formen menschlicher Vergesellschaftung', wie er sich, unter Lüftung seiner kleinen Goldbrille, gern ausdrückte. (V, 61)

(...becoming heated about moral questions – when these were raised he regularly cited the Greeks, Egyptians, Indians and Cherkessans as representatives of every conceivable preference in life and love – he regarded simply as proof of profound ignorance and extreme unfamiliarity with the 'changing forms of human societal organization', as he liked to put it, lifting his small gold-rimmed spectacles.)

In this atmosphere, to decline to enter upon a little extra-marital intrigue would appear philistine. The height of amused cynicism, expressed in the Princess's attitude to 'kleinstädtische Vorgänge' (small-town affairs) in Fredericksborg, places the substantial virtues of Holk's normal provincial existence in a ridiculous light (V, 130). Amorality becomes synonymous with breadth of culture, knowledge of the world, and awareness of the relativity of all standards. Holk is further confused by the observation that, at the court, standards depend not only on a consensus, but also upon the personal whim of royalty: 'Denn Prinzessinnen sind sich selber Gesetz, und was sie gut heißen, das geht und das gilt' ('For princesses are a law unto themselves, and what they approve of is what goes'; Ebba, V, 145). At the same time Holk is undermined by a modern sense of changing values, a simplified version of Fontane's own awareness of the shifting ground beneath his feet; and the court reinforces the Graf's facile sense of the lability of moral standards:

Christine war in allem so sicher; was stand denn aber fest? Nichts, gar nichts, und jedes Gespräch mit der Prinzessin oder gar mit Ebba war nur zu sehr dazu angetan, ihn in dieser Anschauung zu bestärken. Alles war Abkommen auf Zeit, alles jeweiliger Majoritätsbeschluß; Moral, Dogma, Geschmack, alles schwankte...(V, 122)

(Christine was so sure of herself in everything she did; but what *was* certain? Nothing, nothing at all, and every conversation with the Princess, let alone with Ebba, was only too apt to reinforce this view of his. Everything was a provisional consensus, the prevailing majority verdict: morality, dogma, taste, everything was in flux...)

The ultimate 'modern' position is announced by the older Frau Hansen – a suspect enough spokeswoman – in a remark calculated to sustain Holk's folly, and referred to as a *Predigt* (sermon):

Es läßt sich alles schwer nehmen, aber es läßt sich auch alles leicht nehmen. Und wer die Kunst des Leichtnehmens versteht, *der* lebt, und wer alles schwer nimmt, der lebt nicht und ängstigt sich vor Gespenstern, die gar nicht da sind. (V, 199)

(Everything can be taken hard, but it can be taken lightly, too. Someone who knows the art of taking things lightly is *living*, and someone who takes everything seriously is not living and is scared of ghosts that aren't there at all.)

This attitude is very close to Holk's standard response to his wife's gloom, and quite acceptable as an antidote: however, it is *not* justified, Fontane suggests, as an absolute standard. There is perhaps in the word *Gespenster* a subtle reference to Ibsen's play *Ghosts* (reviewed by Fontane at the opening of the new 'Freie Bühne für modernes Leben' in Berlin in September 1889, but also earlier, on the occasion of the play's Berlin première in January 1887, a performance discussed by Fontane in the *Vossische Zeitung* for 13 January); and indirectly, a reference to modern impatience with the trammels of the past in general, the 'ghosts' who dominate our lives and can be shaken off by an act of will-power.

Fontane is on the side of the modern; he could not otherwise (on 31 December 1889) have exchanged his role of theatre critic at the Königliches Schauspielhaus for the job of reviewing the productions of a highly controversial, innovatory institution like the 'Freie Bühne'. But he points out the recklessness of an abrupt dismissal of nineteenth-century 'hypocrisies', especially by those who, like Holk, are not strong enough to play the *Freigeist* (free thinker). So it is, as Reuter says, that we find Fontane allowing modernity to pass him by when needs be:

Wieder schützte Fontane das 'Alter' vor, wenn es ihm darum ging, Positionen zu behaupten, die sich seither als nichts weniger denn überaltert erwiesen haben.[10]

(Once again Fontane pleaded 'old age' when it came to asserting points of view which have since proved to be anything but antiquated.)

Or, as Fontane himself put it: 'Mit klingendem Spiel in das

Lager der "Neuen" überzugehen wäre Kleinigkeit und mir
moralisch unbedenklich, aber dazu fehlen mir einige Zentner
Überzeugung. Ich sehe das Gute, aber auch das Nicht-Gute
und drücke mich in die Sofa-Ecke. Mit 71 darf man das' ('To
beat the big drum and go over to the camp of the "new men"
would be simplicity itself and to me morally harmless, but
what I lack for that is a few hundredweight of conviction. I
can see the good side, but also the not-so-good, and I shrink
back into my sofa-corner. At 71 you're allowed to do that';
letter to Otto Brahm, 4 April 1891). In *Unwiederbringlich,*
Fontane is concerned to point out that the equation of scepticism with cynicism, of the mocking tone with knowledge of
life ('ride si sapis'; V, 61), leaves out of account another vast
area of knowledge.

Even Ebba cannot completely deny this 'knowledge beyond
cynicism', as was evident in her reaction to the Doll Tearsheet
allusion already mentioned: 'Sie war dicht vor einem hys-
terischen Anfall' ('She was close to hysteria'; V, 110).

A further comment on the relationship between Holk and
Ebba, developing the theme of Holk's attraction to the
mysterious and the romantic, is the motif of homeopathy, a
contemporary fashion for the apparently mysterious cure of
like by like. Ebba is Holk's homeopathic cure, as well as the
doctor for the malady of his marriage (like the Schleswig
veterinary surgeon, who is a convert called Lissauer, Ebba has
Jewish blood; she is the granddaughter of the personal physician
of a Swedish monarch, 'des... Lieblings- und Leibjuden König
Gustavs III', 'of Gustav III's favourite and "personal Jew"';
V, 87). She is Holk's counterpart, *similia similibus,* 'the woman
who knows how to laugh': compare Christine's words to Graf
Holk in chapter 6, in reply to his charge of excessive earnest-
ness – '...ich wünschte dir wohl eine Frau, die mehr zu
lachen verstände' ('I could wish you a wife who knew how to
laugh more often'; V, 41). But, with the poetic justice beloved
of Fontane, it transpires that Ebba knows *too* well how to
laugh, and the laughter she finally directs at Holk is the echo

he is left with in exchange for a marriage. With his weak head for such things, both the court in general and Ebba in particular prove too strong a draught for him. He would have done better to confine himself to a smaller, 'homeopathic' dose of freedom, just enough, perhaps, to reconcile him to the continuing ties of marriage. As Seminardirektor Schwarzkoppen tellingly remarks:

Die Homöopathie verzichtet, so viel ich weiß, auf alles Geheimnisvolle oder gar Wunderbare. Es ist einfach eine Frage von viel oder wenig und ob man mit einem Gran so weit kommen kann wie mit einem halben Zentner. (V, 14)

(As far as I know, homeopathy does not rely on anything mysterious, let alone miraculous. It is simply a question of much or little and whether a grain can do as much good as half a hundredweight.)

There, no doubt, speaks the pharmacist along with the artist in Fontane!

It was suggested above that the court itself, like the museum a not-so-innocent repository of the past,[11] offers Graf Holk an easy transition to a radical break with his wife.

With the move of the Princess's court to Fredericksborg Castle, the scene is set for a climax, both of Holk's fever of infatuation with Ebba, and of the theme of the incompatibility of old and new. The journey itself takes the royal entourage through a landscape which even Ebba is obliged to view as mysterious and romantic: 'Alles wirkt so geheimnisvoll, als berge jeder Fußbreit Erde eine Geschichte oder ein Geheimnis' ('It's all so mysterious, as though every foot of earth contained a story or a secret'; V, 126). Here, too, is an 'objective correlative' for Holk's state of attraction to 'das Geheimnisvolle, Mystische' ('the secretive and mysterious'),[12] and the castle itself is an intensification of the mood, 'still und märchenhaft' (still and fairytale-like) as it is (V, 128). It also intensifies the archaic nature of the court, for here there is a reversion to a medieval, gothic milieu:[13] 'Alles in der Ausschmückung der Halle war noch halb mittelaltrig wie die Halle selbst' ('Everything in the decoration of the hall was still half medieval like the hall itself'; V, 131), and the short mid-winter days produce a prevailing atmosphere of impenetrable murkiness, ineffectually combatted with the aid of pine torches.

Fredericksborg has the additional romantic asset of being built upon the site of an earlier castle belonging to Admiral Herluf Trolle. His battles are recorded in the smoke-blackened paintings that adorn the castle hall and provoke much discussion of the heroic past and the nature of heroism. Ebba is unimpressed by the kind of heroism generally ascribed to participants in battles: she shares *this* view, at least, with Christine[14] (and with Fontane). But she substitutes for it, clearly as a provocation to Holk to play the part of the hero, an image of ruthlessness (V, 174), the Romantic heroism of a Childe Harold or a Don Juan. In effect she issues a challenge to Holk to live up to this image, to be what he likes to think he is:

> ...a mortal of the careless kind
> With no great love of learning, or the learned,
> Who chose to go wher'er he had a mind,
> And never dreamed his lady was concerned...
> (Byron, *Don Juan*, Canto I, XIX)[15]

The outdated, military-hero kind of courage was relatively easy, it is suggested; Holk could probably have managed the task of boarding a Swedish flagship under fire and exploding its powder-hold, like the Danish hero Otto Rud (V, 135). So Ebba challenges Holk to demonstrate 'true' courage, daring him, in her mock-heroic tone, to be man enough to 'board' her (another Swede!) and demonstrate *Rücksichtslosigkeit* (ruthlessness) or 'Heldenmut der Leidenschaft' (the courage of passion).

The authentic heroic act, however, is one of restraint or resistance. In accepting Ebba's challenge, Holk becomes a new edition of the unheroic hero, indeed the *ultimate* unheroic hero, more fully developed than Leo Treibel, with less dignity than Botho, and unable to plead an excuse like Waldemar in *Stine*. In the discussion (chapter 25) on the subject of 'what is decadence?', the courtier Lundbye, like Fontane (and surely, if she were honest, like Ebba herself) has no doubt that what Ebba calls a 'weakness' – the *rejection* of sexual temptation, 'ein Dekadenzfall' ('a phenomenon of decadence') – is not much in evidence in this modern age: 'Das Moderne verurteilt solche Schwäche von Grund aus' ('The modern age condemns such weakness entirely'; V, 174). Fontane is combatting in this indirect form a genuine misconception of his modern age, that progressiveness requires immorality, and that immorality is a courageous stance. He is advocating a genuinely old-fashioned, indeed classical, morality of restraint.

The crowning irony of the novel's events is the sequel to Holk's surrender to Ebba's increasingly blatant sexual invitation. Having rescued himself and her from the fire which breaks out in the tower, Holk is acclaimed by the press as 'Der Held des Tages' ('The hero of the hour'). It is understandable that his reaction is to exclaim: 'Der Held! Und wie wenig heldisch war ihm zumute' ('The hero! But he was far from feeling heroic'; V, 185). For, by his light-headed affair with Ebba, he had already forfeited all claim to be a 'hero' in any sense but that of reflex reaction to an emergency. The essence of the heroic, as described in chapter 2 above, is independence of mind and action; but Holk merely *reacts*, in response to the stimuli of Ebba's strategies, or the danger of fire.

The conflagration in the ancient castle is an eloquent symbolic statement of the fire of passion in a subject incapable of containing the heat.[16] Just as the move to Fredericksborg means an intensified awareness of the archaic, historical aspects of the court as an institution, it means also a more concentrated exposure of Holk to the new, in the shape of Ebba and her ultra-modern views. The fire-symbol has a dual aspect. One of its components is implicit in the discussion between Pastor Schleppegrell and Doctor Bie, as to the desirability of heating the old tower to modern standards, the imposition of the new upon the old: ' "Ach", lachte Bie, "Du hast wieder historisches Bedenken. Ein Turm, in dem man zweihundert Jahre gefroren hat, in dem muß weiter gefroren werden... Ich für meine Person, ich bin für warmsitzen"' (" "Oh", laughed Bie, "There you are again with your historical reservations. If people have been freezing in a tower for two hundred years, they must go on freezing there... For my part, I like to be snug"'; V, 169). The other aspect, the suggestion that the heat is that of passion, is made explicit by the information that Ebba's Swedish maid, Karin, has a shrewd idea of what she is doing when she stokes the old iron stove in the tower on the doubly-fateful night: 'Sie war darin überaus erfahren, und Wärme, wie sie wußte, kam der Liebe zustatten' ('She had plenty of experience and knew that warmth was an aid to love'; V, 168–9). And the final comment on the whole affair is supplied by Schleppegrell: 'Es ist der größte Leichtsinn. Und überall Tannäpfel und kienen Holz und die Dielen und Verschläge so wurmstichig wie Pfeifenzunder' ('It is the greatest irresponsibility. And with fir-cones and pinewood everywhere and the floorboards and partitions as worm-eaten as tinder'; V, 170).

In a continuing state of *Leichtsinn* (irresponsibility), Graf Holk reads quite wrongly the 'sign' that has been given him, his escape from the fire. So besotted is he that he assumes he has been spared in order to start a new life with Ebba. Their rescue, he knows, was due to the fact that he had previously happened to spy out the land and spot the possibility of access from the tower to an adjoining roof. 'Was hat uns gerettet?... daß ich, weil alles so hell und klar dalag, in aller Deutlichkeit sehen konnte...', etc. ('What was it that saved us?... the fact that, because everything was so bright and clear, I could see it perfectly plainly...'; V, 182).

Thus the blind man praises his own clear-sightedness, in a failure of self-knowledge which is a central motif of the novel. There is perhaps more and profounder introspection on the part of the protagonists here than in any other Fontane novel, but never the self-knowledge to prevent disaster.

What precludes greater self-knowledge, and the satisfying sublimation of Holk's basic drives, is the lack of sufficient culture and education. To accept this is to submit to one of those periodic shifts of perspective Fontane demands from his reader. It is axiomatic for any student of his works that Fontane is not enthusiastic about formal education. The point is so familiar as to need no elaboration, and it should suffice to quote, as one example of many, Czako's remark on this subject in *Der Stechlin*: 'Waren die Patriarchen examiniert, oder Moses oder Christus? Die Pharisäer waren examiniert. Und da sehen Sie, was dabei herauskommt' ('Had the Patriarchs passed exams, Moses or Christ? The Pharisees passed exams. And you see what comes of it'; VIII, 191), a remark which can safely be taken to carry Fontane's blessing. And yet in *Unwiederbringlich* (as, in the final analysis, in *Frau Jenny Treibel*) education is valued highly, its value manifested chiefly in its absence in the hero. Not only is Holk generally deficient in cultivation of the mind ('denn Holk war ziemlich unliterarisch', 'for Holk was fairly unliterary'; V, 6), but he is also the archetypal dilettante in those things that he *does* turn his hand to, such as gentleman-farming, in which he admits to being less proficient than his brother-in-law, and proud of it: 'Er war kein großer Landwirt wie sein Schwager Arne, ja, tat sich was damit, es *nicht* zu sein' ('He was no great farmer like his brother-in-law Arne, indeed, he even made much of *not* being one'; V, 13). He despises his son's tutor Strehlke, a poor physical specimen, and would prefer to see Axel remain untutored: 'Du wirst noch ein richtiger Holkscher Jäger werden, und offen gestanden, das wäre mir das liebste. Das Lernen ist für andere' ('We can still make a proper Holk and a huntsman out of you, and frankly I'd prefer it. Learning is for others'; V, 53). What Holk really believes in is Nature, the unreformed Old Adam, the natural man. ' "Wie man in die Wiege gelegt wird, so wird man in den Sarg gelegt". Erziehung tut nicht viel' (' "As we're laid in the cradle, so we're laid in the grave." Education doesn't add very much'; V, 35). He is an unconscious primitivist who believes in the pre-intellectual virtues. As Christine rightly says of him: 'du willst dein richtiges irdisches Paradies und willst...die Nachtigallen darin schlagen hören' ('you want your regular earthly paradise and to hear the nightingales give song there'; V, 193). This reference to the earthly paradise is an echo of Holk's description of himself, in his first conversation at court, as 'ein Träger und Bringer alles Idyllischen' ('a bearer and bringer of everything idyllic'), and his subsequent allusion to Arcadia (V, 78: one can follow the metaphor through – Ebba is a Scandinavian version of Eve, she tempts him to partake of the apple of the tree of knowledge, he is expelled from paradise...). While Fontane considers naturalness to be supreme (compare the words of Professor Schmidt at the end of *Frau Jenny Treibel*, 'Natur ist Sittlichkeit und überhaupt die Hauptsache', 'Nature is decency and the thing that matters'; and also the letter to James Morris of 13 May 1898), he maintains that Nature alone is not enough. The letter quoted in the next chapter in connexion with the dénouement of *Frau Jenny Treibel* puts the point succinctly, incidentally acting as an indictment of Holk: 'Wir haben nur das bißchen Kunst und Wissenschaft, das uns, in ehrlicher Arbeit, über uns erhebt und haben als Bestes – die Natur' ('We have only a small portion of art and knowledge which, with honest work, raises us above ourselves, and best of all we have – Nature'; to Mete Fontane, 13 March 1888).

Nature by itself does not achieve much (cf. the implication of old Stechlin that 'die Natur ist dumm', 'Nature is stupid'; VIII, 25). Holk's daughter Asta sums up the essence of the dilettante when she says of her piano-playing 'Ich habe bloß Lust und kein Talent' ('I just have enthusiasm, but no talent'; V, 18). Significantly, she clearly benefits from the (pietist) Gnadenfrei education her mother has insisted upon, in the face of resistance from her father, for in chapter 34 we read 'Asta hatte sich während ihrer Pensionstage zu einer kleinen Virtuosin auf dem Klavier ausgebildet' ('during her time at boarding school, Asta had made herself quite a little virtuoso at the piano'; V, 218). The discipline imposed upon her, it is implied, was necessary to counteract that dangerous wildness which is so like Effi Briest's, and so catastrophic in the case of the latter. (See V, 54: ' "Und alles, was Märchen ist, ist meine Schwärmerei, meine Passion"... Gleich danach hörte man denn auch eine Chopinsche Etüde, freilich nicht recht flüssig und mit vielen Fehlern', ' "I love, I adore anything to do with fairy-tales"... This was immediately followed by the sound of a Chopin *étude*, admittedly not quite fluent and with many mistakes.') The combination of Holk's willingness to let nature take its course, and Asta's romanticism (this too inherited from him) has all the ingredients of an *Effi Briest* tragedy, contained *in nuce* in Asta's words to her friend: 'Wenn es nach dem Papa ginge, so ginge alles ruhig weiter, bis jemand käme und mich haben wollte' ('If it were up to Papa, everything would go on just as it is until somebody came and asked for my hand'; V, 46).

Holk has few skills, very little outlet for his modest talents, and therefore only a limited capacity to extrovert his psychic energies. Ebba as usual puts her finger on the truth:

Alles in allem, *er hat nicht die rechte Schule gehabt* und seine bescheidenen Talente nicht nach der ihm entsprechenden Seite entwickeln können. Er mußte Sammler werden oder Vorstand eines Asyls für gefallene Mädchen oder auch bloß Pomologe. (V, 117; my italics)

(All in all, he has not had the right training to allow him to develop his modest talents in a suitable direction. He should have been a collector or director of an institute for fallen women or even just a pomologist.

Ebba is right: Holk is 'displaced' (a theme which takes us back to an earlier chapter of this book and the suggestion of 'displacement' as an excuse for the unheroic and unpoetic qualities of the nineteenth-century hero). But so is his wife, who should either have been an eighteenth-century 'schöne Seele', or the wife of a hero, or yet again, as Holk suggests, an educationist: '...und wenn du nicht als Baronesse Arne geboren wärest, so wärest du Basedow oder Pestalozzi geworden' ('...and if you hadn't been born Baroness Arne, you would have become a Pestalozzi or a Basedow'; V, 35). It is this latter quality in the Gräfin which creates the extreme discrepancy between the married couple, as proponents of 'nature' and 'nurture' respectively, and this discrepancy it is, above all, which makes the necessary mutual adjustment in the Holks' marriage so very difficult, exacerbated by Christine's tendency to confuse 'mind' with 'soul', religion with education; in turn making education a subject almost impossible for Holk to discuss with his wife.

Christine, who is outwardly pietistic and contemplative, is in fact very aggressively religious. Much as she believes she longs for *Ruhe* (a state which is *her* pseudo-poetic – in fact morbid – affective centre, as the 'romantic–mysterious' is Holk's), her passionate resentment of Holk's behaviour is borne out by the fact that she never achieves resignation and peace after the re-establishment of their marriage, as she might have been expected to do had she been the truly devout soul she thinks herself to be. Her suicide bears witness to the unendurable strength of her feelings, and, paradoxically enough, it is the first occasion on which she bends her inflexible Christian principles, to the dismay of her paid companion, Julie von Dobschütz, who, in a postscript, draws attention to this anomaly inherent in Christine's action. She had harboured suspicions that the Gräfin contemplated suicide,

Ahnungen, die niederzukämpfen mir nur dadurch gelang, daß ich mir den christlichen Sinn und die ganze Glaubensfestigkeit der teuren Entschlafenen vergegenwärtigte, den christlichen Sinn, der das Leben trägt, solange Gott es will. (V, 221)

(. . . forebodings which I could only suppress by recalling the Christian spirit and the strength of faith of the dear departed; the Christian spirit which bears with life for as long as God wills it.)

Even Christine's morbid fixation on her dead child (for the benefit of whose memory she obsessively plans the new vault), unrelieved by her pleasure in the two who live on, demonstrates her lack of Christian resignation; 'to guard one's dead' is a flight *from* death, not a religious acceptance of it.[17] The repression which Christine imposes upon herself turns the preoccupation with death into a destructive anxiety. 'Only if Eros

– the life instinct – can affirm the life of the body can the death instinct affirm death, and in affirming death magnify life.'[18] Christine's affirmation of death is spurious, because she cannot affirm life. Her suicide is not a resigned seeking of death, but a reproach to life.

Nonetheless, Holk concedes at some level of his consciousness that Christine is in the right, at least in the basic tenets of her faith. A dark struggle with his conscience is needed before he can convince himself that his intention to separate from his wife and marry Ebba is justified, and in the course of this struggle, he carefully avoids the naming of two powerful words, *Gott* and *Himmel*:

Er rief beide nicht an, weil er unklar, aber doch ganz bestimmt herausfühlte, daß er im Dienst einer schlechten Sache focht und nicht wagen dürfte, den Namen seines Gottes mißbräuchlich ins Spiel zu ziehen.
(V, 183)

(He did not invoke either, because he felt, obscurely but quite definitely, that he was fighting in a wrong cause and dared not improperly call upon the name of his God.)

There is a network of night and day, light and dark motifs (the seduction and fire scene takes place at night) which suggests that Christine, despite all her shortcomings, is the voice of duty for Holk, while Ebba corresponds to the promptings of instinct (superego versus id). More than once the temptations of the night are driven away by daylight and thoughts of his wife, as for example in chapter 17:

Holk freute sich [am anderen Morgen], weil ihm aufrichtig daran lag, all den unliebsamen Betrachtungen, wie sie diese Weiber, Ebba mit eingerechnet, in ihm angeregt hatten, entrissen zu werden. Und dazu war nichts geeigneter als ein Brief von Christine. (V, 114)

(Holk was glad [next morning] because he genuinely welcomed the distraction from all the unwholesome reflections which these women, Ebba included, had provoked in him. And nothing was better suited to that purpose than a letter from Christine.)

The contrast is more vividly conjured up in chapter 18, however:

Ebba war eine Rakete, die man, solange sie stieg, mit einem staunenden 'ah' begleitete, dann aber war's wieder vorbei, schließlich doch alles nur Feuerwerk, alles künstlich; Christine dagegen war wie das einfache Licht des Tages. (V, 122)

(Ebba was a rocket whose ascent, as long as it lasted, was accompanied by an admiring 'ah', but then it was all over; it was all fireworks, in the end; everything was artificial: Christine by contrast was like the simple light of day.)

The taut construction of the novel can be seen in a prefiguration of this image of Ebba as a rocket exploding against the night sky,[19] which occurs in an early chapter in conjunction with the theme of literary culture, itself to be echoed later during the episode of the Graf's London sojourn. Baron Arne, accompanying Seminardirektor Schwarzkoppen towards his home, comments on a rocket shooting up on the horizon, and connects it with some celebration at the court of the King (V, 29). He uses the opportunity to distance himself from court life and all its degenerate ways, for he shuns all contact with the royal household: 'was mich persönlich angeht, ich lese lieber "David Copperfield" oder die "Drei Musketiere"' ('personally, I'd rather read *David Copperfield* or *The Three Musketeers*'). Unliterary and uncultivated as he is at the beginning of the novel, Graf Holk later, in his London exile, creates a life precisely out of literary and cultural contacts, including Charles Dickens, whose *David Copperfield*[20] (a novel he reads to the exclusion of all others from Dickens's prolific pen) he has the opportunity to praise to the author's face 'bei Gelegenheit eines Whitebait-Diners in Greenwich' ('on the occasion of a whitebait-dinner in Greenwich'; V, 206)! (This development seems more credible if we recall that during an early stay in London Fontane was a neighbour of Dickens in Tavistock Square, and forebore to introduce himself to the great man only because 'ich weiß, daß er von Deutschen überlaufen und mit den üblichen Bewunderungsphrasen gelangweilt wird', 'I know he's overrun with Germans and is bored by the stock expressions of admiration'. See *Aus England und*

Schottland, 'Tavistock-Square und der Straßen-Gudin', XVII, 42.)

In his new conversion to culture, Holk comes closer to a position from which some compromise with Christine might be possible. And there is indeed an apparent resolution, along lines of compromise. Life has taught Holk by hardship, in exile and isolation, some of the lessons he disdained to learn in a less perilous way. What tips the balance against a continued happy outcome is the Gräfin's inability to conquer *her* natural self, the woman's jealousy which will never let her forget she is second best in the eyes of the man she has married (V, 207). Her failed education in the natural, too, can in the last analysis be laid at Holk's door, for the lack of one piece of vital knowledge is perhaps the ultimate cause of his undoing: recurrently throughout the novel he is told 'you do not know women!' (Cf. V, 125, 155, 201.) He failed to perceive and respond to the woman in Christine, and it was the woman in her which wreaked the final vengeance.

Unwiederbringlich is the tragedy of a marriage brought down by lack of knowledge: of self, of the world, of women.[21] The latter, knowledge of women, has for Fontane almost the status of a criterion of civilization itself. Holk did not know that Christine's sermons to him were appeals for his love. Of the crucial conversation in chapter 29, for example, it was said above that Christine's martyr-complex makes her provoke Holk to a confession that he wants to divorce her (V, 192). The martyr-complex is an appeal to Holk for reassurance, for the heroic, manly response that is, sadly, not in him. She, in her repression and unfamiliarity with the ways of Eros, takes the stance of other middle-aged women defending their love and marriage against internal and external onslaughts; anguish and jealousy are expressed through an appeal to principle, and in her case in an unbearable 'unco guid' manner. Failure is almost invariably inherent in this approach, and yet the dignity of a matron and wife of many years standing rules out the disguise of seductress which seems to be the only alternative.

If Holk had read (instead of Walter Scott!) Dickens's novel of marriage, *David Copperfield*, at the right stage, their marriage might have avoided this painful dilemma and achieved more poetry, less disastrous prose. The poetry was there beneath the surface, after all, emerging occasionally, in the Gräfin's assertion that 'eine Ehe, wenn nur noch etwas Liebe da ist, hat doch auch immer noch eine andere Seite' ('a marriage always has another side to it as long as there is still some love'; V, 57); or in her description (ibid.) of moments of warmth and affection, unfortunately suppressed: 'Und dann ...möchte ich auf ihn zufliegen und ihm sagen: "Bester Holk". Sieh Julie, das kommt auch vor; aber niemand sieht es und niemand hört es' ('And then...I'd like to run to him and say: "dearest Holk". You see, Julie, that does happen; but nobody sees it and nobody hears it') (including, of course – and this is the point – Holk himself!). The submerged poetry surfaces above all in glimpses of Holk's frustrated poetic aspirations (awakened from their dormant state first of all by Ebba), expressed in images of 'die Nachtigallen schlagen hören' ('hearing the nightingales sing') and 'Blumen auf unsren Weg streuen' ('strewing flowers in our path'). The latter metaphor, particularly, recurs as a contrast to the increasingly sober, prosaic tone of the correspondence between the couple. Christine having failed to 'strew flowers in their path' (V, 193), Holk turns to the 'romantic' in the shape of Ebba, who hurls the very same phrase back in his face ('Statt alle Treibhäuser des Landes zu plündern und mir Blumen auf den Weg zu streuen...', 'Instead of raiding all the hothouses in the country and strewing flowers in my path'; V, 202).

Belatedly, after his London exile and the education he undergoes there, Graf Holk seeks to resurrect the poetry of his marriage. On the route to the ceremony of rededication in Holkeby Church, 'Alle hielten Körbe in den Händen und streuten Blumen über den Weg' ('Everyone carried baskets and strewed flowers over the path'; V, 213), a symbolic gesture all too soon repeated, for the last time, at Christine's funeral: 'die Mädchen

von Holkeby standen, wie damals beim Erscheinen des hoch-
zeitlichen Zuges, das Dorf entlang und streuten ihre Blumen.
Aber heute waren es weiße Astern, die sie streuten...' ('the
girls of Holkeby stood, as they had earlier when the wedding
procession appeared, along the village street and strewed their
flowers. But today it was white asters that they strewed...';
V, 220). The gesture now conveys mourning for the lost possibility of poetry. 'Ein Herz, das sich nach Ruhe sehnte, hatte
Ruhe gefunden' ('A heart that longed for peace had found
peace'; V, 221). Christine has silenced the yearning for peace
which spoke to her so powerfully and seductively in Waib-
linger's poem, 'Die Ruh' ist wohl das Beste' ('Peace is surely
best'; V, 42). But true poetry should be for the living, not for
the dead. It is a tragedy both for Graf Holk and for Christine
that the promise of poetry is fulfilled only by death.

6 · FRAU JENNY TREIBEL

Frau Jenny Treibel, like *Mathilde Möhring*, stands at the opposite pole from the balladesque Novellen. We saw that in *Effi Briest* the poetic elements of *Ellernklipp* had been transmuted, but were still present, conveyed through the medium of the novel of society. In *Frau Jenny Treibel*, however, Fontane took up, as he did at about the same time in his *Mathilde Möhring*, the challenge of the completely prosaic milieu. This book, perhaps more than any other, raises to a conscious level a question that recurs in many nineteenth-century contexts, that of the survival of the poetic in a prosaic age. Edmund Burke made the classic statement on the victory of the prosaic, in his *Reflections on the Revolution in France*: 'But the age of chivalry is gone. That of sophisters, economists, and calculators, has succeeded; and the glory of Europe is extinguished for ever.' This fear was certainly no less oppressive in late nineteenth-century Germany than it had been at the end of the previous century in an England experiencing the first far-reaching effects of the Industrial Revolution.

'Poetry or prose?': the question is one of the most obvious themes of the novel. Frau Jenny herself, with her persistent claim to a poetic nature attuned to 'higher' things, never lets us forget the theme, although her claim to poetry is in fact merely another aspect of her profound philistinism.

To say that Fontane presents a prosaic milieu, and predominantly prosaic characters, is not to say that he himself succumbs to prose. The poetic yield of unpoetic material can be seen in the sheer exuberance of this novel; its pastiche of bourgeois styles, for example, in passages of soliloquy or in letters, like the superb epistle Jenny addresses to her Hamburg in-law Helene (VII, 133), when Treibels and Munk-Thompsons bury their differences in the face of a determined attack from Corinna. The exuberance can be seen in dialogue such as that in which Corinna manipulates Leopold Treibel into proposing

131

to her at Halensee (VII, 113), a *jeu d'esprit* on Corinna's part which, with its cool use of foreign words (*confessions, fait accompli*), its clever tactics, its mock-modest confession ('denn die Liebe, das seh ich klar, ist demütig, und ich fühle, wie meine Fehler von mir abfallen', 'for love, I see clearly, is humble, and I can feel my faults dropping away from me'), and its sentimental and stylized references to Nature ('hier unter diesem Waldesdom, drin es geheimnisvoll rauscht und dämmert', 'here beneath this forest canopy, with its mysterious twilight and rustling sounds...'), is set off by Leopold's words 'ich habe nie große Worte gemacht' ('I have never used grand phrases'), and by the fact that his passionate declaration of love finds its way into reported speech, which undermines it even more effectively than does its obvious element of self-delusion ('Leopold beteuerte, daß er nicht bloß wolle, daß er es auch werde. Denn wenn die Liebe demütig und bescheiden mache, was gewiß richtig sei, so mache sie sicherlich auch stark...', etc., 'Leopold declared that it was not only his wish but his intention. For if love made one humble and modest, which was surely true, it certainly also made one strong...'.

Such scenes can be relished despite the prosaic and calculating aim Corinna has in mind, the annexation of Leopold and, ultimately, the Treibel villa. The poetic quality of the novel, despite its prosaic setting, lies also in its muted satire, which, because ironic, indirect and humorous, is never as biting as Fontane's well-known stated intention for the book suggests: 'Zweck der Geschichte: das Hohle, Phrasenhafte, Lügnerische, Hochmütige, Hartherzige des Bourgeois-Standpkunktes zu zeigen' ('The aim of the story: to expose the hollowness, emptiness, mendaciousness, arrogance and hard-heartedness of the bourgeois standpoint'; letter to his son Theodor, 9 May 1888).

The central theme of the novel is aspirations of one sort or another, and its exploration of this theme within a fairly restricted range is remarkably coherent. Characters attempt to find their level, in keeping with the true motto of the book, Pindar's 'werde, der du bist', one of Professor Schmidt's favourite quotations. Critics are fond of pointing out the similarity to the *Lustspiel* (stage comedy) tradition, and correspondingly the theme is explored both on the serious and the comic levels, though the seriousness is never more than implicit. The results of floundering, philistine attempts on the part of the bourgeois to find the *bon ton* and the elegance they think fitting to their wealth and station are hilariously evident in their very language, epitomized by Jenny's remonstration to her husband, 'du könntest dich mit deinen Vergleichen etwas höher hinaufschrauben' ('you might try to raise the tone of your comparisons a notch or two'). The exchange in which this remark occurs, Jenny's and Treibel's contretemps in chapter 12 over the news of Leopold's engagement to Corinna, is surely one of the best reproductions of a marital row in nineteenth-century fiction (VII, 128–32). From her point of view, his response is linguistically totally inappropriate, representing for her the threat of a deflation of her status (a threat as real as if Treibel were to plunge a pin into that air-cushion which literally raises her above all her fellows at the dinner table in chapter 3, VII, 24). Jenny falls back on the forms of good language, but she matches Treibel's inappropriateness with her own, with the difference that, while his tone is too low, hers is too high. And her high-falutin' tone is all the more comic since her own earlier reaction to the news of the engagement was couched in language even more vulgar than Treibel's: she expostulates that 'die Treibels wachsen nicht auf Bäumen und können nicht von jedem, der vorbeigeht, heruntergeschüttelt werden' ('the Treibels don't grow on trees and they can't be shaken down by just any passer-by'; VII, 126).

Comparatives in general, and 'high' and 'low' comparisons in particular, recur on practically every page of the book and form its texture. As in *Mathilde Möhring*, characters define their status, to their own satisfaction, by reference to others above and below them. Jenny confuses the issue by insisting on the identification of high social standing with spiritual and aesthetic aspirations. In a manner typical of the petty-bourgeois, snobbery and sentimentality conflate 'higher things' with social superiority (see VII, 109 – 'Leopold...soll höher hinaus', 'Leopold is intended for higher things').

Comparisons abound on every page: of Schmidts and Bürstenbinders, of Hamburg and Berlin, Prussia and England, crabs and lobsters, blondes and brunettes, Halensee and Capri, the present and the past, 'das Ethische' and 'das Moralische' (the 'ethical' and the 'moral'; VII, 10), envy and love (VII, 122), the poetic and the historic (VII, 63) and the poetic and the prosaic (VII, 10, 26, and *passim*). Superlatives are used just as liberally, if not more so, as though to settle any possible arguments raised by comparisons. As 'das Höhere' (the 'higher') is the key term of comparison, so 'das Höchste' (the 'highest') represents the absolute, only to be trumped by a facetious use of the super-superlative 'das Idealste' (the 'most ideal') by Treibel ('das Idealste bleibt doch immer eine Soubrette', 'a soubrette is still the most ideal'; VII, 39). Comparatives and superlatives imply choices, and choice is inevitably involved both in the maintenance of a life-style and in attempting to break away from it, to realize aspirations.

The framework of the novel is provided by three such problems of choice and aspiration. All three are formulated in terms of a campaign directed against Frau Jenny Treibel. Corinna Schmidt faces the choice of maintaining, as a teacher's wife, the rather limited life-style of a teacher's daughter, or of exploiting her talents to acquire the grand style of a bourgeoise in the *Gründerzeit* (the post-unification period of business expansion). The initial campaign to catch Leopold is easily won, but real victory would lie in deflating Jenny's colossal ego, and this implies a power-struggle that Corinna could only win at the expense of all that really matters to her. It is only in the course of the war with Jenny, however, that Corinna learns to recognize what *is* of value to her.

Similarly, Leopold's attempt to marry Corinna is a move essentially directed against Jenny. Having failed to assert himself in so trivial a matter of choice as 'coffee or milk' during his solitary breakfasts at Treptow, Leopold elects to join battle on the rather more important ground of his choice of a bride. He only gains the courage to do so because Corinna seems to be mettlesome enough to protect the two of them from Jenny's wrath.

Treibel senior creates for himself a similar option, the decision to enter politics: and this, too, is an act of defiance of Jenny as well as an attempt (in which she has no faith) to fulfil her ambition, and his own, to improve on the title of *Kommerzienrat* (Commercial Counsellor) with which they have had to content themselves so far. All three attempts are initiatives on the part of the participants which the respective sequels show to have been false moves, out of character for each of them. Like his father, in his parliamentary candidature for Tirpitz-Zossen, Leopold conducts his campaign from a distance (a fatal flaw seen also in Innstetten's wooing of Effi Briest by correspondence) and, again like Treibel senior, he takes the word for the deed. Once he has talked the enterprise out of his system, Leopold takes no further action. The same, very Fontane-esque, character-trait is to be found also in Corinna, however.

All three allow their relationship to Frau Jenny Treibel to dominate their actions. She is 'was fest steht' ('what stands fast') ('unentwegt', 'constant', is one of her favourite words), the rock around which the movement in the novel flows. The most limited character in the novel thus conditions the attitudes of the rest. It is in relation to the stream flowing around it that we judge the rock's massiveness and its powers of resistance. By the same token, the individual initiatives of the three characters, Corinna, Leo and Treibel senior, are not individual at all but mere reactions. It is in their retreat from their respective initiatives that the real qualities of the three are differentiated. Individualism, as we saw in the chapter on '*Poesie* and *Prosa*', is one of Fontane's highest values. Leo and his father cannot be said to reassert their individualism by renouncing their aspirations, for the former never possessed any distinctive personality in the first place; and the latter simply withdraws from politics because his very first political act, his disastrous choice of an agent, revealed that by temperament he is totally unsuited to political life. Corinna, on the other hand, comes from a family and a class of individualists. Schmidt and his circle, as schoolmasters, are independent to the point of eccentricity, in the long tradition of dominies accustomed to the unchallenged airing of their opinions in the classroom. In their gatherings, 'wie sich von selbst versteht, zerfiel die Gesellschaft in fast ebenso viele Parteien, wie sie Mitglieder zählte. . . ' ('as is self-evident, the group fell into almost as many different parties as there were members present. . . '; VII, 51). *Quot homines, tot sententiae*: the appropriate classical quotation (from Terence) is only thinly disguised by Fontane's free German rendering. The typical professional deformation of the schoolmasters, the fault of their virtue – in the phrase of George Sand quoted by Schmidt, VII, 61 – is 'knowing better', and the conviction that they can invariably improve on whatever their colleagues are trying to express. The comparisons *they* care about are kept within their class; their standards are self-satisfied internalized ones. Corinna is the full heir to their self-sufficiency. Unlike the other two initiators of action, she has a genuine choice, in that she could undoubtedly have her way and marry into the class of industrialists if she really wanted to. But, unlike Leo and Treibel in this also, she reasserts her individualism in rejecting her 'trophy', Leo. Her decision does not have personal implications only, but symbolic ones too. She becomes the standard-bearer of individualism in defiance of the pressures of late nineteenth-century mammonism.

As a novel of aspiration, *Frau Jenny Treibel* is a product of the German *Gründerzeit*, and its thematic concerns go to the heart of the age. It is an era in which the tune is called by the prosaic bourgeois, a period not so much of rattling ballot-boxes (in Carlyle's phrase) as of rustling bank-books. Thus it is Jenny, with her habit of imperious command, who begins the action of the novel by venturing forth in full bourgeois state[1] to summon Corinna to a dinner party given for the sake of Mr Nelson, a business contact of her son Otto. The resolution of the novel, in the traditional comedy-form of a wedding scene, is a genuine one, but it does not disguise the brute fact that the most benighted members of society continue to condition the reactions of the rest. Professor Schmidt's famous parting words, 'Geld is Unsinn, Wissenschaft ist Unsinn, Professor auch' ('Money is nonsense, learning is nonsense, professors too') – whose context, we should bear in mind, includes his happily drunken state, the fact that the Treibels are on his territory, and that he has got what he has always wanted – point to the relief of being able for once to drop snobbish distinctions which Schmidt would by nature and calling prefer to see abolished (as well as some others dearer to him: we shall return to the point later). But we can take it that *Jenny* would never let these distinctions go, for she is the spirit of the 'verdammte neue Zeit' ('the damned new age'; VII, 69), whose very soul is the observation of nuances of social snobbery. Outsiders like Corinna can envy the bourgeois, feel vexed, irritated, exasperated by them, but they are powerless. Unless they are gifted with natural stupidity and a spirit as profoundly prosaic as Jenny's, they cannot enjoy having what Jenny has.

Yet to turn one's back on the present and ignore it is no solution. There is no wholly intact moral position from which to condemn this age. Schmidt, for example, is no dinosaur, but is fully aware of the shortcomings of the past. Schoolmasters in earlier generations claimed an authority which had less to do with substance than with externals, like those very (bourgeois) *Äußerlichkeiten* (surface appearances) which are one of the most repugnant aspects of the *new* age. Professor Schmidt has a certain poetic sensitivity to the necessity of change, an awareness of the fact that to idealize the past is only to reveal weakness, an inadequacy in adapting to the present.

Schmidt demonstrates the same awareness that was described above as the wisdom of *Effi Briest*; as we feel ourselves superior to the past, he remarks, so will the future see itself as superior to us (VII, 55), suggesting by implication that 'what we live so completely is a myth – which will appear as such to men of a future century, and perhaps to ourselves a few years hence...' (see chapter 3, p. 75 above). This is more than a political awareness: it is a poetic view of life conditioned by time. Schmidt embodies the spirit of Fontane's writing, and the attraction which makes him more accessible than some other nineteenth-century novelists, especially German ones: the complexity and flexibility of his approach, the absence of moralizing and didacticism, and above all the sophisticated demonstration of the relativity of all social forms and conventions. He has already built into his works the relativization that – to the detriment of lesser writers – the passage of time always effects. Schmidt refuses to make a fetish out of the collective past, as the other teachers do – in a way that recalls, even to the very words, Jenny's idealizing of her *own* past. (Compare VII, 54, 'Ja, Schmidt, *das* waren Zeiten, da verlohnte sich's, ein Lehrer und ein Direktor zu sein', 'Yes, Schmidt, *those* were the days, it was worth being a teacher and a headmaster then'; and Jenny's reminiscence in chapter 1 – 'Ach, waren das Zeiten gewesen!', 'Ah, what days those were!'; VII, 8.) Schmidt is prepared to concede, too, the possibility that 'die höhere Wissenschaft' (the higher learning) – another comparative phrase, suspiciously reminiscent of the role of 'das Höhere' (higher things) in Jenny's pseudo-poetic vocabulary – is outmoded, even moribund:

Ich glaub es nicht. Aber wenn es wäre, wenn die höhere Weltanschauung, das heißt das, was wir so nennen, wenn das alles fallen müßte, nun, so laß es fallen. Schon Attinghausen, der doch selber alt war, sagte: 'Das Alte stürzt, es ändert sich die Zeit.' Und wir stehen sehr stark vor solchem Umwandlungsprozeß, oder richtiger wir sind schon drin.

(VII, 56)

(I don't believe it. But if it were so, if the higher *Weltanschauung*, that is to say what we call by that name, if all that had to go, well, then let it go. Even Attinghausen, who was old himself, said 'The old world is foundering; times are changing.' And we shall see that process of change very soon indeed, or, more correctly, we are already in the midst of it.)

There is a prefiguration, in the Schmidt–Corinna constellation, of old Stechlin's relationship to his son, in Fontane's last novel. If Schmidt is prepared, however reluctantly, to accept the new age, it is not surprising that the next generation of Schmidts, represented by Corinna, should positively embrace it. It is made clear that Corinna herself is a child of progress, the intelligent and emancipated – but not *too* emancipated – young woman who can make the character of the times an excuse for her materialist ambitions: '. . . ein Hang nach Wohlleben, der jetzt alle Welt beherrscht, hat mich auch in der Gewalt, ganz so wie alle anderen. . .' ('. . . just like everybody else, I'm in the grip of a fondness for luxurious living – the whole world's dominated by it nowadays'; VII, 49). The mammonism which Fontane had foreseen many years earlier would spread from England to Germany, has now conquered.

Corinna, then, becomes a kind of natural test-case providing evidence towards an answer to the question: why *not* adopt the prevailing standards of the new plutocracy? What standpoint can a modern young woman like Corinna perceive from which to condemn the present age? After all, the pursuit of an affluent life-style, at the level of the Treibels, is only a modest reflection of the self-indulgent European 'belle époque', that Age of Extravagance from the late nineteenth century to the outbreak of the Great War, an age which stressed the glitter of external appearances (*Äußerlichkeiten*) and sartorial elegance above all; an emphasis reflected in the many references to dress and smart turn-out in *Frau Jenny Treibel*.[2]

Certainly, Corinna will need all the histrionic talent she commands in order to overcome her natural good sense and play the part of a Frau Jenny Treibel: but the dinner party and the proposal scene at Halensee indicate that she has no lack of that talent, among others (cf. VII, 68). However, in a Prussian context, the question that Fontane is raising may be a more serious one than whether or not Corinna might be able to sustain the role of a *nouvelle riche*. Corinna seeks wealth and social advantage inevitably at somebody else's expense, in this case Jenny's, for her declared aim is territorial expansion. She calculates that when Treibel dies (which can only be a matter of a decade or so), as Leo's wife she will take over the villa, ousting Jenny from power (VII, 68).

We are reminded that in its earliest origins, i.e. Brandenburg, the Prussian State had recurrently been faced with a choice: either that it should be absorbed by its more powerful neighbours, above all by Poland, or that it should continue to grow at the expense of others.[3] This was the dynamic of earlier Prussian history: the law of survival left little room for moral scruples. Much later, the very formation of the Second Reich was still predicated upon territorial aggression. During the years 1864–6 the Schleswig-Holstein question (over which, as it happens, Fontane believed Prussia to be in the right: see p. 109 above) was used by Bismarck to subserve his diplomacy, the chief end of which was the aggrandisement of Prussia. The duchies were occupied and eventually annexed to Prussia in 1865. Another spectacular annexation took place after the defeat of France in 1870 when the French, though German-speaking, province of Alsace, together with part of Lorraine, was ceded to Prussia. Only then, in January 1871, was the work of expansion crowned with the proclamation of the German Reich by King Wilhelm I of Prussia. I should not have dwelt so explicitly on this theme of Prussian expansionism were it not that, in an age of comparative political stability, when the slogan 'expand or go under' was no longer an excuse, Fontane was profoundly disturbed by the legacy of Prussian aggression and what he saw as the treachery involved in the furtherance of Prussian interests. (Compare Baron Osten's tirade, in chapter 7 of *Irrungen, Wirrungen*, against Bismarck and the standpoint of 'Macht gehe vor Recht', 'Might before Right'.) To quote the highly relevant sentiments of Lewin in *Vor dem Sturm*: 'wer nicht Treue hält, der ist des Todes' (I, 552). It is no surprise in *Frau Jenny Treibel* when Marcell (VII, 46) draws Corinna's attention to the carillon of the Berlin *Parochialkirche*, which at that moment is doing its best to remind her of the old teutonic virtues by chiming out the venerable tune 'Üb' immer Treu' und Redlichkeit'. ('Be always loyal and honest.' Compare Schmidt's words, VII, 59: 'Denn die Treue, von der heutzutage jeder red't, wird in Wahrheit immer rarer', 'for loyalty, on everybody's lips nowadays, is in fact becoming rarer all the time'.) Corinna chooses to misunderstand Marcell, suggesting that he is only accusing her of breaking a vow to him which she has not specifically made, since their engagement to marry rests only on a long-established tacit understanding:

'Treu' und Redlichkeit. Meinst du wirklich, daß die mir fehlen? Gegen wen versünd'ge ich mich denn durch Untreue? Gegen dich. Hab ich Gelöbnisse gemacht? Hab ich dir etwas versprochen und das Versprechen nicht gehalten?'
Marcell schwieg. (VII, 47)

('Loyalty and honesty. Do you really think I lack them? Against whom have I sinned by disloyalty? Against you. Did I make any vows? Did I promise you something and fail to keep my promise?'
Marcell was silent.)

He is accusing her principally of treason to her better self, of capitulation to the *mores* of *Gründerzeit* Prussia. In so far as she, a Schmidt, stands for the old German virtues of loyalty, *Dichtung* (poetry), and idealism (all epitomized, certainly, by her father) she is betraying the old Germany in favour of the new, for the new era meant a transition from the philosophical-literary values of Classical/Romantic German culture (Schmidt is a dedicated teacher both of the Classics and the Romantics) to the practical and materialist. The betrayal of the 'Land der Dichter und Denker' (land of writers and thinkers) by the prosaic interests of Siemens and Krupp may be a cliché, but it is one which has a solid basis in German historical consciousness, confirmed by the synopsis of modern German history provided by Lorenzen (here, if anywhere, surely Fontane's spokesman) in *Der Stechlin*:

Und dann kam die dritte Zeit...Da war das arme, elende, halb dem Untergange verfallene Land nicht von Genie, wohl aber von Begeisterung durchleuchtet, von dem Glauben an die höhere Macht des Geistigen, des Wissens und der Freiheit...Aber...die Begeisterung ist tot. Eine rückläufige Bewegung ist da...(VIII, 252–3)[4]

(And then came the third age...The poor, miserable country, half given up to its demise, was irradiated with the light, not of genius, but certainly of enthusiasm, of belief in the higher power of the intellect, knowledge and freedom...But...the enthusiasm is dead. A decline has set in.) Frau Jenny marks the transition, combining literary pretensions with hard-headed materialism.

The tension between the humanities and the new model of practical, technical or commercial man is symbolized historically in the opposition of the 'humanistische Gymnasien' (grammar schools) and the innovatory *Realschulen* (modern schools). The traditional *Gymnasien* had been engaged, prior to German unification, in an attempt to turn the clock back, replying to attacks from those of a more '*real*' (practical) and modern persuasion by reinforcing, rather than reducing, the pre-eminence of classical studies in the curriculum. It is against this sort of rearguard action, presumably, that Professor Schmidt is protesting in the speech already quoted (chapter 6, VII, 56), when he declares himself unwilling to defend the traditional stance of 'höhere Wissenschaft' (higher learning). For all his idealism and enthusiasm for his subject, he is realist enough to recognize that classical humanist education must be a lost cause, faced as it is by an invincible, and ultimately lethal, combination of commercialism and nationalism. To quote a standard Wilhelminian work on German education in the Second Reich:

Je entschiedener nun dieser humanistische Geist das Gymnasium beherrschte, je einseitiger damit die Vorbildung für die gelehrten Berufe und das akademische Studium auf die Beschäftigung mit dem klassischen Altertum gegründet war, desto lebhafter trat das Bedürfnis hervor, für diejenigen Berufsarten, die auf eine engere Fühlung mit dem praktischen Leben angewiesen waren, vor allem für Kaufleute und Techniker, eine Vorbildung moderneren und praktischeren Inhalts zu schaffen.[5]

(The more decisively this humanistic spirit dominated the grammar school, the more narrowly preparation for the learned professions and for higher education was based on the study of classical antiquity, the more pressing the need appeared to create a more modern and practical educational background, especially for those whose careers required close contact with practical life, such as businessmen and engineers.)

At a pedagogical conference in 1890, no less a spokesman than Wilhelm II himself stressed not only the practical but also the national element which classical studies had long kept at bay: German subjects, language, literature and history, had been almost entirely missing from the old *Gymnasium* syllabus. The events of 1870/71 mark a clear turning-point, after which a commercial boom combined with a surge of national pride increased the pressure for an educational system based on practical aims as well as the new national consciousness.[6]

Here is the central problem of *Frau Jenny Treibel*: to concede the inevitable eclipse of the old (as Schmidt reluctantly does) is not necessarily the same as endorsing everything that replaces it. And yet it is not easy to disentangle the fashionable identification of commerce with national progress, modernity and success. In the effort to do so, the only aid that can be relied upon is an inherited outlook which, innately, Corinna shares with her father, an attitude lying so deep as to be almost instinctive, but surfacing to combat Corinna's conscious desires – wealth, power and comfort – when the need arises. The ultimate triumph of Corinna's better self can be read as a token of Fontane's hope that the German soul is not beyond saving. That it is in jeopardy is an understandable assumption in reaction to the *Gründerzeit*.

The initiative in capitalist development was taken, and the pace set, by a rapidly expanding Berlin. The expansion of heavy industry, in Berlin and elsewhere, led to a novel expansion of the German economy, but also to a speculative and self-deceptive boom, and this in turn led to repercussions in the moral sphere in everyday social life; something which Fontane's novels both display and correct, as in *Stine*, for example, where the working-class moral outlook is in marked contrast to the degeneracy of the aristocrats and the traditional governing classes. Before the big crash of 1873, there were symptoms of moral corruption in business ethics, bank frauds and speculative fever (*Gründungsmanie*), and the prevailing Manchester liberalism was justified by a fashionable theory of social Darwinism, reflected in *Frau Jenny Treibel* as well as in *Stine*, *Die Poggenpuhls* and other Fontane novels. Certainly in *Frau Jenny Treibel* there still prevails an atmosphere of opportunism, new wealth and ruthless competition.

In this light, the question posed by the novel, however humorously, is a serious one: can the qualities of 'Treu' und Redlichkeit' survive in an age when there are no valid authorities to impose them, and when the example set at the top (Bismarck's policy of 'Macht gehe vor Recht': see *Irrungen, Wirrungen*, III, 127) is a deplorable one? The answer lies in loyalty to the self: 'werde, der du bist' ('become what you are'). But Fontane is not content simply to lay this down as a pedagogical principle. Through the example of Corinna he shows the principle in action.

The central doubt about her plan to carry off Leo is whether what is gained by intelligence can be *sustained* by intelligence. The very power of the imagination that Corinna displays in the service of *Berechnung* to achieve the engagement to Leo (VII, 111) suggests that she must eventually abandon her aim of marriage to him, or face an unhappy life after its achievement. Her fantasy is inherently in conflict with her prosaic plans. She reveals as much when, in admitting the defeat of these plans by renouncing Leo, she paints a picture of the life she *might* have led had she married him, a fantasy projection which moves further and further away from the bourgeois norms:

Ich...wäre...nach Korsika oder nach Sizilien gefahren, immer der Blutrache nach. Denn ein Bedürfnis nach Aufregung würd ich doch wohl zeitlebens gehabt haben; Leopold ist etwas schläfrig. (VIII, 161)

(I would have gone to Corsica or Sicily, following the blood-feuds. For I would always have had a need for excitement; Leopold is rather lethargic.)

The engagement itself was nothing but the expression of her

'Bedürfnis nach Aufregung' (need for excitement); the subsequent marriage would have been its opposite (as, in the case of Effi Briest, the craving for love and excitement leads to her adultery, but the subsequent affair is prosaic). Corinna undoubtedly craves power and position, but she cannot in the end go against her natural instincts.

Fontane neatly sidesteps the question of moral criteria by this equation of *Natur* with *Sittlichkeit* (cf. Schmidt's words at the end of the novel: 'Natur ist Sittlichkeit und überhaupt die Hauptsache', 'Nature is decency and the thing that matters'). As with Mathilde Möhring, there is no moral law that demands that she should hide her light under a bushel: indeed, there *is* a moral law that permits her to do the opposite – 'Das war mein gutes Recht' ('It was my perfect right'). Because Corinna's cleverness is a talent given her by nature, as in *Mathilde Möhring*, she cannot be condemned for using it. 'Soll ich mich dessen entkleiden? Soll ich mein Pfund vergraben? Soll ich das bißchen Licht, das *mir* geworden, unter den Scheffel stellen?' ('Shall I divest myself of it? Shall I bury my talent? Shall I hide the small light I am endowed with under a bushel?'; VII, 140). She goes on to give the answer herself, however, in the very assertion of her defiance of Jenny – 'ich, ich bin eine Schmidt' ('I, I am a Schmidt'). Being a Schmidt gives her gifts enough to enable her to seduce Leo and defy Jenny, but it also firmly places her in the milieu of the intelligentsia represented by her father and Marcell. Mathilde Möhring, too, belonged by nature in the schoolteaching sphere, but life offered her no such convenient alternative as that held out to Corinna by the loyal Marcell, and in that novel the heroine's true quality cannot easily emerge.

In pulling back from her 'unnatural' plans, Corinna also, incidentally, steps out of a conventional comedy role, that of the female who pursues the male while pretending not to do so. The fact that she had found her way into such a stereotype role is in itself indicative of the rather dehumanizing effect that her resort to cunning and calculation had had upon her. It underlines the point that wilful distortion of the personality has to be paid for, and that to abandon one's natural discrimination is to become in a sense *unmenschlich* (inhuman) and to move towards the ranks of those characters who, whether by choice or not, play out roles so limited as to be almost dehumanized: Honig, Lizzi, Nelson (a 'Zappelheld', puppet-hero!), Vogelsang – who is equated, in name, in appearance and in the monotony of his refrain, with the parrot that adorns the Treibels' garden – and even Helene, who denies nature completely in favour of appearances to the extent of refusing to breast-feed Lizzi because to do so is 'nicht schön' ('not nice'; VII, 78), and elevates external trivia to an almost religious status (Lizzi is 'ein Engel', 'an angel').

Discrimination is choice, and in coming back to the topic of choice we return to a function which characterizes individuals at the most basic level. The power-struggle which takes place between Jenny and Corinna is unequal from the beginning, because, as emerges in the course of the story, Jenny has a choice available to her which Corinna lacks, and that is the choice of discarding her 'ideals' in an emergency. Idealism and the poetic are dispensable luxuries. The second call Jenny pays on the Schmidts, after the engagement between Leo and Corinna, is in marked contrast to her visit in chapter 1. She is stripped for action this time, without her stage props, 'diesmal allein, ohne Fräulein Honig und ohne den Bologneser' ('alone this time, without Fräulein Honig and the Bologna dog'; VII, 137), and by implication she has also left behind all her sentimental pretensions to poetic *Bildung* (culture). The true version of this *Bildung*, however, is indivisible, not a matter of choice, but an integral part of the personality, which Corinna proves unable to discard when it comes to the final decision. What sways Corinna is a matter of instinct, once more, rather than of morality, and a matter of the aesthetic sense derived from a refinement of instinct. These, fortunately, ensure her defeat in the pitched battle with Jenny:

Wenn Geld alles ist und Herz und Sinn verengt und zum Überfluß
Hand in Hand geht mit Sentimentalität und Tränen – dann empört
sich's hier, und das hinzunehmen, wäre mir hart angekommen, wenn
ich's auch vielleicht ertragen hätte. (VII, 161)

(When money is everything and closes the heart and mind and, for good
measure, goes hand in hand with sentimentality and tears – then the
anger rises here [in my heart], and to accept all that would have come
hard to me, even if I might perhaps have endured it.)

The metaphor of battle comes readily to hand when talking of
Frau Jenny Treibel, for battle metaphors and military language
abound in the novel, a reflection of the status of the military in
the period; and more specifically, perhaps, a reflection of the
new note of menace that crept into Prussian and European
political life after 1888, when the threat of preparations for
war began to increase. Fontane's letters caught this ominous
note and accurately prophesied the conflict to come. In the
period of outward peace and stability which followed unification, during which there were no further wars between great
powers, no frontier in Europe was changed outside the Balkans,
and the German constitution remained unaltered until 1918,
the prevailing economic policy was a sinister and aggressive
one, that of protectionism and economic war of all against all.

These weighty matters may seem somewhat remote from the
Lustspiel world of *Frau Jenny Treibel*. But Fontane largely
agreed with Stifter in the contention that 'differences between
"big" and "small", or "good" and "bad", were not to be
endowed with particular emphasis'.[7] For Stifter – conducting
a polemic, as Erich Heller says, against the dramatist Hebbel
and his Hegelian themes of historical grandeur – the eruption
of a volcano is not 'greater' than a milk-pan boiling over: both
are expressions of the same natural law. So, for Fontane, the
battle between Jenny and Corinna is not a 'lesser' event than
the Battle of Trafalgar, much referred to at the dinner party
given for the mock-heroically named Mr Nelson. For Jenny, it
is a struggle for existence itself, since what is at stake is the villa
with which her existence is completely bound up. The same

qualities decide the outcome as in a 'real' battle, namely 'geniale Disposition oder ein heroischer Mut' ('a brilliant plan of battle or heroic courage'; VII, 30), the former quality being Corinna's, and the latter Jenny's. The result of the struggle will have consequences for the two contestants of a kind as far-reaching on their personal level as wars have for the lives of nations. If one cares to follow up the suggestion that the Corinna–Jenny fight implies the struggle for the soul of Germany, however, then Corinna appears as the bearer of a message to Germany to renounce, in the name of her better, less chauvinist self.

Broadly speaking, what happens in the novel is that the chief characters are made to bring their emotions or ideals into line with the reality of their everyday lives. Until Corinna takes up the challenge issued by Jenny, that is the challenge to test the authenticity of Jenny's 'poetic' sentiments, the characters inhabit a realm of open possibilities, where the imagination has free play. In the course of the novel they are forced to abandon an idealized conception of their room to manoeuvre, and accept the reality of actual choices. Treibel has to accept that politics are not for him; Corinna's dreams of wealth are abandoned. Some things only exist when kept at a distance; proximity automatically destroys them. One exceptional case is mentioned in the novel, as if to prove the rule: the example of the archaeologist Schliemann, self-educated discoverer of the site of Troy, who stands for the vision triumphantly vindicated, the ideal realized, or in other words reality brought into line with vision, rather than the reverse process demanded of the figures in Fontane's novels, that of vision reconciled with reality. (Our latter-day doubts about Schliemann are immaterial.)

A neat opposition between characters is apparent, however. Whereas both Jenny and Leopold contrive to maintain their *idealized* self-image (poetic and heroic, respectively) only at the cost of restricting their self-knowledge to a mere nodding acquaintance, Corinna by contrast can manage to be her *worse* self only in the realm of the imagination. The contrast is carried through in linguistic terms, for, where the prosaic characters (Jenny, Leo) play with poetic and heroic language and sentiments, only to discard them when life begins in earnest, their opposite numbers (the 'poetic' characters, Schmidt and Corinna) play with the prosaic, only to assert their genuinely poetic values when a vital choice is demanded of them. But even the use to which they put the prosaic argues their more poetic natures. Corinna combines prosaic material with imaginative power in a superb *tour de force* at the Treibel dinner table, in her play upon the art of *Kunststopferei* or invisible mending, which becomes a modern metaphor for the art of coquetry, and neatly expresses Corinna's calculated view of her ability to handle Leopold Treibel, in whose expensive coat (*Äußerlichkeiten*, external appearances, once more) she proposes to burn a cigarette-hole, exactly in the *heart* region, in order to return the coat next day mended so that not a mark is visible:

Und dann werd ich auftreten wie eine Künstlerin, die ich in der Tat auch bin, und werde den Rock herumgehen lassen, und wenn Sie, dear Mr Nelson, dann noch imstande sind, die Stelle zu finden, wo das Loch war, so will ich Ihnen einen Kuß geben und Ihnen als Sklavin nach Liverpool hin folgen. (VII, 33)

(And then I'll make my entrance like an artiste, which indeed I really am, and have the coat passed round, and if you, dear Mr Nelson, are still able to find the place where the hole was, then I'll give you a kiss and follow you back to Liverpool as a slave.)

She is certainly an artiste, in the same sense that Mathilde Möhring is, 'eine Tochter der Luft' (acrobat, daughter of the air) who performs dazzling tricks of verbal acrobatics (VII, 46), all in the service of prosaic aims. Her image of mending the damage to Leopold's heart which she herself has created is, however, a sure prediction of the outcome of the story, on two levels: a literal one (what she undoes, she can also mend) and a metaphorical one; the poetry of her imagination triumphs over the prose of her intentions.

Professor Schmidt, too, takes up some attitudes that apparently place him in the camp of the prosaic. For example, according to Corinna, 'seine Bequemlichkeit und seine Pfeife sind ihm lieber, als ein junger Engländer, der vielleicht dreimal um die Welt gefahren ist' ('he prefers his comfort and his pipe to a young Englishman who may have been round the world three times'; VII, 11). (The sequel shows Mr Nelson, in fact, to be rather more prosaic than Professor Schmidt; thus the Professor is vindicated!) Similarly, Schmidt seems to place himself on a par with the philistines in his interest in incidentals, in the petty and anecdotal details of history, for example. Compare Helene's homily to Lizzi and her governess on the importance of trivia ('wer Großes hüten will, muß auch das Kleine zu hüten verstehen...ich möchte Sie doch bitten, auf diese Kleinigkeit, die keine Kleinigkeit ist, mehr achten zu wollen', 'if you wish to take care of the big things in life, you must also know how to look after the small things...could you please pay more attention to this trivial matter, which is actually not trivial at all'; VII, 78–9) with Schmidt's remark to Distelkamp in chapter 7: 'Das Nebensächliche...ist...die Hauptsache, denn es gibt einem dann immer das eigentlich Menschliche' ('Incidentals are the most important thing, for they always give you what is really human'). 'Poetisch magst du recht haben' ('Poetically, you may be right'), replies his professorial colleague (VII, 62). It is hardly necessary for Schmidt to add (but he does) that by 'poetisch' is to be understood something rather different from what Jenny has in mind! If what is great can be desecrated by Jenny, the insignificant can equally be celebrated by Schmidt, who is accused of talking indiscriminately about Homer, Schliemann and *Menufragen* (culinary questions), all on the same level (VII, 64). But this is a *classical* levelling, in contrast to the trivializing of which Helene – and more spectacularly, Jenny – are guilty. Schmidt's interest in 'inessentials' is the classical sentiment of Terence's 'Homo sum: humani nil a me alienum puto', nobly represented also by Fontane's favourite character, Stechlin, of whom it is said: 'Nichts Menschliches war ihm fremd, weil er sich selbst als Mensch empfand und sich eigner menschlicher Schwäche jederzeit bewußt war' ('Nothing human was alien to him, because he was aware of his humanity and constantly mindful of his own human weakness'; VIII, 351). Where Jenny can phrase an ugly threat to Leopold, the loss of his inheritance, in her inimitably 'poetic' language ('bringe dich nicht um einer gefährlichen Person und einer flüchtigen Laune willen um die Fundamente, die das Leben tragen, und ohne die es kein rechtes Glück gibt', 'for the sake of an untrustworthy person and a fleeting fancy, do not rob yourself of the foundations on which life rests, and without which there can be no real happiness' – i.e. money: VII, 127), Schmidt utters a hymn to life couched in the form of a paean to the humble crab (VII, 64). Likewise, the Professor is not seriously worried about Corinna's rebellion against 'das Schmidtsche' (the Schmidt way of life) until he hears that she has also rejected one of his favourite dishes: in the next breath, the very suggestion that she might do such a thing convinces him she cannot possibly be serious (VII, 69).

Through this intellectual character, who is certainly no mandarin, Fontane asserts once more, be it noted, the primacy of 'das Kreatürliche' (the natural, the animal). Schmidt represents a healthy, Goethean view of the wholeness of perceptual and conceptual knowledge. So, for example, in his reaction to Corinna's sudden rejection of a favourite dish, he displays a good empirical knowledge of ethnology, since questions of diet have always had an interesting part to play in marriage exchanges, especially in difficult problems of exogamous versus endogamous marriage transactions. In *Frau Jenny Treibel*, all parties eventually fall back on safe endogamous unions, the solution favoured also in *Irrungen, Wirrungen* (there is more than a hint in *Effi Briest*, too, that Effi might have done well to marry her cousin rather than Innstetten).

The important theme of 'das Kreatürliche' is extended to include Treibel senior, whose saving grace, bringing him close to the Schmidt ambit, is his instinctive and genial eye for the natural and the unnatural in his fellow-creatures' behaviour.

Though impressed by Vogelsang's *Sprechanismus* (loquacity), Treibel is warned by his instinctive knowledge of humanity that the man is untrustworthy. A glorious example of his grip on 'das Kreatürliche' occurs during the excursion to Halensee. It is at the same time a prime example of Fontane's humorous method of indirect comment on his characters. The broken-down cab-horse which carries Leo out to the excursion rendez-vous, like the sad old hack which takes him for his morning rides, is by extension a part of the characterization of Leo himself. Treibel, a pitiless judge of character, is aware of the similarity between man and beast, but confines his comments to the horse. It is left to the reader to recognize in the 'schwaches Freudengewicher', the weak whinny of joy which the creature gives forth on downing the beer donated to it by Treibel, the temporary fit of liveliness induced in Leopold by a heady draught of Corinna's attentions (VII, 101), and the complete absence in him of a psychic dynamo to drive him along once he is deprived of the fiery steed of Corinna, that *Junker generis femini* whom he had counted upon to abduct him (cf. VII, 76, 138).

Treibel, for all his bourgeois faults, is clearly a character who enjoys Fontane's approval, and the reason is that he is a Fontane-esque character; a man of the middle (though not mediocre), prone to see things from two sides (VII, 131), given to *Phantasie* (VII, 143), and altogether commendably human. It is all the more ironic that he, as the archetype of middle-class man opposed to all extremes (which are, among other things, bad for business), should recruit the services of the fanatical Vogelsang to represent him, Treibel, on a platform of *Royaldemokratie*, an abstruse doctrine which would lead to a dangerous bi-partite division of power. Vogelsang's ideal is expressed in the image of a plateau (the people) dominated by a single peak (the monarchy). He stands, therefore, at the very opposite pole from the classical standard of all life as a spectrum, a *continuum*, in which no part is worthy of greater emphasis than any other, a naturally democratic view which rejects 'das Höhere', be it Vogelsang's monarch in his splendid isolation, or the peaks of Jenny's combined cultural and social pretensions. 'Humani nil a me alienum puto': Treibel would surely endorse this standard as readily as his friend Schmidt, without ever consciously elevating it to the level of a *Weltanschauung*. Schmidt's kind of classical 'levelling down', which can just as well be seen as a levelling up, is carried through in the various familiar references by Schmidt to family relationships in the royal households of Greek antiquity. Discussing in chapter 9 the question of which members of the royal family are represented by the golden masks disinterred by Schliemann, Schmidt:

> ...entschied sich...auf das bestimmteste hinsichtlich der einen für Aegisth. Aegisth sei doch immerhin sieben Jahre Klytämnestras Gemahl gewesen, außerdem naher Anverwandter des Hauses, und wenn er, Schmidt, auch seinerseits zugeben müsse, daß der Mord Agamemnons einigermaßen gegen seine Aegisth-Hypothese spreche, so sei doch andererseits nicht zu vergessen, daß die ganze Mordaffäre mehr oder weniger etwas Internes, sozusagen eine reine Familienangelegenheit gewesen sei, wodurch die nach außen hin auf Volk und Staat berechnete Beisetzungs- und Zeremonialfrage nicht eigentlich berührt werden könne. (VII, 89)

> (...in the case of one of them, most emphatically decided in favour of Aegisthus. After all, Aegisthus *had* been Clytemnestra's husband for seven years, as well as being closely related to the Royal House. And if Schmidt was obliged to admit that the murder of Agamemnon ran somewhat counter to his Aegisthus-theory, on the other hand it must not be forgotten (he said), that the whole murder incident was more or less an internal business, a purely family affair, so to speak, which could not really affect the external question of the funeral and its protocol, which were designed for the needs of state and nation.)

Archaeology, a nineteenth-century science, has brought an immediacy and freshness into the study of the humanities to counterbalance the tendency to overidealize the world of the hallowed classics. To talk of the murder of Agamemnon on the level of a feud between the Treibels and the Schmidts does not diminish the classics, but revitalizes them. It brings the classical world down to the plane of the present, and makes the past as vivid and intelligible as today's world, a mere matter of *Familienangelegenheiten* (family affairs). But then *Familienangelegenheiten* are *not* 'mere' to those involved in them, and one can equally well speak of bringing modern family affairs *up* (within an intimate circle) to the level of importance universally enjoyed by events of the order of Agamemnon's death.

The classics provide the answer to the question raised earlier: why *not* adopt the standards of the *nouveaux riches* of the German *Gründerzeit*? The classical is pre-Christian yet moral, relevant to the time and yet universal, incorporating valuable lessons learnt from the past. 'Glaube mir', says Professor Schmidt to his daughter in chapter 10, 'das Klassische, was sie jetzt verspotten, das ist das, was die Seele freimacht, das Kleinliche nicht kennt und das Christliche vorahnt und vergessen und vergeben lehrt, weil wir alle des Ruhmes mangeln' ('Believe me...the classical, which they deride nowadays, is what emancipates the soul: it is innocent of pettiness, while it anticipates Christianity by teaching us to forgive and forget, for we all come short of the glory of God'; VII, 158–9). The classical ideal has the potential genuinely to achieve what Vogelsang's ludicrous political theory promises. Vogelsang proposes to 'square the circle' (VII, 92), to abolish the victory of *Prosa* ('der Prosa gehört die Welt', 'the world belongs to prose', he declares (VII, 27), though his policy is pure fantasy) by excluding from political life the centre, the *Mittelpunkt*, by implication the very bourgeoisie to whom that victory belongs. As Vogelsang's policy *claims* to combine the reactionary and the radical, in a programme of simplistic conservative revolution that foreshadows some of the political themes raised in *Der Stechlin*, as well the later historical development of Fascism (even down to the capitalist's – e.g. Treibel's – support for it on the mistaken grounds that it offers business advantages), so the nobility of the classical ideal, embodied in some of the most venerable poetry, is in truth capable of 'squaring the circle', or genuinely reconciling in humane values the modern and the traditional, helping to bring about the necessary adjustment of ideals to reality. The manly generosity of Marcell's letter to Corinna is a model of classical restraint and *virtus*.

Professor Schmidt's reaction to the letter offers a resolution of Jenny's favourite theme:

Du bist ein Glückskind. Sieh, das ist das, was man das Höhere nennt, das wirklich Ideale, nicht das von meiner Freundin Jenny. (VII, 158)

(You are a child of Fortune. You see, that is what they call higher things, the genuine ideal, not my friend Jenny's version.)

Marcell is Corinna's higher reality. He represents a resolution of the themes of reality and the ideal (he is a cousin *and* an intellectual) lying mid-way between Jenny's high-sounding hypocrisy and the cheerful philistinism of Treibel, whose notion of combining adjustment to reality with 'das Höhere' (higher things) is to raise his factory chimney a few feet every year to deflect smoke away from the environs of the nearby villa! (VII, 16).

Marcell's letter itself resolves another theme much harped on by Jenny, the one betokened by the key-word *Herz* (heart), which apart from its appearance in the book's sub-title ('Wo sich Herz zum Herzen find't', 'Where one heart finds another') is employed frequently throughout the novel. One example to stand for many is Jenny's gesture in chapter 10 – '"Das Glück, es ruht *hier* allein". Und dabei legte sie die Hand aufs Herz' ('"Happiness lies only *here*." And she laid her hand on her heart'; VII, 109). It is an empty gesture repeated by Corinna – but this time sincerely and without histrionics – for Marcell's benefit, when she definitively rejects all that Jenny stands for (VII, 161). She thereby responds to Marcell's own, equally sincere invocation of *Herz*. Of the four occurrences of the word in his letter to her, the most significant is the conjunction of *Herz* with *Vernunft* (reason) (Romantic *and* classical?), yet another indication of the marriage of ideal and reality: 'die rechte Vernunft käme aus dem Herzen' ('true reason comes from the heart'),[8] Professor Schmidt is quoted as saying (VII, 158).

For Jenny, by contrast, *Herz* in its (pseudo-) ideal sense is in opposition to *Vernunft*. When Corinna proves deaf to all her more rhetorical arguments, Jenny finally descends to plain-speaking language to persuade her rival to relinquish Leopold ('lassen Sie den Jungen los', 'let the lad go'), and prefaces this 'speaking from the heart' – in the *genuine* sense of 'heart', for once – with the request 'Corinna, lassen Sie uns vernünftig reden' ('Corinna, let's talk sensibly'; VII, 141). If Jenny wishes to preserve *Herz* and yet still be *vernünftig*, she must redefine *Herz*, and this is precisely what begins to happen in her letter to Hildegard, the counterpart of Marcell's to Corinna. When Jenny accepts Helene's help and the latest Hamburg in-law, the leitmotif-word *Herz* and the frequent reference to sentimental tears at last become related, not to 'das Höhere', but to class and family solidarity, a sphere in which the ideal can comfortably be achieved: 'angesichts dieser Tatsache [i.e. Helene's prompt and 'selfless' response to Jenny's SOS] fühlte Jenny das Eis hinschmelzen, das acht Jahre lang ihr Schwieger-mutterherz umgürtet hatte. Zugleich traten ihr Tränen in die Augen' ('in view of this fact, Jenny felt that the ice which had encircled her mother-in-law heart for the last eight years was melting. At that moment her eyes filled with tears'; VII, 135). The incongruous compound *Schwiegermutterherz* (mother-in-law heart) tells the whole tale of her conversion. As Brecht might have said, there is no friendship to compare with that where economic interests converge completely. The sentimental words that Jenny likes to sing also now come true: 'Wo sich Herz zum Herzen find't' is borne out by her 'finding' of Helene, or, in another sense, the identifying of interests with sentiment.

In accordance with the motto 'werde, der du bist', each of the main characters is made to discover who he or she really is, by becoming it: not always a pleasant discovery, of course, as Schmidt implies in his gloss on Pindar's aphorism: 'Freilich, dieser Werdeprozeß, der hier gefordert wird, muß sich verlohnen...' ('Certainly, this process of becoming which is being exhorted here must be worthwhile'; VII, 159). This is where Corinna has an advantage over Jenny; 'bei *dir* verlohnt es sich' ('in *your* case it's worthwhile'), declares Schmidt, with paternal pride in his daughter. If Corinna is brought to her senses, Jenny, on the other hand, is simply humbled, by being forced to ingratiate herself with Helene and the Hamburg in-laws, originally viewed as the worst possible fate. For Jenny's class, it seems (as for Prussia in her historical development) there is no standing still; there is a dynamic at work which inexorably pushes her forward, like a dictator on the way up, if she is not to sink back into her obscure origins. Thus the Treibel family is pushed towards the seemingly inevitable transition from comfortable middle-class to grande-bourgeoisie status. *Per contra*, Corinna must not leave her natural ambience, for her cleverness could be fatal if she were to move out of the schoolmaster-intellectual Schmidt circle. Her salvation is that she does *not* marry Leopold, and that Schmidt family life can continue to smooth down the sharper edges of her personality. The major irony of the novel is that Jenny helps Corinna to her salvation by frustrating her will. One is tempted to add 'and vice-versa', but the effect of Corinna on Jenny is less straightforward. Jenny ostensibly triumphs, but at the same time she is forced to accept the logical conclusion of her own snobbery, and become, by virtue of the sheer overwhelming strength of numbers and prestige of the Hamburg in-laws, a satellite of the Munk-Thompsons. In that ambience, Jenny is fated to discover who she is. Although with Hildegard's arrival a moratorium has been declared upon all comparisons ('keine Parallelen werden gezogen', 'no parallels will be drawn'; VII, 144), this state of affairs cannot last, and Professor Schmidt's irony, ostensibly aimed at his daughter and therefore pro-Jenny in import, foretells the many invidious

Hamburg–Berlin comparisons that Jenny will undoubtedly have to swallow from now on ('...alles will über sich hinaus und strebt höheren Staffeln zu, die die Vorsehung sichtbarlich nicht wollte', '...everyone is trying to better himself; everyone is striving to reach heights providence clearly did not intend him for'; VII, 142).

This remark can be interpreted as a general epilogue to the novel, as well as a verdict on the *Gründerzeit* in general. Above all it applies to Corinna, Leopold and Jenny, and to Treibel with his misconceived political ambitions. This is a relative world, where Schmidts and Treibels define themselves by their differences from each other, and in terms of nuances. A common understanding for such nuances lies behind a recurrent formula such as 'Engel und Engel ist ein Unterschied', 'Kaufmann und Kaufmann ist ein Unterschied', 'bewerben und bewerben...' ('There are angels and angels', 'there are businessmen and businessmen'), etc. The difference between Schmidts and Treibels is not, after all, very great.[9] It is so much a matter of definitions, 'was man darunter versteht' ('what you mean by it'). Most of the criticisms that can be made of the Treibels can also be levelled, in some form or other, at the Schmidts. Jenny has money, but no education. Corinna has education, but no money. Both want to lay claim to what they have not got, but not at the expense of what they *have*. The chief characters unite to form a neat comic circle, where each attempts to achieve his aims through an intermediary or a *Nebenperson*. Leo thinks he has gained a victory over his mother by becoming engaged to Corinna. Corinna momentarily believes the same of *her* engagement. Jenny mistakenly believes that Professor Schmidt will make Corinna break off the engagement, while Marcell thinks that Schmidt's approval ought to be enough to gain him the hand of Corinna. Treibel believes Vogelsang can win for him the hearts of Tirpitz-Zossen. Corinna at the Treibel dinner party devises such a complex stratagem of angling for one male by apparently playing for another, that even she is unaware that Marcell appears to be her real quarry. By transforming him from a prosaic cousin to a more ardent, more poetic suitor (there is a hint of this underlying, probably unconscious aim in chapter 5, VII, 67: 'ein Mädchen wirbt nicht, um ein Mädchen *wird* geworben', 'a girl does not pay court, she is courted'), she helps *him* to fulfil the humanist commandment 'werde, der du bist'. Vogelsang helps Treibel to do the same on the political level, for, as the Majorin von Ziegenhals points out to him, 'Industrielle sind fortschrittlich' ('industrialists are progressive'). The Vogelsang episode very clearly points out to Treibel what he is *not*, and in the case of a relatively stereotype (however jovial and likeable) figure such as Treibel, this is tantamount to telling him also what he *is*: 'das Produkt dreier, im Fabrikbetrieb immer reicher gewordenen Generationen' ('the product of three generations growing progressively richer through factory ownership'; VII, 132), a bourgeois through and through.

The Schmidt circle itself represents a sub-species of bourgeois man, and this is not entirely disguised by its idealism, which can sometimes come very close to a snobbery of antimaterialism. Corinna remarks with justice that her father 'unterschätzt alles Äußerliche' ('underestimates externals'; VII, 11). And yet, at the same time, there *are* appearances that matter to him, as evidenced by Frau Schmolke's complaints about the many heavy tomes that she has to dust, but which nobody reads. The professorial circle, for all its saving grace of *Selbstironie* (self-ironizing), comes perilously close at times, in its academic smugness, to the kind of 'süße Selbsttäuschung' (sweet self-deception) that Jenny indulges in: and even self-ironization itself can become smug. Nor are the pride and ambitions of the two groups intrinsically so different. All cherish or covet certain 'trophies': an impressive collection of books and a Zeus from Mycenae for Schmidt; Leopold, his money and the Treibel villa for Corinna; a title, for both Marcell and Treibel (and for Schmidt, on his daughter's and Marcell's behalf: I mean of course the professorial title which

Marcell gains by the end of the book); her money, her villa, and a volume of poems bound in green morocco for Jenny... The social pretensions of the two circles are similarly touching in the way that reality falls short of pretensions. The guests at the Treibel dinner party (admittedly an occasion wished upon Jenny by her daughter-in-law) cannot possibly advance Jenny's or Treibel's interests, but amount in the main to a collection of social misfits, has-beens and charity cases, a token of Jenny's social ineptitude and of an inability to shift for herself which makes the second Hamburg marriage inevitable. As for the Schmidt evening, those present are only there because they have nothing better to do, though thread-bare etiquette demands that they uphold the social lie that they set great store by these gatherings.

What most significantly distinguishes the Schmidts from the Treibels, in the end, is the defeat of *Kabale* by *Liebe* (intrigue by love) in Corinna's heart. (Schiller's play is alluded to on a number of occasions: see e.g. VII, 147, 155.) Corinna's reaction to the bourgeois cult of sentimentality, which led her to assume a hard, 'realistic' persona, leads also to the rediscovery of genuine feeling. Corinna renounces prose in favour of poetry; Jenny renounces poetry (as understood by her) in favour of prose. That the sentimental is acceptable in the right place, and that Corinna is susceptible to such genuine senti- ment, was beautifully demonstrated earlier by Frau Schmolke's account of the late Herr Schmolke's reaction, that of a decent, ordinary man, no saint but a Berlin policeman of the vice- squad, when confronted by the daily moral degradation of nineteenth-century prostitution:

Denn ich sage dir, wer da so tagaus tagein in der Sitte sitzen muß, dem vergeht es, dem stehen die Haare zu Berge über all das Elend und all den Jammer,...ich sage dir, Rosalie, wenn man das jeden Tag sehen muß, un man hat ein *Herz* im Leibe un hat bei's erste Garderegiment gedient un is für Proppertät und Strammheit und Gesundheit, na, ich sage dir, denn is es mit Verführung un all so was vorbei, un man möchte 'raus gehn und *weinen*, un ein paar mal hab ich's auch, alter Kerl, der ich bin...(VII, 119–20; my italics)

(For I tell you, when you're stuck there day in and day out in the vice
squad, you lose your appetite, your hair stands on end at the sight of all
that misery and heartbreak,...I tell you, Rosalie, when you've got to
see that every day and you've got a heart in your body and you've served
in the First Guards Regiment and believe in clean living and uprightness
and healthiness, well, I can tell you, you forget about seduction and all
that, and you feel like going outside and crying, and I've done that a
few times too, even an old so-and-so like me...)

Herz and *weinen* (heart and tears), Jenny's sentimental motifs,
are meaningful and appropriate here, powerful enough to
drive out even Corinna's modern cynicism: 'Um Corinnas
Mund verlor sich jeder Ausdruck von Spott' ('All signs of
mockery disappeared from Corinna's expression'; VII, 119).
The note of permissible, genuine and appropriate sentimentality dominates the end of the novel. The song that
Professor Schmidt wrote for Jenny in his poetic youth, before
she betrayed him, his song which has been misappropriated and
vulgarized by Jenny, is sung for the last time by Krola (*not* by
Jenny) at Schmidt's request and to the accompaniment of his
sentimental tears. Be it noted that they are tears of happiness
for the future, on behalf of Marcell and Corinna, as well as
tears of nostalgia (as Jenny's *always* are) for the lost youthful
ideal.

It is the context and the application of the sentiment that
matters, not its intrinsic quality; like Treibel's admonition at
Halensee, 'genieße fröhlich, was du hast' ('enjoy cheerfully
what you've got'; VII, 102) – a sentiment open either to poetic
or prosaic interpretation, meaning either 'selfishly enjoy money
and material possessions while you can', or 'be true to your
best self': 'werde, der du bist'.

The singing of Schmidt's song, on Schmidt territory,[10] to
celebrate the marriage of two members of the Schmidt family,
represents the final triumph of 'echte Lyrik' ('true lyricism';
VII, 166) in the battle between true and false poetics throughout the novel. The reinstatement of the song *as* poem, as a
genuine youthful outpouring, freed from all the social accre-
tions associated with it by Jenny, is the reinstatement of the

poetic in general, an expression of 'das Schmidtsche in höchster Potenz' ('the Schmidt quality to the highest degree'), as Schmidt once described Corinna. It is, by suggestion and extension, the German tradition of culture and poetry reclaimed from the philistines of the *Gründerzeit*. The subject of the poem is, appropriately, matters of individual choice:

> Glück, von allen deinen Losen
> Eines nur erwähl' ich mir.
> Was soll Gold? Ich liebe Rosen
> Und der Blumen schlichte Zier.
>
> (Happiness, of all your chances
> For myself I choose but one.
> What use is gold? My love is roses,
> The simple beauty of a flower.)

Ordinary life is raised again to the level of rededication of the self to the chosen way, not money, not merely the pursuit of a profession or of one's bread and butter, but the way of the mind. In the light of this victory of poetry, Schmidt can permit himself the luxury of the highest *Selbstironie*, and the denial of distinctions that mean a good deal to him: 'Geld ist Unsinn, Wissenschaft ist Unsinn, alles ist Unsinn. Professor auch' ('Money is nonsense, learning is nonsense, everything is nonsense. Professors too').[11] It is an attitude of extreme lyricism (tempered, of course, by the comedy of the Professor's mildly intoxicated condition) worthy of Schmidt in his careless, rapturous youth, the counterpart to the extremes of calculation and self-seeking that permit the prosaic Jenny the luxury of her false-poetic flights of sentiment. The message of Schmidt's song, 'Wo sich Herz zum Herzen find't' ('Where one heart finds another'), is no longer satirical. Jenny has won the battle against Corinna, but in losing, Corinna has achieved a victory of poetry over prose.

7 · DIE POGGENPUHLS

'Nichts dauert. Was ist aus dem Spanien Karls des Fünften geworden! Und schließlich ist doch alles gerecht.' ('Nothing lasts. What became of Charles V's Spain! And in the end it is all right and proper.') So wrote Fontane in a letter to James Morris in the last year of his life (13 May 1898). In *Die Poggenpuhls* decline is seen without too much regret as *gerecht* (just) and natural. Regret at the end of the Junker class, and more particularly the type of the '*Schwertadel*' or *Militäradel* (military aristocracy),[1] as epitomized by the Poggenpuhls, is outweighed by Fontane's enjoyment in exploring the historical moment at which this minor aristocratic class becomes aware of its own demise.

There is some embarrassment in historical consciousness, because one of the qualities of the Junker class is its unquestioning acceptance of traditional or unintellectual values. Leo is the best example in *Die Poggenpuhls*, and notable cases of the natural lack of historical awareness in the Junker class are to be found in *Der Stechlin*, among the cronies gathered around Dubslav von Stechlin on election day. (He himself is an exception, as in so many other ways; a glorified version of the Junker-type.) When conscious reference has to be made to the past, as the only method of establishing and justifying values, the Poggenpuhl family are obliged to expose these values to intellectual scrutiny, with the result that they increasingly lack content. As want of money (both the reason for their decline as a class, and the outward evidence of it) forces the family to spend most of their time trying to make ends meet, so concern about their lack of status and recognition in society becomes the chief content of their imaginative lives.

The undermining of their position has two main effects. On the one hand it reinforces their sense of pride in their origins, leading them to redouble their efforts to maintain what status is left to them. (Therese is the one who makes most effort in this direction, and pays the price for over-concentration on pride of ancestry by frequently becoming ridiculous.) This phenomenon, at a national level, had been remarked upon by Fontane in another letter to James Morris, of 6 January 1898, with reference to England's power: 'Überall schwere Gefahr. Aber wie immer, wenn die Gefahren sich mehren, ja, wenn "decay and fall" als Möglichkeiten am Horizonte sichtbar werden, raffen sich die Völker noch mal zu größten Leistungen auf...' ('Serious danger everywhere. But as always when dangers multiply, indeed, when "decay and fall" appears on the horizon as a possibility, nations rouse themselves once more for their greatest efforts...').

The other effect of the undermining of the Junkers' position is a positive one: they are forced out of their isolation and self-sufficiency into the wider world, with results that are, on the whole, humanizing for them. So, for example, they begin to refine their beliefs about other groups in society and to apply criteria of relativity. Whereas Jews used to be simply Jews, with all the unthinking dismissiveness that the phrase implies, the Poggenpuhls now find themselves making distinctions between the (affluent) Jewish families with whom they are newly forced to consort. The very circumstance that the family has moved, seven years before the story opens, from the provinces into Berlin, means an inevitable *de facto* democratization of their lives; Fontane often deployed the power of metropolitan life (within certain strict limits) to break down social distinctions. In the city, all forms of life are interdependent, for most people, apart from the very rich, share the same public amenities, above all transport and recreation, *Pferdebahn* (horse-drawn trams) and public parks. It is Baronin Berchtesgaden in *Der Stechlin* who formulates the natural democracy of the big city, in chapter 14 of the novel: 'Es ist, mein ich, nicht passend, auf einem Pferdebahnperron zu stehen, zwischen einem Schaffner und einer Kiepenfrau' ('It does not seem fitting to stand on a tram-platform between a conductor and a woman with a pannier'; VIII, 132). Such contact demo-

cratizes not only by its very nature, but because it implants
questions in the minds of the aristocrats which disturb their
age-old assumptions: 'es ist noch weniger passend', continues
the Baronin, 'in einem Fünfzigpfennigbasar allerhand Ein-
käufe zu machen und an der dabei sich aufdrängenden Frage:
"wodurch ermöglichen sich diese Preise?" still vorbeizugehen'
('it is even less fitting to make all sorts of purchases in a six-
penny bazaar and to pass silently by the insistent question:
"how are these prices possible?"'). City life is not only democratic but indeed revolutionary, by its very nature, and whether
the Globsower (the employees of the glass-factory in *Der
Stechlin*) vote Social Democrat or not is irrelevant: the revolutionary influence of the big city will inevitably penetrate, in
the end, even to Lake Stechlin.

Both *Der Stechlin* and *Die Poggenpuhls* are concerned with
the decline of the aristocratic class, but a very great difference
between them lies in Dubslav von Stechlin's powerful sense of
identity with his surroundings, epitomized by his ability, to the
end of his life, to use the feudal possessive pronoun, and to
speak of the village schoolteacher as 'mein Lehrer' ('my
teacher'; VIII, 48), and even of the proletarians as 'meine
Globsower' (VIII, 61: the adjustment of balance that occurs
after Dubslav's death is indicated by the fact that his successor
Woldemar, who would surely never dream of referring to the
glass-workers so intimately, is actually claimed by them as
'einer der "Ihrigen"', one of their own; VIII, 361). Dubslav
is a genuine survival, the most highly-developed representative
of his type, and one of the last. He needs no civilizing, no
humanizing, and he can do without the city. But for others,
the metropolis *is* a civilizing influence. Here, of course, Fontane is swimming very much against the tide of traditional
German attitudes, which have always been notoriously anti-
metropolitan. In *Irrungen, Wirrungen*, in the evocations of
London street life in *Der Stechlin*, and in Onkel Eberhard's
enthusiasm for Berlin in *Die Poggenpuhls*, there is a hymn to
the colour and complexity of life itself, implied in old General

Poggenpuhl's exclamation: 'Ja, Kinder, wenn ich das vor mir habe, da wird mir wohl, da weiß ich, daß ich mal wieder unter Menschen bin, und darauf mag ich nicht gern verzichten' ('Yes, children, when I have all that in front of me, I feel fine, I know I'm back among people again; that's something I don't like to do without'; IV, 317). *Menschen* (people) is surely a term to be understood qualitatively as well as quantitatively, and *verzichten* (renounce, do without) already casts forward the shadow of the old man's death, so that his hymn to Berlin becomes a farewell to life itself, and thus one of those many valedictory statements Fontane makes by proxy in the novels of his last years.

While humanizing, life in the city also, paradoxically, reinforces the need to maintain a class identity, at the same time, and for the very reason, that it makes it more difficult to do so. The metropolitan melting-pot makes for anonymity and blurring of class-demarcations. (Both Agnes Nebelung, the daughter of the *Portier* at the Poggenpuhls' apartment-house, and Manfred von Klessentin, the aristocratic ex-officer cadet, gravitate towards careers in the theatre, a metropolitan institution which would easily allow them to meet on something like equal terms.) And because, in the city, the individual is an island in a sea of anonymous humanity, he lives very much in his imagination; his life is very largely constituted by his *Gesinnung* (outlook), alongside the common reality imposed on him, impersonally, as it is upon all his fellow city-dwellers.

Whereas Dubslav von Stechlin's identity is in everything around him, *his* castle, *his* lake, *his* villagers, the urbanized Junker (certainly if he is a Poggenpuhl) has no property, and therefore no identity save that which lives in his imagination and in the collective family memory. The Poggenpuhls have been stripped of their outer identity.[2] Like their ancestor, old General Poggenpuhl, known as 'der Hochkircher', who was surprised by the enemy before he had time to dress, they bravely defend their position to the end, despite the disadvantage of their state of 'undress'. For all the symbolic relationship between them and their ancestor, however, the very existence of the battle-picture, featuring the old General in his semi-clad condition, makes a statement about the past which implies the extent of the changes that have taken place since it was painted; for the fact that it was ever thought appropriate to record the General's plight in such frank terms indicates precisely the kind of unselfconsciousness and naïveté the Poggenpuhls can never again recapture. Any assertion by the present-day generation of their rightful Poggenpuhl status tends only to emphasize their metaphorical state of 'undress'; or in other words, to bring them perilously close to an 'Emperor's clothes' situation. The exercise of the imagination is once again a central theme. The Poggenpuhls live in a manner practically indistinguishable from the petty bourgeois. For example, despite their cramped circumstances in the Großgörschenstraße, they maintain one room as an *Empfangssalon* (reception room, salon), an aristocratic-sounding description which barely conceals the familiar lower-middle-class 'gute Stube' (front parlour) (IV, 288). Despite all their best efforts, style is inevitably an expression of the means available, and so their style approximates to the bourgeois. (Compare the arrangements in the Möhring flat in *Mathilde Möhring*.) And yet they *feel* powerfully different. Their fight against the prosaic world encroaching daily upon them explains their interest for Fontane, who created so many variations upon the theme of the prosaic forces pulling the imaginative individual down. His defence lies in the power of the imagination itself, and this force I have chosen to include under the general term 'poetic'.

With the possible exception of Mathilde Möhring, none of Fontane's creations is in quite so precarious a position as the Poggenpuhls. The fear of becoming *déclassé*, and indeed the knowledge that this has to some extent already happened, encourages a reaction which is in imminent danger of 'ins Ridiküle fallen' ('becoming ridiculous'; IV, 359), as well as a devotion to cheeseparing and wick-trimming that blurs the fine distinction between *Rechnen* (economizing), which is honourable, and *Berechnen* (skimping and scheming), which is not (IV, 289–90). What particularly sharpens the pain of the Poggenpuhls' difficulties is the contrast between their condition of reduction and contraction, and the expansion that is taking place all around them, for 'Berlin wird Weltstadt' ('Berlin's becoming a metropolis'; IV, 319). One can go further and say that the expansion associated with the era of capitalist enterprise, symbolized by Berlin's rise in the world, is directly related to the declining power of their class in its broadest sense, for the Junkers were essentially an agrarian caste, and with the world-wide agrarian crisis of the 1870s the old agrarian order, undercapitalized as it was, 'was compelled to take the helping hand offered by industry, thus accepting a capitalist industrial society and all it stood for',[3] and so signing its own death-warrant.

But on the other hand, little as they might desire it, their condition of decline makes the Poggenpuhls sympathetic material for the writer. There is even (at least in the case of Sophie) a compensating process at work, as in Thomas Mann, by which material decline is symbiotically related to spiritual growth: and there is poetic potential in their condition, if only because it puts them, like Fontane, out of step and out of sympathy with the material boom at whose centre they live. Fontane is always interested in those who see things differently from the crowd.[4] He is also aware of the dangers inherent in being banished to the periphery of society.

We have seen that Fontane frequently stresses the power of the imagination to create the world we want, in defiance, or as a conquest, of reality. (See the chapter on *Irrungen, Wirrungen*, above.) But admirable though that power is, Fontane shares Frau Dörr's apprehension, expressed on behalf of Lene in *Irrungen, Wirrungen*, about the dangers of *Einbildung*. He is aware, as ever, of the need to redress the balance whenever any particular faculty is developed at the expense of a fundamental, stabilizing grasp of proper perspective. The wholesome ability to put a positive construction on unpromising circumstances becomes in *Die Poggenpuhls* at times a refusal to see what is not welcome. Leo's bourgeois mother points out to him that 'was dir nicht paßt, das siehst du nicht, willst du nicht sehen, und was dir schmeichelt und gefällt, daraus machst du *Wahrscheinlichkeiten*' ('What does not suit you, you don't see, you don't want to see, and out of whatever flatters and pleases you, you create *probabilities*'; IV, 305). Therese's aunt says of her, likewise, in an ad hominem generalization, 'was einem nicht paßt, das glaubt man nicht gern' ('one does not like to believe what does not suit oneself'; IV, 354). The context in which this remark is made demonstrates the perils of wishful thinking, which is to be distinguished, at least in its less innocuous forms, from the power of *Gesinnung* (basic convictions) or *Vorstellung* (vision) in other novels. Until this point, in chapter 12, we have not been in a position to know the truth about the aunt's financial affairs. The chief source of information has been the prejudiced conclusions prematurely arrived at by Leo and Therese Poggenpuhl (rather in the way that, in the related world of Jane Austen's *Pride and Prejudice*, for a long time we see D'Arcy only through the prejudiced eyes of Elizabeth Bennett and her family). Leo and Therese feel that their uncle, General Eberhard Poggenpuhl, who has made a good match, has never done as much to ease their dire poverty as family honour requires, and that their aunt, by birth a bourgeoise, is responsible for curbing the generous impulses they are sure the General has towards them. The truth is that the aunt's estate is entailed and will return on her death to the family of her first husband, the aristocratic Leysewitzes, and that she therefore only has the usufruct of it. What is more, her own inheritance has long since been dissipated. In short, 'Therese, wie das so oft geschieht, hat eine falsche Vorstellung von meiner Vermögenslage' ('Therese, as so often happens, has a mistaken view of the state of my fortunes'; IV, 354).

The danger of the misuse of *Vorstellung*, that it will turn to the bad in the service of 'nach unten rechnen', calculating downwards rather than upwards, 'nach oben' (see the chapter on *Der Stechlin*, p. 197 below), is always present where conditions have deteriorated and there is a surplus of *Vorstellung* available, – an excess generated, in this case, by an overestimation of what the world owes the Poggenpuhls. But for the most part the form taken by the imagination in the novel is much more innocent, though always responsive to the precariousness of the Poggenpuhls' reduced circumstances. This response is discernible in a contrast between Stechlin's imaginative excursions, which, like the one quoted on p. 206 below, are free exercises of the imagination, almost embryonic works of art, and Leo's similar flights. The difference is that in almost every case Leo's inner vision is employed in the service of wish-fulfilment or compensation; in other words, we see a lively imagination not exercising its powers freely, but harnessed to a particular object. The aesthetic drive, the *Spieltrieb* of Schiller's Fourteenth Aesthetic Letter, is channelled and distorted. An example from Leo, to parallel the example of the Bavarian mountain inn conjured up so vividly by Dubslav von Stechlin, is the picture of a *Stiftsdame* (canoness), a benevolent, fairy-godmother version of Tante Adelheid, Domina of Kloster Wutz in *Der Stechlin*, who is surrounded by rural plenty, whose needs are few, and whose generous instincts towards her impoverished relations are limitless (IV, 302). There is an element of patronage in Fontane's presentation of Leo which is entirely absent from that of Dubslav, a pathos arising from Leo's compensatory daydreams and compounded by the fact that his charm, and his ability to remain hopeful and courageous, seem to depend (again in contrast to Dubslav von Stechlin) on nothing more enduring than his youth. Assuredly, Leo has a sympathetic role when, in chapter 4, he talks of the need to believe in mirages:

Wer was hat, nun ja, der kann das Leben so nehmen, wie's wirklich ist, der kann das sein, was sie jetzt einen Realisten nennen; wer aber nichts hat, wer immer in einer Wüste Sahara lebt, der kann ohne Fata Morgana mit Palmen und Odalisken und all dergleichen nicht existieren. (IV, 307)

(A man of means, well, he can afford to take life as it really is, he can be what they call nowadays 'a realist': but if you haven't got anything, if you live constantly in a Sahara Desert, you can't exist without mirages, palms and odalisques and all that.)

But the mother's point of view is just as valid, when she replies that only youth can so believe.

If pathos implies an invitation to the reader to be condescending, then Leo is pathetic. Not that he makes any plea for sympathy on his own behalf; but his courage and cheerfulness are offset by a certain quality of helplessness. The symbol of his circumstances is the Edam cheese of chapter 5. His imaginative ability to turn this hollowed-out remnant, literal evidence of cheeseparing, into the globe's Northern hemisphere, indicates the capacity of youth to regard the world as its own to exploit, but also that too many hands have been there before him, so that his world is already hollow (IV, 312). However, if Leo is the most vividly imaginative member of the family (his imagination and charm being his only assets), Fontane also endows him with more insight than the other younger members of the family into the reality of Poggenpuhl life in modern Berlin. Thus Fontane counteracts any sentimental effect he might fear to be creating through Leo. It is Leo who refers to 'unerbittliche Wirklichkeit' ('inexorable reality'; IV, 296), declares (albeit facetiously) that 'Wahrheiten drängen sich immer wieder auf' ('truths are always intruding'; IV, 299), and satirizes the Christmas-tide sentimentality of his landlord in Thorn, a butcher, while praising the meat which this sentimentality has moved the slaughterer to present to Leo (IV, 296: however, the snobbish Therese's attitude to her rich Jewish friends is not dissimilar – 'Therese [stand] zwar kritisch zu den Bartensteins, [war] aber schließlich froh, daß sie existierten', 'Therese's attitude to the Bartensteins was certainly critical, but when all was said and done she was glad that they existed'; IV, 298).

Above all, it is Leo who faces reality most squarely and robustly by exposing the decline of the heroic tradition and its incongruousness in the modern world.[5] Coats of arms and a heroic past no longer suffice to preserve a name. The present is dominated by soap, cocoa, and chocolate brand-names, by the useful, the commercial and the vulgar. Here we are taken a step further away from the heroic and towards the ultra-prosaic than we are in *Der Stechlin*, where Pastor Lorenzen is content to assert that 'James Watt und Siemens bedeuten uns mehr als du Guesclin und Bayard' ('James Watt and Siemens mean more to us than du Guesclin and Bayard').[6] He goes on to say that 'das Heldische hat nicht direkt abgewirtschaftet..., aber sein Kurs hat nun mal seine besondere Höhe verloren...' ('the heroic is not quite finished...but it has passed its highest peak...'; VIII, 253). Watt and Siemens are still relatively heroic names, however, compared to 'Pears Soap und Blookers Cacao' (IV, 331)! (Though he lamented the passing of the heroic, as we saw in an earlier chapter, Fontane was no Don Quixote, and could appreciate some of the inventiveness and wit channelled into modern commercial promotion. On receipt of a copy of the *Illustrated London News* from James Morris, he expressed his admiration (14 March 1898) for a Bovril advertisement which he described as 'beneidenswert glücklich', enviably felicitous.)

Again, the sympathy which Fontane displays for his subject is prevented from falling into sentimentality by the amusing contrasts of attitudes among the Poggenpuhls themselves (as well as by his own irony). Their separate awareness of decline is subtly graded. All of them are concerned to preserve the appearance of aristocratic status, and all can therefore appear comic, for the aristocratic stance is either genuine and free, or it is role-playing, and the family are perceived to be battling to achieve what is at best an 'almost':

So wohnten die Poggenpuhls und gaben der Welt den Beweis, daß man auch in ganz kleinen Verhältnissen, wenn man nur die rechte Gesinnung und dann freilich auch die nötige Geschicklichkeit mitbringe, zufrieden und *beinahe standesgemäß* leben könne...(chapter 1, IV, 289; my italics)

(This was how the Poggenpuhls lived, proving to the world that, given the right frame of mind and then, of course, the necessary skill, even in reduced circumstances one could live contentedly and almost in the manner proper to one's class.)

There is also a hard core of ruthless snobbery (*Gesinnung* once more in its negative sense), both in Therese's inflated view of the family as a 'pillar of society', and in her older brother Wendelin's grim determination to carve out a career in the army. Therese in her class-consciousness has the most pronounced ruthlessness within the family circle, as we see in her treatment of the bourgeois mother, of whom she is ashamed. The figure of the mother is the repository of any sentimentality attaching to the Poggenpuhl situation, allowing the rest of them to escape this charge. They view their position as following directly in an old tradition of service without complaint. Frau von Poggenpuhl is the only one to give vent to her feelings ('Sämtliche Poggenpuhls – die Mutter freilich weniger – besaßen die schöne Gabe, nie zu klagen...'; 'All the Poggenpuhls – although, admittedly, their mother to a lesser degree – possessed the fine gift of never complaining'; IV, 290); she is the one who is most aware of decline and transition. The *double* aspect of the view from the window, the sweet-factory on one side and the churchyard on the other, belongs to her and not to the family as a whole, for she it is who relies on cough-lozenges to ease her chronic cough, and who has a sentimental fondness for the subject of death; while it is implied that for the rest of the family the churchyard view alone is the acceptable one, not for sentimental reasons, but because its monuments and its family vaults strengthen their sense of a proud family past (IV, 287: compare my remarks, in the chapter on *Ellern-klipp* and *Effi Briest*, p. 67 above, about the role of churchyards in Fontane). But symbolic of the Poggenpuhls' precarious existence, sustained by the good will of the bourgeois class, is the fact that the mother, the bourgeoise, is the one who acts as intermediary between the family and the outside world. She is the only one who is really aware that the roof over their heads is granted them at a bargain rate by the good grace of an erstwhile proletarian, now a *Rentier*, who happens to be aware of his feudal obligation to his superiors and has by implication a shrewd idea of their 'letter-heading' value, that is to say the respectability which they profitably lend to his premises (IV, 288). And Fontane introduces through the character of the mother, especially at the end of the novel, the makings of a natural aristocracy through restraint and humility, suggesting of her, as he did of Lene Nimptsch in *Irrungen, Wirrungen*, that possession of an *Ahnengalerie* (gallery of distinguished ancestors) is not always a necessary or sufficient condition for nobility. Frau Majorin von Poggenpuhl comes as close as any of his heroines to the quiet heroism for which he professes admiration in the letter of 31 January 1896 to James Morris: 'Es gibt ein ganz stilles Heldentum, das mir imponiert' ('There is a very private heroism by which I am impressed').

And yet, praiseworthy as she is, Fontane witholds absolute approval from her. Her prosaic concern for day-to-day survival, while it enables her Poggenpuhl brood to continue to indulge in its mirages, cannot prevail against the poetic appeal of the genuine aristocrats' enjoyment of life. She is the prose whose contrast makes their poetry possible. The celebration of her fifty-seventh birthday ought hardly to justify the phrase 'die alte Frau' ('the old lady') which is nonetheless used of her in chapter 6 (IV, 315), but she is brought down by care and prematurely aged by her lone struggle. Uncle Eberhard, who is sixty-seven, remains by contrast what Lorenzen said of Dubslav von Stechlin in his funeral address, 'das Beste, was wir sein können, ein Mann und ein Kind' ('the best thing it is possible for us to be: a man and a child'; VIII, 351). Essential to the preclusion of mundane anxiety, and thus to the preservation of youth in the aristocrat, is a sense of being the master of fate and not its victim. As Uncle Eberhard remarks, 'man hat immer das Spiel in der Hand und ist gerade so jung wie man sein will' ('the game is always in one's own hands, and one is as young as one wants to be'; IV, 336). The contrast is a recurrent one in Fontane, so that (to take two extremes) while the bourgeois Leopold Treibel was never really young, Dubslav von Stechlin was never really old.

The younger Poggenpuhls divide into two groups: Leo, Sophie and Manon on the one hand, and Wendelin and Therese on the other. The former group inherits the youthfulness of Uncle Eberhard. The two solemn older children, however, for all that they appear to be the strongest upholders of Poggenpuhl dignity, are bourgeois in aristocratic guise. The future belongs to the prosaic, to the mother's side of the family, while General Eberhard Poggenpuhl is clearly a survival from the past. He rejects his sister-in-law Albertine's (i.e. Majorin von Poggenpuhl's) bourgeois vocabulary, containing such items as 'sich versagen', 'Verhältnisse', 'Glück' and 'so gut wir's haben' ('self-denial', 'circumstances', 'good fortune', 'what little we can offer'; IV, 337–8): and yet he too is dependent for the maintenance of his Junker life-style upon a bourgeoise (his wife), albeit one who has risen to the occasion by developing, more graciously than Frau Albertine, a natural aristocracy. He is, however, the last of his line who can be a genuine, traditional Poggenpuhl and enjoy effortless status as well, although, as he himself recognizes, even his claim to Junker independence is a façade ('Selbst ist der Mann. Aber nein, nein, ich will dies nicht gesagt haben...', 'A man makes his own life. But no, I take that back...'; IV, 338) and his position is very similar to that of his nephews and nieces in their Berlin flat, since he does nothing more than to lend his good name to his wife's estate: 'er gibt nur den Namen dazu her und auch das kaum...' ('all he supplies is his name, and hardly even that'; IV, 306). He is only a tenant of the Silesian property, and moreover he has no direct heir.

As measured by the standards of Uncle Eberhard or Dubslav von Stechlin, Leo, Manon and Sophie are the genuine heirs to the Poggenpuhl tradition. It is true of them that they have 'das Spiel in der Hand' ('the game in their own hands'), a phrase perhaps casually thrown out by the old Uncle, but reminding us of Dubslav's *Spielerei* (love of play) in *Der Stechlin* (VIII, 192: see p. 200 below). Stechlin and Barby enjoy, to antici- pate a later point, the freedom to imagine the demise of their class and even of the world-dominating position of their continent, and some such freedom of the imagination is the property of the three younger Poggenpuhls. What is meant is the sovereign exercise of the imagination in order to retain control and equilibrium in the face of decline: or, in poetic terms, the Faustian ability to shake off 'Sorge', care (see *Faust*, Part One, 1. 644: 'Die Sorge nistet gleich im tiefen Herzen', 'Full soon in deepest hearts care finds a nest'; and compare IV, 342-3) as a life-denying force. Uncle Eberhard demonstrates this power when he accepts the, at first sight, scandalous spectacle of Manfred von Klessentin as an aristocrat turned actor. He even goes so far as to make the entirely Fontane-esque suggestion that we are all actors in our various roles, and certainly his 'guest role' on the Leysewitz estate gives him a good basis for this observation.

The true quality of Leo, Manon and Sophie lies in their ability and willingness to diversify, although there is a degree of irony in the fact that by doing so they are likely to have to forego their traditional aristocratic trappings and status in order to sustain their true aristocratic heritage. And we must differentiate among them. Manon and Leo are the most care- less about jettisoning the external properties of the Poggenpuhl past, and this is especially understandable in the case of Manon, since she never knew her father (the last real link with the heroic past) but was born after his hero's death at Gravelotte. These two are prepared to accept relatively demeaning escape- routes from their poverty: for Leo, the pursuit of the Golden Calf is by no means ruled out (IV, 317: we recall that in Lorenzen's funeral address in *Der Stechlin*, a chief point of praise for Dubslav is 'Das goldene Kalb anbeten war nicht seine Sache', 'Worshipping the Golden Calf was not for him'; VIII, 351 - but his options were better than Leo's). Manon seeks to arrange a rescue of the family fortunes through marriage to the rich Jewish Bartensteins, which, though it would solve the financial problem, would at the same time, in terms of the aristocratic code, deprive the Poggenpuhl line of its good name and heritage. Evolution and adaptation are necessary, but this can be an evolution upwards or downwards, and Sophie is the purest heir of the old Poggenpuhl tradition, for hers is an adaptation *upwards*. Like Elizabeth Bennett, she does not calculate an advantageous marriage for herself; nonetheless, through her great naturalness and charm she wins the affection of her aunt and gains for her family at least some relief from their penury, as well as the promise of a secure future for herself, thanks to her aunt's generosity. But more than this, Sophie develops certain talents, which were never necessary to earlier generations of her ancestors, and which would have been frowned upon and suppressed by them as 'unstandesgemäß', unsuited to her class status (IV, 290). Sophie is the most able 'diversifier' of all; the other two possess no assets but their personality, whereas Sophie can turn her hand to anything and do it supremely well. She is both a *Lebenskünstlerin* (artist of life) and an artist in the purer sense. Nowhere else in Fontane do we recognize so clearly the legacy he was to pass on to Thomas Mann. And yet, unlike the artistic qualities of that product of the *Dekadenz*, Hanno in *Buddenbrooks*, the final flowering of *Geist* (spirit) and art which brings the Buddenbrook line to an end, Sophie's artistic talents are seen as entirely positive. Where they would, in an earlier era, simply have been either a decoration or an encumbrance, now they are the means of survival itself; and more than merely survival, for Sophie's art is triumphantly placed in the service of the highest spiritual cause, symbolized by the painting of a church mural. We shall return to this subject.

The inclination towards art as an alternative to a heroic–aristocratic stance, now a faintly ridiculous anachronism (cf. Therese's ambition, 'die Poggenpuhlsche Fahne hochzuhalten', 'to hold high the Poggenpuhl banner'; IV, 290) was of course prefigured by the appearance of the aristocrat-actor 'Manfred' in chapter 7. The theatre evening is highly educational for the more receptive of the Poggenpuhls, for it teaches them the aesthetic nature of the current phase of Junker existence. There had been an allusion to role-playing in the first chapter – 'so war die Rollenverteilung im Hause Poggenpuhl' ('this was the distribution of roles in the House of Poggenpuhl') – but at that point consciousness of their own role was not heavily emphasized. In chapter 7, however, the question of which play to go to is a very delicate one, for it brings out all the precariousness of their situation. Both *Snow White* and *Cinderella* are turned down (IV, 317), the former because the prominence of a glass coffin has altogether too funereal an association for the old General's liking, as well as being, perhaps, a symbolic if unrecognized allusion for the family, in that they too are encased in a kind of hermetic glass coffin, and, as a class, await a reawakening, which will never come in their generation. (There are other allusions to a possible resurrection, as in the reference to *Auferstehung* in chapter 14 (IV, 365), and at the end of chapter 6: 'Vielleicht kommt es noch mal wieder', 'Perhaps it will all come back', says Leo, to which Uncle Eberhard replies 'glaub ich auch. Nur nicht bei uns', 'I think so too. Only not for us'; IV, 318.) *Cinderella* is clearly equally unsuitable, having too close a resemblance to the *Aschenbrödeltum*, the Cinderella-like deprivations of the Poggenpuhls' existence, and to Leo's fantasy-solution to their problems, his constant yearning for a fairy godmother. The choice now is between the genuine or the parody version of *Die Quitzows*.[7] Leo is for the parody, and for a moment the dialogue hovers on the brink of a painful exposure of the Poggenpuhls' sham position, the white lie of their existence. It is a moment which exemplifies the family's ability, so well captured in the novel, to balance on the edge of dignity and absurdity. Of course, for the most part they see through their own hollow pretensions; but to go as a family to a parody of their own Junker past would be altogether too much. Nonetheless, they are not saved from a self-recognition, beyond the dignified one created for them by

the stirring, 'straight' version of *Die Quitzows*; for, by courtesy
of Manfred von Klessentin, a perspective opens up which is
interpreted existentially by Uncle Eberhard ('all life is role-
playing') and sociologically by Sophie. Manfred's acting career
is, for her, only an extension of a *de facto* situation, for the
Poggenpuhls can only survive in the modern world *as* the
Poggenpuhls by acting the part of themselves, by a self-
production which trades on the aristocratic cachet found so
desirable by *nouveau riche* Jewish families and bourgeois
widows with large estates (IV, 334).

Such a role is a highly transitional one, belonging only to a
brief moment in history, and in the end self-defeating. If the
aristocratic class is worth anything at all, then it can see
through its own pretence – which is in fact the case with the
more realistic members of the family – and therefore does not
ultimately want self-preservation. The present-day aristocratic
talent *par excellence* is, logically, an aesthetic one, the ability
to act out a role despite knowledge of its inauthenticity: and
from there, it is only a short step to an acting career proper,
like Manfred's. The theatre, a world parallel to the aristocratic
one, is illuminating for the old General, for within it he
discerns distinctions of rank as clear as any in the Army, and is
even reminded that the link between aristocracy and theatre
has a distinguished antecedent (if not in Prussia) in the shape
of Lord Byron. As Klessentin the actor remarks: 'Der Byronsche
Manfred ist eine Pyramidalrolle, groß, erhaben wie Lord Byron
selbst, während ich durchaus auf einer Anfängerstufe stehe'
('Byron's Manfred is a star role, great, sublime like Lord Byron
himself, whereas I am very much a beginner'; IV, 323). The
fascination of the minor aristocracy for Fontane in the late
1890s is the aesthetic quality of their existence; a poetic but
ephemeral survival in a prosaic world.

Not to embrace this poetic role is, as we see with Therese
and Wendelin, to capitulate to the prosaic. They are a humourless pair, and that in itself is indicative of their failing on
the human level. These two will, in contrast to the other

Poggenpuhl offspring, strive to maintain their aristocratic status intact in its narrow traditional sense, fighting back against its diffusion by financial opportunism (Leo and Manon) or by an opening out to the human and universal (Sophie). But they, Therese and Wendelin, while maintaining the outer appearances of their caste, will have lost its inner content. Wendelin is the only Poggenpuhl who does not appear in person in the story, and this shadowy existence of his conveys a sense of his alienation from the rest of the family. The most successful of the Poggenpuhls is *not* one of them, as Leo observes: 'Er heißt Poggenpuhl, aber er ist keiner, oder doch ganz auf seine Weise, die von der unsrigen sehr abweicht' ('His name is Poggenpuhl, but he isn't one, or if he is, it is entirely after his own fashion, which is very different from ours'; IV, 349). The aristocratic ideal is nothing if not a declaration of independence, which, as we have seen, is also one of Fontane's highest values (he sacrificed a good deal in his life in order to remain his own man), and in the very effort to maintain his status, Wendelin must discard it, for by definition the ambitious careerist is not his own man. Like Innstetten, Wendelin von Poggenpuhl sells his Junker birthright, in this case for brilliant prospects in a General Staff appointment. Ambition is anathema to Fontane's most attractive characters: Uncle Eberhard agrees with Klessentin's rejection of *Strebertum* (careerism): 'Bravo, bravo. Ganz mein Fall. Nur nicht andre beiseite schieben, nur nicht über Leichen' ('Well said, well said. I'm exactly the same. Anything but elbowing other people out of the way, anything but stepping over dead bodies'; IV, 324); and even more weight can be given to the various negative remarks about ambition in *Der Stechlin*, for example the verdicts on Rex and Koseleger (cf. VIII, 20, 162, 168). Wendelin is the New Man of the age, who regards himself, significantly, not as the last of a long line, but as the *first* of the Poggenpuhls, 'weil seiner aufrichtigen Meinung nach das Poggenpuhlsche nicht mit den Kreuzzügen, sondern einfach mit Wendelin von Poggenpuhl anfängt' ('because in his sincere opinion the Poggenpuhl quality does not begin with the Crusades, but simply with Wendelin von Poggenpuhl'; Leo: IV, 349). He is one of the more dangerous-looking characters to appear in Fontane's fiction, and it may well be that Fontane is suggesting through him the thrusting, arrogant militarism which, to his dismay, flourished almost unchecked in Prussia in the last decades of his life (see the letter to Georg Friedländer of 3 April 1887: 'Besonders die militärische Welt überschlägt sich...Der Rest der Welt...ist nur dazu da, gescholten und verdächtigt, unter allen Umständen aber angepumpt zu werden', 'The military in particular are getting carried away...The rest of the world ...is only there to be abused and distrusted, but above all to have money squeezed out of it'). Leo sums up his brother's ruthlessness thus: 'wenn es ihm so vorkommt, daß er persönlich damit bei hohen Vorgesetzten anstoßen oder wohl gar in einem fragwürdigen Lichte dastehen könnte, so ist es mit allem Familiengefühl und aller Bereitwilligkeit rasch vorbei' ('if he feels he might offend highly placed superiors or even be put in a dubious light, then it's short shrift for all family feeling and willingness to help'; ibid.).

The loss of independence is the loss of a certain admirable style, and this is one of the aspects in which Fontane seems to see most potential for regret in the passing of the aristocratic class. He conveys loss of quality in a familiar observation, that the sad and undeniable concomitant of the sharing of privileged amenities is that these things thereby become devalued. This is not a reason for keeping privilege in the hands of the few, but it does underline a quality in the aristocratic life which Fontane aesthetically admires. (Once again, Eberhard expresses Fontane's position: 'Na, wir brauchen es nicht abzuschaffen; aber wenn andre sich dran machen, offen gestanden, ich kann nicht viel dagegen sagen', 'Well, there's no need for us to abolish it; but if others set about doing so, quite frankly I haven't much to say against it'; IV, 336–7.) Manon and Therese are agreed that the park of the Leysewitz estate is superior to the fine public parks in Berlin, because what is publicly accessible is devalued simply by the quality of 'das Öffentliche' (public-ness), which affects the aesthetic response to a work of art (IV, 364). The new, prosaic world in which there is – quite rightly, as Fontane would see it – no room for aristocratic privilege, nonetheless runs the well-known risk of the leveller or fanatical democrat, that of pulling down the mountains to fill in the valleys. This is not a note on which Fontane would wish to dwell, and he places the discussion in the context of Leysewitz, not Berlin, thus underlining his detached aesthetic interest in the subject and removing it from the real world of the metropolis in which, as he knows full well, the future of Germany is actually being forged.

Herein lies, perhaps, some part of the reason for that abrupt change of emphasis and milieu in the novel which has puzzled the commentators on *Die Poggenpuhls*. Until Sophie's move to Adamsdorf, Leo tends to dominate such action as there is, with the preparation for his homecoming, his arrival, the visit to the theatre, and his departure. Thereafter the scene shifts to Silesia, enabling Fontane to break out of the Berlin milieu, in which little development of his themes is possible. The death of Uncle Eberhard serves to take the three women – Manon, Therese and the mother – who have so far been tied to their Berlin flat, out of their own secure and isolated environment, and make them measure themselves against something greater. So that although the novel has as one of its central themes the increasing 'bourgeoisification' of the nineteenth-century world, the climax itself transcends this theme and places the Poggenpuhls in contrast with the magnificence of the Leysewitz estate, no longer with the bourgeoisie. The episode of the funeral once more emphasizes their precarious position between two worlds. The funeral clothes are paid for by the bourgeois aunt (whereby the 'undress' of the family – see the discussion of the 'Hochkircher' picture, above – is temporarily relieved), thus enabling the women to celebrate in *standesgemäß* (fitting) style the glory and greatness of their own family, and so summing up the white lie of their position. On the other hand we are reminded

that they are not even *real* aristocracy, in comparison with the
Leysewitzes: a Poggenpuhl family portrait would be out of
place, for more reasons than one, in the Leysewitz ancestral
home. In this setting, the loss to the world represented by the
decline of 'das Poggenpuhlsche' seems much reduced. They are
placed in the perspective suggested by their name ('frog-pool')
as against the grander setting of a genuine lake, the Stechlinsee
for example.

But the change of milieu also has strong positive justification,
as does the change of emphasis from Leo to Sophie. The name
of the locality, Adamsdorf, in itself prefigures Sophie's Old
Testament inspiration in her church painting, and points to an
opening-out to a universal perspective, a move away from the
cramped, self-obsessed existence of the Poggenpuhls in Berlin.
Here, Sophie might be said to assert to the full her independence and freedom of the imagination – in the world of art. As
Thomas Mann felt that in his own person, as an artist, he was
usefully releasing to the world the *Bürger* qualities developed
and previously locked up within the narrow streets of his home
town of Lübeck, so Sophie now chooses not to 'employ her
talents in the service of the family' by producing, as was first
suggested, a version of the Poggenpuhl coat of arms, intended
to replace the Leysewitz ones on the household plate (IV, 339);
but instead to serve, so to speak, the family of man (in *Adamsdorf* church) by an act of celebration. Her paintings for the
church are a celebration of the Creation itself, 'eine kleine
Schöpfung', as her uncle says (IV, 356). Unlike Leo and
Therese, who concentrate on what the world owes them as a
class and as a family, but refuses to concede them, Sophie
'pays back' to life in general and Prussia in particular what the
Poggenpuhls have enjoyed in the course of their privileged
history.

Sophie's pictures provoke in Uncle Eberhard, very shortly
before his death, an affirmation of the goodness of life similar
to that of Dubslav von Stechlin in his last hours (VIII, 314).
The old General's English-style understatement is very much

to Fontane's taste: 'Wenigstens kann ich mir nicht denken, daß Gott die Welt aus Verdrießlichkeit geschaffen hat' ('At any rate, I can't imagine that God created the world in a fit of peevishness'; IV, 356). Sophie's church-painting, then, is a return to simplicity and a renunciation of pretension which builds up to the old General's death. The figure of General Poggenpuhl, after all, lends the novel what unity it has. His simple humility relates him to Sophie; his good nature, liking for social life, emphatic renunciation of bourgeois limitations, his ability to compromise with principle for the sake of comfort – these bring Leo and Manon close to him. He combines in his person the two aspects which the novel as a whole (as a preamble to *Der Stechlin*) aspires to reconcile: the particular, in his individuality and the very marked characteristics of a military member of the Junker caste in the late nineteenth century; and the universal, in his self-effacing ability to see the world from the perspective of others, his sense of role-playing and of the ephemeral nature of social systems. Precisely these qualities of the universal and the particular are present in Sophie's paintings, for they combine Bible stories with local scenes which serve as the landscape background in the pictures. The childlike quality of Eberhard (similar to that of Dubslav von Stechlin) and of the old aristocratic type is present in his suggestion – inspired by a Brandenburg model he has seen – that she depict the village church itself, on a second mountaintop next to Mount Ararat, where the Ark perches above the receding waters of the Flood. It is a final note of resurrection, of poetic hope that the old Prussian values can one day come into their own again, or, as Sophie puts it in a letter to Manon in chapter 12:

So kindlich es mir anfänglich vorkam und auch noch vorkommt, so hat es doch zugleich eine tiefe Bedeutung; als die alte Sündenwelt unterging und die neue, bessere, sich aufbaute, war das erste, was neu erschien... die Kirche jenes kleinen märkischen Dorfes und jetzt also die von Adamsdorf. Es war, als ob Gott sie gleich dahin gestellt habe. Natürlich kann man darüber lachen, aber man kann sich auch darüber freuen.

(IV, 352)

(Childish as it appeared to me at first, and still does, all the same it has a deeper meaning; when the old sinful world was destroyed and the new, better one began to emerge, the first thing that appeared...was the church of that little village in the Mark, and, now, the Adamsdorf one. It was as though God had immediately placed them there. Of course one can laugh about it, but one can enjoy it too.)

True to the sense of this conciliatory ending, Fontane concludes his novel with a series of satisfying conversions. The old General is converted before his death to an appreciation of the possibilities of art. The haughty Therese begs her mother's pardon for some arrogant 'aristocratic' remarks, and is said to be 'nicht eigentlich eigensinnig' (not really obstinate). Manon develops a new, reasonable approach to life; and the mother for once becomes the defender of Poggenpuhl pride *and* makes a powerful statement on her own behalf which combines her natural modesty with an assertion of her genuine claim to respect, despite her bourgeois shortcomings (IV, 372). Even the scornful *Portier*, Nebelung, forgets his own, proletarian, class-consciousness for a moment and helps unload the trunk from the cab when the Poggenpuhl ladies arrive home in Berlin. Since there has already been a reconciliation with the bourgeois aunt at Leysewitz, the Poggenpuhls have now made their peace with the two rival classes by whom they are threatened. The legacy from the uncle and the settlement by the aunt do not amount to much, but are enough to put an end to grandiose imaginings of good fortune which had only served to distract the family from the business of living. In their case, as representatives of their class, this is tantamount to the business of dying (*aussterben*). At its best, as Fontane went on to show in *Der Stechlin*, there is no business more poetic.

8 · DER STECHLIN

It is very easy to describe Fontane's last novel as poetic simply because it is concerned with atmosphere rather than event, belonging to the timeless realm of the contemplative lyric rather than the bustling world of the realist novel: it is, to quote Flaubert's phrase again, *le roman sur rien* or novel of pure circumstance. And yet there is a danger that this is a definition by default, as though, since very little happens in *Der Stechlin*, it must for want of any other description be called a 'poetic novel'. But that label suggests something rather different from what *Der Stechlin* actually reveals itself to be. Its essence is unpretentiousness. Almost all of Fontane's familiar preoccupations recur here, but in an abstract pattern where no one theme is heavily dominant. Motifs which, in other novels, had a power of symbolic or metaphorical suggestion, recur in *Stechlin* digressively, without the accustomed poetic concentration. One example is the nocturnal reflection of lights in water, a very familiar motif in Fontane, often suggesting romantic associations, and sometimes the dangerous lure of the illicit, as, for instance, in chapter 10 of *Unwiederbringlich*, when Graf Holk arrives for the first time in Copenhagen: 'Über ihm funkelten die Sterne in fast schon winterlicher Klarheit, und mit ihnen spiegelten sich die Uferlichter in der schimmernden Wasserfläche' ('Above him the stars glittered with an almost wintery clarity, and they and the lights on the shore were reflected in the shimmering expanse of water'; V, 59: the motif is echoed in a minor key on his second journey to Copenhagen by the lights reflected in the water of Flensburg Bay, chapter 29, V, 197). The figure is employed on a number of occasions in *Der Stechlin* (cf. VIII, 126, 142, 190, 282), but never with quite the poetic or metaphorical import of its function in the *Unwiederbringlich* examples.

The novel as a whole is characterized by the digressive style of gossip, *Klatschen*, although of course an elevated kind

of gossip. (Compare Czako's defence of *Klatschen*, VIII, 191,
against Rex's critical attitude: '...das sagen Sie so spöttisch
und überheblich, weil Sie glauben, Klatschen sei was Inferiores
und für mich gerade gut genug. Aber da machen Sie meiner
Meinung nach einen doppelten Fehler. Denn erstlich ist
Klatschen überhaupt nicht inferior, und zweitens klatschen
Sie gerade so gern wie ich und vielleicht noch ein bißchen
lieber', '...you say that so derisively and arrogantly because
you think that gossip is inferior, just about good enough for
me. But there, in my opinion, you are making a two-fold
mistake. For first of all gossip is not inferior at all, and
secondly you like gossiping just as much as I do and perhaps
a bit more'.) It is as though Fontane has become impatient
with his own familiar techniques, or with the will to form and
to interpret, and has resorted to a Turner-esque, though
muted, colour-tone (the tone would be that of a quiet sunset)
and to an impressionistic concentration on surfaces. 'Lights on
water' make a good subject, as the Impressionist painters dis-
covered. The reference to Turner and the Impressionists is not
as fanciful as it might seem, remembering the discussion on
contemporary art which takes place at the Barbys' social
gathering. The pompous academic painter, Professor Cujacius,
slaps down Woldemar von Stechlin's enthusiasm for 'die
Phantastika des Malers William Turner' ('the hallucinations of
the painter William Turner'), for, in the Professor's view, 'die
Koloristen sind das Unglück in der Kunst' ('the colourists are
a disaster for art'), and the only salvation lies in a return to the
past: 'Umkehr, Rückkehr zur keuschen Linie' ('turning back
to pure line'; VIII, 221). Correcting Woldemar's howler in
confusing Millais with Millet, Cujacius is utterly scornful of
the latter (not surprisingly, in view of Millet's humble realism)
but expresses grudging approval of Millais in his purest Pre-
Raphaelite period. To equate the technique of *Der Stechlin*
with the colourist approach in visual art would, of course, mean
taking a metaphor much too far. But what *can* be said is that
the dichotomy between Turner, the Impressionists, and the

realists like Millet on the one hand, and the English Pre-Raphaelites on the other, is merely the continuation of a nineteenth-century opposition of realism and idealism. In the discussion on art, Fontane's characters recapitulate familiar arguments. His novel is the literary equivalent of Impressionism, standing at the opposite pole from German idealism, which maintains that the 'reality' around us is mere appearance, and that the real is transcendental, manifested in the visible world only as a shadowy reflection. The Pre-Raphaelite Brotherhood is a backward-looking group of idealists seeking a conservative revolution in art as well as a return to a more 'natural' life. They are descendants of another idealistic group of brethren, the German Nazarenes; and, significantly, Professor Cujacius's real enthusiasm is reserved for a prominent Nazarene, Peter Cornelius (VIII, 189: the similarity of names is surely not coincidental). It is not at all surprising that, with a German Romantic tendency to identify the archaic with the aesthetic, the Professor uses his views on art as a bridge to his political convictions, which are equally in favour of a conservative revolution to put the emerging Fourth Estate back in its rightful humble place (VIII, 190). The notion of a return to the past as a route to progress is a theme that is treated in various ways in *Der Stechlin*, and it will be taken up again later.[1]

We can say at this point that *Der Stechlin* is itself a case of progress-by-regress, for it is broader in scope than any novel since *Vor dem Sturm*; but Fontane's last novel possesses a kind of breadth very different from that of his first. It is an epic like *Vor dem Sturm*, but an epic of characterization and not of momentous historical events. In contrast to the intense study of character under stress in *Effi Briest* or *Unwiederbringlich*, the chief quality of *Der Stechlin* is breadth, not depth. Like the Impressionists, Fontane here finds the interest and meaning of life in the depiction of an apparently unremarkable surface; and also like them, his novel brings about a conversion of quantity into quality. As Monet, for example, challenges nineteenth-century high art with apparently prosaic themes like railway stations and locomotives, so Fontane's uneventful and prosaic subject-matter is merely a starting-point for the accumulation of observations adding up to a powerful impression. To Alfred Sisley, 'even a flood was a kind of festive occasion, for in purely visual terms it is an intensification of light, and the great sheet of water provides a vast surface area acting like a mirror to reflect colour'.[2] So, in *Der Stechlin*, the more surface, the more light, the more colour. Like a flood, a death is usually conceived as a calamity, and yet, seen with the impartial yet sympathetic eye of the artist, the period leading up to Stechlin's death serves as a celebration of his life and as a suitable panoramic reflection of the Mark Brandenburg, synchronically and diachronically. The purely visual is the basis of Impressionist art, precisely *because* no interpretation is implied. But value-judgment is implied by fascination with the subject-matter, and so it is with old Stechlin, in the setting of his house, his village and his lake.

The setting subordinates him spatially: the novel opens with an introduction to the name *Stechlin*, which becomes known to us first of all as the name of the lake, and then ripples out like the effect of a stone splashing in water, so that it designates in turn the wood, the village, the 'Schloß', and finally its owner (VIII, 5, 6). He belongs to all these Stechlins, therefore, rather than they to him. This is important, for it is his sense of complete subordination to and identification with his native area that gives his life harmony and a natural combination of humility and sense of place. (These are, incidentally, the virtues of Fontane's ideal vision of England; cf. VIII, 236. Like Dubslav von Stechlin, the English nation incorporates civilization as second nature, in complete contrast to Prussia's insecurity, notwithstanding her military successes: like Dubslav again, the self-confidence of the English allows them to put a 'Fragezeichen hinter alles', 'a question mark after everything', simply because they *are* so secure.)

Dubslav is subordinated temporally, as well as spatially, for the novel begins and ends with the name of the lake, which literally has the last word, implying a continuity that counteracts any impression of finality his death might have produced. The lake can do better than this, though, by way of creating its own spatial and chronological scales, for it is linked to geological time and space-scales by its connexions with unstable spots on the earth's crust, whose volcanic or seismic eruptions are registered by the lake in the form of a geyser. It is linked by repute with historical time, and synchronically with global events, too, for superstition has it that at times of great disruptions in the world outside, a red cockerel appears and crows, in place of the water-spout. The air of uneventfulness created by the novel and by Dubslav's life is a surface impression. The lake supplies symbolic acknowledgment of the role played by unexpected events welling up from the depths. Thus Dubslav's life is subordinated in another sense, too, to a broader range of historical and potential future occurrences than those recorded in his own relatively short history. The limited treatment of an individual existence is supplied with epic breadth. Fontane is at great pains to link the particular with the universal, as the Stechlin symbol clearly indicates. Once again he is making the point that concentration on the particular is the only way to knowledge of the general. When he retreats into the local and regional setting of Brandenburg he does not do so as an exponent of familiar German particularism, but because he believes that universal validity is to be found in accurate knowledge of the particular, informed by sympathy.

It was said in connexion with *Effi Briest* that it is when Fontane, like other nineteenth-century artists, dares to be prosaic and deal with apparently unexalted themes, that he achieves poetry. This suggestion becomes almost an axiom in *Der Stechlin*, where a good deal of stress is placed upon the prosaic qualities of the *Mittelmark*, a name implying in itself the 'middle way' of moderation and sobriety: 'weil wir in unsrer Mittelmark nicht so bloß äußerlich in der Mitte liegen, sondern weil wir auch in allem die rechte Mitte haben und halten' ('for we in our Mid-Mark do not just outwardly occupy a middle position, but know and maintain the middle course in everything'; Tante Adelheid, VIII, 148).³ Yet it is strongly suggested that this astringency (compare Corinna's remarks on the *Adstringens* (astringent) in fruit as 'das, was zusammenzieht..., was alles wieder in Ordnung bringt und vor Schaden bewahrt', 'that which draws together..., which puts everything to rights and protects from harm'; *Frau Jenny Treibel*, VII, 149) is the precondition for true poetry. Fontane presents us here with the complete reverse of Frau Jenny Treibel's ostentatious, and therefore prosaic, display of poetry in a green morocco binding. Apart from the properties of the lake itself and the red cockerel of popular legend, everything in the Stechlin area contributes to the surface impression of an entire lack of poetry. Even the red of the legendary cockerel is linked directly with the prosaic red of the roofs of the Globsower glassworkers' cottages. Red is the revolutionary colour, but the Globsowers, though they vote Social Democrat, are as prosaic in their politics as in their product, so that in both cases expectations which have been raised are lowered again. Czako, in the role of sightseer, is excited by the glass-factory's appellation of 'die grüne Glashütte' ('the green glassworks'), which 'klingt ja wie aus 'nem Märchen' ('sounds like something out of a fairy-tale'). Dubslav von Stechlin is quick to pour cold water on his fantasy, however, in a refutation exemplifying the whole area:

Ist aber eher das Gegenteil davon. Sie heißt nämlich so, weil man da grünes Glas macht, allergewöhnlichstes Flaschenglas. An Rubinglas mit Goldrand dürfen Sie hier nicht denken. Das ist nichts für unsre Gegend.
(VIII, 51)

(It's more the opposite. It's called that because they make green glass there, common-or-garden bottle glass. You mustn't think of ruby glass with gold rims here. That's not for us, in these parts.)

In Koseleger's words, 'alles nackte Prosa'...'aufgesteifte Leute, geschwollen und hartherzig, und natürlich so trocken und trivial, wie die Leute hier alle sind' ('all barest prose'...

191

'starchy people, pompous and hard-hearted, and naturally as dry and trite as everybody here'; VIII, 160, 161). Dubslav himself subscribes to the popular self-image of the *Mittel-märker*, with remarks like 'Ich bin nicht für's Poetische, das ist für Gouvernanten und arme Lehrer...' ('I'm not one for the poetic, that's for governesses and impoverished school-teachers...'; VIII, 45), or, *à propos* of the so-called *Poeten-steig* (poet's walk) in his grounds, his comment on the inappropriateness of the term in an area never graced by poets – adding 'und ist auch recht gut so', for 'bei den Kürassieren war keiner...' ('and a good thing too... there weren't any in the cuirassiers'; VIII, 50). Thomas Mann would have heartily agreed that a poet among the dragoons would be a bad sign indeed for the health of the nation, and one is put in mind of Mann again much later, when Dubslav tacitly admits the gravity of his illness by resorting to reading a novel (VIII, 291). Like Hans Hansen in *Tonio Kröger*, Dubslav is not to be won over to literature, except *in extremis*, and it is implied by the novelist Fontane, with a self-irony which pre-figures Mann, that the healthy have no need of novels.

Throughout *Der Stechlin* the refined and the aesthetic are rejected. Fancy foreign loan-words, for example, are 'nie was Feines, auch wenn es so aussieht. Dunkle Gefühle, die sind fein' ('never refined, even if it looks like it. Obscure feelings are refined'; VIII, 62). These are Dubslav's words, but their sentiments are echoed by Czako when he speaks of art as 'feine Dinge' ('cultivated things') not suitable for someone like himself 'aus Ostrowo' ('from Ostrovo'; VIII, 98). Aesthetic qualities, 'für manchen ein Unglück' ('for many people a misfortune'; Superintendent Koseleger) are pointedly absent from Stechlin's typically Prussian schoolroom (VIII, 157–8); and Armgard von Barby defends her adopted Mark Brandenburg against her sister Melusine and against Woldemar, in her criticism of their inordinate stress on external aesthetics:

'Ich glaube', sagte Armgard, 'du legst zu viel Gewicht auf das, was du das Ästhetische nennst. Und Woldemar tut es leider auch. Er läßt auf seine Mark Brandenburg sonst nichts kommen, aber in diesem Punkte spricht er beinah so wie du. Wohin er blickt, überall vermißt er das Schönheitliche.' (VIII, 267)

('I think', said Armgard, 'that you put too much stress on what you call the aesthetic. And I'm afraid Woldemar does too. He won't usually hear anything against his beloved Mark Brandenburg, but on this point he talks in much the same way as you do. Wherever he looks there is a lack of beauty.')

Armgard's views are borne out by Melusine's reply, which launches into a wildly romantic excursion on the theme of 'archaic equals poetic' (almost a self-parody of the earlier, enthusiastic ballad-writing Fontane), only to founder in its own extravagance – 'Und selbst unser "dunkles Mittelalter" – schönheitlich stand es höher als wir, und seine Scheiterhaufen, wenn man nicht gleich selbst an die Reihe kam, waren gar nicht so schlimm' ('And even our "dark Middle Ages" – aesthetically they were superior to us, and their burnings at the stake were not so bad, as long as it wasn't your turn'; VIII, 268). The novel overall goes further than Armgard. While she is content simply to maintain that aesthetics do not apply to the Mark, Fontane clearly wants to suggest that, on the contrary, the discerning eye, once it abandons the search for conventional aesthetic appeal, will find in the area a very rare kind of beauty, as the reader will find a rare kind of moral beauty in the voice of the Mark, Dubslav von Stechlin, a man as astringent as his native land ('der alte Dubslav war nicht sehr für Freundschaften. Er sah zu sehr, was jedem einzelnen fehlte', 'old Dubslav was not much of a man for friendships. He saw only too clearly the failings of every individual'; VIII, 171), and, by extension, will also find an uncommon pleasure in a novel that departs so far from the conventional aesthetic rules of the day.

There is at one point a suggestion by Dubslav himself that beauty and morality are one and the same thing (VIII, 303) – as long as morality is understood in the right sense, one that is probably 'kirchlich falsch' ('wrong according to the Church'). The moral law of an area so outwardly impoverished as the

Stechlin is 'man behilft sich mit dem, was man hat' ('you make do with what you have'; VIII, 305). The imagination, too, must make do with what it has, and the surprising result is that, when it is not distracted by such mirages as Melusine's medievalism, it discerns beauty where it is least expected. It takes a man from the rich, picturesque German South, Baron Berchtesgaden, to drive home the object lesson at the end of the novel, in simple but highly significant words: ' "Wie schön", sagte Baron Berchtesgaden, "und dabei spricht man immer von der Dürftigkeit und der Prosa dieser Gegenden" ' (' "How lovely", said Baron Berchtesgaden, "and yet people talk of the poverty and drabness of these regions" '). That it is not only the scenery which the reader should have in mind is implied in Graf Barby's response, at first sight a rather surprising one, coming from a mourner driving away from a funeral: 'Alles stimmte zu, zumeist der alte Graf, der die Frühlingsluft einsog und immer wieder aussprach, wie glücklich ihn diese Stunde mache' ('Everyone agreed, particularly the old Graf, who drank in the spring air and kept repeating how happy this hour had made him'; VIII, 355). Dubslav von Stechlin's death is not an occasion for gloom, but a celebration, because his life was a celebration, above all of the power of the imagination over mere limitations of money, freedom or geography.

Any temptation to think of Dubslav as what he pretends to be – a limited, prosaic Junker from the Mark – is checked not only by the self-revelation of his conversation, but also by a typical Fontane use of contrast. His sister, the Domina, is all that he is not; indeed, she embodies negative qualities that are the conditions for *his* development, 'eine Armut des Bodens, die den Mut...steigert' ('a poverty of the soil which heightens fortitude'):[4]

Was aber...den Verkehr mit ihr so schwer machte, das war die tiefe Prosa ihrer Natur, das märkisch Enge, das Mißtrauen gegen alles, was die Welt der Schönheit oder der Freiheit auch nur streifte. (VIII, 75)

(But what made dealings with her so difficult was her deeply prosaic

nature, the typical narrow-mindedness of the Mark, the distrust of every-thing even remotely connected with the world of beauty or freedom.)
Limitation may induce limited vision, but, as Dubslav demon-strates, it can produce its opposite. Liberty must be limited in order to be possessed. Whereas his sister's circumscribed existence is composed of nothing more than the sum of all the limitations imposed upon its growth, Dubslav's quality can be measured in terms of what he lacks, or does not need. (That these two categories are usually synonymous is a sign of his success as a personality.) Although a good part of the novel is taken up with preparations for travelling and reports of jour-neys, Dubslav has never travelled much (VIII, 285). But he is no less a 'wirklicher Mensch' (real person) for that (VIII, 272). His reaction to Armgard's letter from her Italian honeymoon makes the point: 'Ja, reisen und in den Krieg ziehen, da lernt man, da wird man anders' ('Yes, travelling and going to war; you learn from them, you become different'; VIII, 314). So much is he the man of renunciation, *Entbehrungen*, that it is almost unnecessary to add that he has never seen action in war, either! ('Seine Jahre bei den Kürassieren waren im wesentlichen Friedensjahre gewesen; nur Anno vierundsechzig war er mit in Schleswig, aber auch hier, ohne "zur Aktion" zu kommen', 'His years with the cuirassiers had been essentially peace-time years, except for '64, when he had been with the Army in Schleswig; but even there, he never saw action'; VIII, 8.) And yet he has the capacity to appreciate the changes that these formative events bring about in others. He has no need of education in this sense, or perhaps in any. In this too, Fontane diverges from a German idealist tradition, that of the *Bildungs-roman*, the novel of education.[5] Dubslav partakes of nature itself, and (in contrast to Graf Holk in *Unwiederbringlich*) is in no need of improvement. Another of Dubslav's renunciations is a second marriage: he has been a widower for thirty years. The reason why he did not marry again is hinted at in an understatement implying a true asceticism. In reviewing the course of his life he summarizes: 'Dann kam ein Lichtblick

[his marriage]. Aber gleich danach starb sie, die mir Stab und Stütze hätte sein können...' ('Then came a beam of light. But soon afterwards she died, who might have been a staff and a support to me...'; VIII, 288). His wife meant so much to him that it has been a self-imposed spiritual discipline – though clearly not of a morbid kind; he is too much the lover of life for that – never to remarry, hard though this was at the beginning ('Anfangs war's ihm schwer geworden...', VIII, 9). His reasons are typical of him:

Sich eine neue zu nehmen, widerstand ihm, halb aus Ordnungssinn und halb aus ästhetischer Rücksicht. 'Wir glauben doch alle mehr oder weniger an eine Auferstehung' (das heißt, er persönlich glaubte eigentlich nicht daran), 'und wenn ich dann oben ankomme mit einer rechts und einer links, so is das doch immer eine genierliche Sache.' (VIII, 8)

(To take a new wife did not appeal to him, partly because of his sense of order, and partly because of aesthetic considerations. 'We all believe more or less in a Resurrection' (that is, he personally did not really believe in it), 'and if I arrive up there with one on the right and one on the left, it will be an embarrassing business.')

The fact is, surely, that he possesses a finely developed 'sittliche Natur' (moral nature), inherited by his son (VIII, 67), which is at home in such an ascetic self-denial; though he would never dream of accepting as relevant to himself the pretentious foreign word *Askese* (asceticism), applied by Rex to Woldemar (VIII, 67). To confirm this judgment of Dubslav's 'sittliche Natur', Lorenzen tells him at the end of his life of one last renunciation he can afford to make, one which above all others emphasizes the fact that what he lacks or can do without is what recommends him: 'Herr von Stechlin, Ihre Seele macht mir... keine Sorge, denn sie zählt zu denen, die jeder Spezialempfehlung entbehren können' ('Herr von Stechlin, your soul gives me no cause for concern, for it is one of those that can manage without any special recommendation'; VIII, 315).

Melusine's views on celibacy (VIII, 354) make explicit the virtues of a morality of renunciation which we noted as implicit in *Unwiederbringlich*. Discussing the bachelor Pastor Lorenzen,

Adelheid (ironically, herself a spinster) has insisted that the single state is unnatural, especially for a clergyman. 'Es widerspricht dem Beispiel, das unser Gottesmann gegeben, und widerspricht auch wohl der Natur.' ('It contradicts the example set us by our Man of God [Luther], and it also surely contradicts nature.') Melusine agrees, but only up to a point: 'Ja, der Durchschnittsnatur. Es gibt aber, Gott sei Dank, Ausnahmen. Und das sind die eigentlich Berufenen. Eine Frau nehmen, ist alltäglich...', 'Yes, the nature of the average person. But there are, thank God, exceptions. And they are the ones with a real vocation. Taking a wife is commonplace...'. What Fontane does here, and by extension in the whole novel, is to redefine the currently fashionable Nietzschean concept of the *Übermensch*, already dismissed by Dubslav von Stechlin in an earlier chapter (chapter 33, VIII, 272):[6] 'Jetzt hat man statt des wirklichen Menschen den sogenannten Übermenschen etabliert; eigentlich gibt es bloß noch Untermenschen, und mitunter sind es gerade die, die man durchaus zu seinem "Über" machen will' ('Now, instead of real Man, the so-called Superman has been set up; actually there are only sub-humans left, and sometimes it is those in particular whom people are determined to elevate to "Super" status'). The same play with *oben* and *unten* (above and below) recurs in the continuation of Melusine's and Adelheid's disagreement in chapter 45. Accused of being an advocate of 'das Unnatürliche' ('the unnatural'), Melusine replies:

'In gewissem Sinne "ja", Frau Domina. Was entscheidet, ist, ob man dabei nach oben oder nach unten rechnet.'
'Das Leben rechnet nach unten.'
'Oder nach oben; je nachdem.'

('In a sense "yes", Frau Domina. The decisive thing is whether that involves calculating upwards or downwards.'
'Life calculates downwards.'
'Or upwards: it all depends.')

The function of *Der Stechlin*, and one which summarizes and crowns the achievement of all Fontane's work, is 'nach oben zu rechnen' ('to calculate upwards'). To achieve this aim Fontane repeatedly inverts normal assumptions about what is 'higher' (and emphatically inverts arrogant Prussian assumptions about the *Übermensch*).[7] What is commonly regarded as 'fine', 'profound' or 'beautiful' is almost never superior, 'das Höhere'. In Fontane, spiritual pride is always close to a fall. The aristocratic, high-principled and deeply religious character, Rex, in *Der Stechlin*, is a prime target. He is thinking of becoming an *Irvingianer* (Irvingian), and sectarianism, because of its exaggeration of religious commitment, is almost invariably the subject of humour in Fontane's works. Not only is Rex brought down from the refined heights he normally inhabits, by being forced to take his boots off to obtain relief during the visit to Kloster Wutz, but aristocratic pretensions are subjected to some typical oblique criticism through the introduction of a character with parallel and independent comic value. Fräulein von Triglaff, one of the inmates of the convent, bears, like Rex, an aristocratic name of awe-inspiring antiquity and enormous prestige – so great that she has become the total victim of her 'stupende Triglaffvorstellung' ('tremendous Triglaff pretensions'; VIII, 83), an exaggerated version of Rex's own almost unlimited aristocratic pride of lineage, intimately connected with his religiosity: 'Die Triglaff... verband in sich den Ausdruck höchster Tiefsinnigkeit mit ganz ungewöhnlicher Umnachtung' ('The Triglaff lady... combined an expression of the greatest profundity with a most uncommon degree of mental derangement').

The ideal of humanity, *Menschlichkeit*, in *Der Stechlin*, in so far as one can talk about an ideal in a novel by a writer who rejects absolutes (as does Dubslav von Stechlin himself), bears some relationship to the *sancta simplicitas* of Tolstoyan humanism, summed up a little dismissively by Melusine as 'etwas mit viel Opfer und Entsagung. Anpreisung von Askese' ('Something to do with a lot of sacrifice and renunciation. Extolling asceticism'; VIII, 144). But Melusine's preference for 'nach oben rechnen' and suggestion of a naturalness superior to the average, an *Übernatürlichkeit* (super-naturalness) which is the complete antithesis of the *Übermensch*-idea, complements Woldemar von Stechlin's confessed enthusiasm for Tolstoy (VIII, 119); and Woldemar, in turn, tends to hold views which are a more conscious and intellectualized version of his father's instinctive beliefs. Although Fontane (not to speak of Dubslav von Stechlin!) would never use such language, and would forfeit the very virtues it extolls if he did, there is something in the following summary of the humane vision of Russian literature which is not entirely inappropriate to the author of *Der Stechlin*:

Die reinigende, heiligende Wirkung der Literatur, die Zerstörung der Leidenschaften durch die Erkenntnis und das Wort, die Literatur als Weg zum Verstehen, zum Vergeben und zur Liebe, die erlösende Macht der Sprache, der literarische Geist als die edelste Erscheinung des Menschengeistes überhaupt, der Literat als vollkommener Mensch, als Heiliger... (Lisaweta Iwanowna in chapter 4 of Thomas Mann's *Tonio Kröger*)

(The cleansing, hallowing effect of literature, the destruction of the passions through knowledge and the word, literature as a path to understanding, to forgiveness and love, the redeeming power of language, the literary spirit as the noblest manifestation of the human spirit in general, the man of letters as perfect human being, as saint...)

Lorenzen, Woldemar's mentor, is clearly another Tolstoyan type, who has decided to employ his considerable talents in a Brandenburg backwater (like Tolstoy at Yasnaya Polyana), in clear contrast to the discontented and worldly Superintendent Koseleger, who desires to climb higher, 'höher hinauf' (VIII, 161, and cf. 26–7). In the sphere of the Tolstoyan, too, belongs the old schoolteacher Krippenstapel, who admires his bees as the model of a utopian state, and, in the old tradition of impecunious Prussian schoolmasters, is not above undertaking peasant labour for the sake of self-sufficiency (VIII, 65). His independence, like Lorenzen's, parallels Dubslav's; and, like Dubslav, neither Lorenzen nor Krippenstapel is married. All three are strangers to ambition, which is seen in a negative light throughout the novel (e.g. VIII, 20, 338) – even heroism in battle tends to be looked down upon by Dubslav as a kind of thrusting oneself forward, *Strebertum*; see p. 8. The *Streber* (careerists), like Rex (VIII, 20), and Innstetten in *Effi Briest*, climb career ladders at the expense of their independence, and as we have seen, independence is Fontane's highest poetic value. It is much easier to be independent, and therefore human, *menschlich*, in a backwater than in the city: as Czako says of Woldemar as early as chapter 2, 'Wenn unser Freund Stechlin sich in diese seine alte Schloßkate zurückzieht, so darf er Mensch sein, aber als Gardedragoner kommt er damit nicht aus' ('When our friend Stechlin retires to this old castle-cottage of his, he can afford to be human; but that will not take him far in the Dragoon Guards'; VIII, 19). Among a number of indications at the end of the novel that Dubslav's death is not the end of the Stechlin spirit, is Woldemar's entirely Dubslavian remark in chapter 45 that 'Eigner freier Entschluß wiegt hundert Erziehungsmaximen auf' ('One's own free decision is worth a hundred educational maxims'; VIII, 359: compare Dubslav's reference to 'Freiheit und Selbstentschließung', 'freedom and self-determination'; VIII, 283). Woldemar gives up his ambition to become a major (VIII, 269) and thus effectively decides to become a *Mensch* instead. Both Woldemar and Dubslav have one talent, and nothing else, the talent to be human, and as Junkers they can develop this talent to the full, for they are fortunate enough to belong to the last non-specialist group in a world of professionalism and division of labour. Woldemar is relieved when his father is defeated in the election, for politics, too, are becoming a specialist area, and Dubslav is no village Hampden: he has no talent to be a Bismarck except in Stechlin. Dubslav fulfils that 'aesthetic imperative' enshrined in the fifteenth of Schiller's Aesthetic Letters (a work which takes as its lodestar the state of mankind before the onset of specialization, and therefore of division): 'Der Mensch spielt nur, wo er in voller Bedeutung des Worts Mensch ist, und er ist nur da ganz Mensch, wo er spielt' ('Man plays only when he is human in the fullest sense of the word, and is only human when he plays'). In some of his little self-ironizing poems, such as 'Großes Kind' ('Grown-up Child'), or 'Was mir fehlte' ('What I lacked'), Fontane humorously deprecates a personal trait which, in reality, he esteems highly – 'der fehlende Sinn für Feierlichkeit' ('the lack of a sense of solemnity'; XX, 31), or in other words the ability to take only the right things seriously. The specialist, by definition, suffers a loss of vital room for manoeuvre or *Spielraum*, is forced to take himself and his role seriously, and thereby suffers a deformation, like that suffered by Innstetten, the only dedicated specialist among Fontane's major characters (women, being excluded from most serious pursuits, are relatively intact). Two minor examples of *déformation professionnelle* in *Der Stechlin* are Cujacius and the musician Wrschowitz, both prisoners of their own dogma.

Complementary to Woldemar's decision to quit the professional Army is the independent decision of his new wife, Armgard, to take up residence in Stechlin and to forsake Berlin (VIII, 360). Thus she complies with Czako's maxim in chapter 10: '...die wirklich Vornehmen, die gehorchen, nicht einem Machthaber, sondern dem Gefühl ihrer Pflicht' ('...really noble people obey, not an authority-figure, but their own feeling of duty'; VIII, 95).

But the ideal of humanity, *Menschlichkeit*, is not completely exhausted by Tolstoyan concepts of the search for personal salvation in a life spent among ordinary people. At the opposite extreme (but extremes tend to meet in *Der Stechlin*) is a pragmatic, sceptical and also exuberant frame of mind closer to the English novel than to the Russian. A distinct colour-tone is created by the many references to the variety of life in England, the self-confidence that breeds an ability to question basic assumptions in a way that is poles apart from the agonizing Russian tendency to take nothing on trust.

This 'English' aspect includes a delight in sheer observation of social nuance and of human idiosyncracy, and a healthy rejection of any inclination to overestimate human motives – for example, Dubslav's remark in chapter 6, 'Der Mensch stiehlt wie 'n Rabe' ('People thieve like magpies'; VIII, 59). In this category too falls the tendency to generalize, prevalent throughout Fontane but almost reaching the proportions of a mannerism in *Der Stechlin*. Examples include 'alle Lehrer sind verrückt' ('all teachers are mad'; VIII, 48); 'alle Klosteruhren gehen nach' ('all convent clocks are slow'; VIII, 71); or a real gem in chapter 14, a generalization *within* a generalization: 'Frau Imme, die wie die meisten kinderlosen Frauen (und Frauen mit Sappeurbartmännern sind fast immer kinderlos), einen großen Wirtschafts- und Sauberkeitssinn hatte...' ('Frau Imme, who, like most childless women (and women with husbands with Pioneer Corps beards are nearly always childless) had a highly-developed feeling for housekeeping and cleaning...'; VIII, 132).

Dubslav's pragmatism has a dual aspect: on the one hand it corresponds to the stability and enduring, honest quality of the Mark, and on the other it delights in the freedom 'hinter alles ein Fragezeichen zu machen' ('to put a question-mark after everything'; VIII, 7). Age and youth are combined in the seemingly contradictory tendencies to generalize, on the one hand, and to question, on the other. At the age of sixty-seven it would be unnatural not to claim enough experience to be able to formulate general truths; and yet to qualify as a real human being, a 'wirklicher Mensch', as he does, Dubslav must have a mind that is open to new ideas. Paradox is the poetry of the independent mind, a means by which contradictory statements can be held together, grammatically at least. At its best paradox is a formulation that achieves sovereignty over contradiction and hence over life, which is nothing if not contradictory. This is probably what Emerson had in mind when he said in his essay on Self-Reliance that 'a foolish consistency is the hobgoblin of petty minds'. And, one might add, the demand for consistency at all times is a kind of vanity, the reduction of vexatious irreconcilables to manageable proportions. Stechlin's self-contradiction, in essence, signifies modesty, not arrogance, as might at first appear to be the case. We are told of Dubslav in the first chapter that 'Paradoxen waren seine Passion' ('paradoxes were his passion'). To prove the point, he is made to say, 'Ich bin nicht klug genug, selber welche zu machen, aber ich freue mich, wenn's andere tun.' He then goes on to create the most complex paradox: 'Unanfechtbare Wahrheiten gibt es überhaupt nicht, und wenn es welche gibt, so sind sie langweilig' ('I'm not clever enough to invent any myself, but I'm glad when others do'. . . . 'There are no unassailable truths, and if there are they're boring'; VIII, 7–8). Dubslav's sublime acceptance of paradox helps him to achieve the reconciliation, or at the very least the frictionless juxtaposition, of old and new, so that, for example, although he is intensely provoked by the products of the Globsow glass-factory, the bottles and carboys destined to hold chemicals associated with ugly modern industrialization (VIII, 61), Stechlin has nonetheless given one of the factory's products pride of place in the forecourt at Schloß Stechlin (VIII, 57).

The reconciliation of old and new which Dubslav achieves is, it was said above, a theme of the book, occurring contentiously for example in the crass notion of a conservative revolution and a Pre-Raphaelite return to the 'natural' favoured by Professor Cujacius; more positively in the admiration for England as a *stable* combination of tradition and modernity (VIII, 236) and in Lorenzen's faith that 'dies neue Christentum ist gerade das alte' ('this new Christianity is precisely the old one'; VIII, 343). Old and new blend naturally in Dubslav's ambience, so that Stechlin lake is geologically ancient, yet 'revolutionary' at the same time. Dubslav is nostalgic for the good old days of the Quitzows, when Junker power outweighed that of the monarchy, yet he can say that it would be best for modern Prussia 'wenn ein einziger Alter-Fritzen-Verstand die ganze Geschichte regieren könnte' ('if the good sense of just one Frederick the Great could take control of the whole situation'; VIII, 39). This last paradox or self-contradiction is a good example of his lack of cumbersome idealism and his common-sense pragmatism. While as a Junker he is suspicious of the nature of the monarchy, his flexibility can easily overcome such scruples. Pragmatically, he recognizes the virtues of a system by which kings are legally endowed with the right to act as the collective ego of all the private egos of their subjects, provided the collective ego of the monarch is sufficiently close to the Junker ego – that is to say, close to his own, for Dubslav is not unlike a self-appointed monarch in his willingness to claim representative status; and after all, were his ancestors not among those who 'schon vor den Hohenzollern da waren' ('were there before the Hohenzollerns'; VIII, 7)? Dubslav, in his own person, ensures that political extremes (among others) meet by coming full circle, so that 'der alte Dubslav, . . . der hat das im Leibe, was die richtigen Junker alle haben: ein Stück Sozialdemokratie' ('old Dubslav . . . has in him what all proper Junkers have: a touch of Social Democracy'; VIII, 192; cf. also 107, 343). Dubslav's home is at one and the same time both a *Schloß* and a *Kate* (castle and cottage; VIII, 19).

The best example of Dubslav's almost royal ability to reconcile extremes in his own person, to an even greater extent than in his opinions, is his funeral, at which all factions and classes pay their last respects. He is a centre on to which all can hinge. As he unites them all in love and respect, so the parvenu middle-class Gundermann, with his disloyalty and his lack of any redeeming qualities, acts as a foil to Dubslav, uniting by contrast both Right and Left in hatred (VIII, 162). If Gundermann, far more than Frau Jenny Treibel, is the living embodiment of the late nineteenth-century mammonism that Fontane so intensely abhorred, then Dubslav, at the opposing extreme, is the embodiment of a poetic quality attaching to aristocracy or monarchy in its highest manifestation. But, as Dubslav would be the first to concede, the most trivial concerns of the living far outweigh even the most important death, and he would sympathize with his fellow-Junkers' complaint of the shocking draughts they have been exposed to at his funeral

(VIII, 352: 'Zug', a draught, is the most potent remainder of human frailty throughout Fontane's works. Cf. Hugo's death in *Mathilde Möhring*).

Fontane places his poetry in a framework of prose which reminds us that he is, after all, a realist, and in the real world there is nothing more absorbing than one's own life, not even court gossip, however much titillation that provides. Armgard remarks in chapter 24: 'Unsre teure Baronin findet unser Leben langweilig und solche Chronik interessant. Ich, umgekehrt, finde solche Chronik langweilig und unser tägliches Leben interessant' ('Our dear Baroness finds our life boring and such a chronicle interesting. I, on the contrary, find the chronicle boring and our daily life interesting'; VIII, 213).[8] Melusine fundamentally disagrees, and the friendly difference of opinion between the two sisters on this issue exemplifies something very important in the novel, two views on the proper use of the imagination. Armgard tends a little to the strait-laced, the slightly over-moral outlook, taking rather too intolerant a view of gossip, *Klatsch*, which, it was pointed out above, is a central organizing principle of the novel. (To redress the balance, as is his wont, Fontane makes her unbend somewhat and become quite promisingly *risqué* in her remark, in the letter home from honeymoon, that she is glad not to be in a nunnery – VIII, 348.) More important, however, is the fact that she is basically in sympathy with the feeling of Stechlin and the Mark that 'man behilft sich mit dem, was man hat' ('you make do with what you have'), to quote again Dubslav's words to Melusine in chapter 37 (VIII, 305). That Armgard is of this persuasion is one of the reasons why it is a foregone conclusion that Woldemar, who, as events show, is a *Märker* (native of the Mark) at heart despite his highly successful foray into the brilliant world of Berlin, London and Windsor, will choose Armgard as his bride and not Melusine. For Melusine's imagination has a kind of divine discontent which, at times, comes dangerously close to Koseleger's combination of ambition and aestheticism (Melusine, VIII, 268: 'wer kein feines Gefühl

hat, sei's in Kunst, sei's in Leben, der existiert für mich überhaupt ·nicht', 'anyone who doesn't have sensitivity, either towards art or life, simply doesn't exist as far as I'm concerned')
or Cujacius's 'große Revolution, die Rückkehr heißt' ('great
revolution that is a return to the past') (Melusine: 'Unser ganzer
Gesellschaftszustand, der sich wunder wie hoch dünkt, ist
mehr oder weniger Barbarei;...Ach wie voraus war uns doch
die Heidenzeit...', 'The whole condition of our civilization,
which thinks itself goodness knows how highly developed, is
more or less barbaric;...Oh, how far in advance of us was the
heathen age'; ibid.). With the possible exception of Czako, she
is the only character in the novel possessed of an imagination
that can compete with Dubslav's. However, the quality of their
mental life is very different. She inclines to the sensational, the
highly dramatic, whereas Dubslav can conjure up sudden
pictures of life free of such drama, but startling in their vivid-
ness, such as the little vignette of an unpretentious hotel in
Bavaria, mentioned above in my chapter on *Die Poggenpuhls*,
almost a whole Novelle in embryo:

Übrigens darf ich bei allem Respekt vor meinem berühmten Hotel Bristol
in Berlin sagen, unberühmte sind meist interessanter. So zum Beispiel
bayrische Wirtshäuser im Gebirge, wo man eine dicke Wirtin hat, von
der es heißt, sie sei mal schön gewesen, und ein Kaiser oder König habe
ihr den Hof gemacht. Und dazu dann Forellen und ein Landjäger, der
eben einen Wilderer oder Haberfeldtreiber über den stillen See bringt.
An solchen Stellen ist es am schönsten. Und ist der See aufgeregt, so ist
es noch schöner. (VIII, 272)

(Anyway, with all due respect for my famous Hotel Bristol in Berlin,
I might say that undistinguished ones are more interesting. For example,
Bavarian mountain inns, where you have a fat landlady of whom it is
said that she was once beautiful and was courted by a king or an
emperor. And then there are trout and a gendarme who is just bringing
back a mob leader* or a poacher across the calm lake. Those are the
nicest places. And if the lake is rough, it's even better.)

* Haberfeldtreiben = (In Bavaria) a 'people's court' or mob justice
applied to unpopular individuals.

There is no lack of material, no obstacle to the fertile
imagination, Fontane suggests, though its vehicle may be

restricted to a remote, land-locked area. Lake Stechlin's ability
to 'telegraph to Java' symbolizes Dubslav's breadth of imaginative power. The mind can encircle the globe, for, as Lorenzen
says, it is the state of mind that matters, 'Gesinnung entscheidet'
(VIII, 317).

The plot of *Der Stechlin*, attenuated as it is, is well designed
to illustrate the importance of the quality of the imagination.
Discounting the non-event of the election, only two significant
events occur; and even in confining his action to these very
limited elements of plot Fontane is making the statement that
constraint is productive and is not always to be identified with
loss of freedom. (Compare Woldemar's formulation in chapter 46: 'Die Scholle daheim, die dir Freiheit gibt, ist doch das
Beste', 'There's nothing better than your proper home soil,
which gives you liberty'; VIII, 360-1). For with these two
occurrences, Woldemar's choice of a bride and Dubslav's death,
Fontane can say all that he wants to say about the power of the
healthy human mind to shape its own world according to the
needs of the whole organism. Woldemar, in choosing between
Melusine and Armgard, must decide who he is. It is perhaps
the most momentous choice of his life, and one of the most
important occurrences of the 'choice' motif in Fontane's novels.
Dubslav's imagination, on the other hand, is faced with its
greatest task yet, the imaginative effort to encompass his own
demise. The strength required is the power of *Selbstüberwind-
ung* (self-conquest).

Fontane is making use of a very well established Romantic
motif when he makes Woldemar choose between the two
women: a conflict between the claims of the imagination
(promising both genuine insight and also the possibility of fatal
confusion) and those of common reality – a choice very often
presented as a choice between two females embodying these
opposing qualities: between Serpentina and Veronica in Hoffmann's *Der Goldne Topf* (The Golden Pot), or between Lady
Venus and Bianka in Eichendorff's story *Das Marmorbild* (The
Marble Image).[9] In a novel which so largely concerns itself

with restraint and the theme of freedom within limitation, it is hardly surprising that Woldemar is made to choose, not the alluring and highly imaginative Melusine, but the quieter Armgard, more earnest and less colourful than her divorcée sister (Armgard is often referred to as pale, *blaß*: VIII, 288, 344). In emphasizing restraint, moreover, Fontane seems to be putting a distance between his present self and his literary beginnings in the 'romantisch-phantastisch' world of the ballad. Such a distance is suggested when, *Northanger Abbey*-style, he twice leads overnight visitors in Schloß Stechlin to expect ghosts in the old building, thus recalling the spooky atmosphere of Schloß Hohen-Vietz in *Vor dem Sturm* (VIII, 43, 240). Such sensational expectations run completely counter to the spirit of the place and the atmosphere of serenity that prevails throughout the novel. In the same anti-Gothic vein is Woldemar's preference, while sightseeing in England, for Waltham Abbey over the Traitor's Gate at the Tower, recommended to him in such imaginative language by Melusine. Fontane's ballad 'Der Tower-Brand' ('The Fire in the Tower') was his first great success at the meetings of the 'Tunnel', and it is significant that, surveying London once more through the eyes of Woldemar, he chooses to dwell upon the very different scene of Waltham Abbey, about which, surprisingly, he had never written a ballad (although he published a description of his visit there in the *Kreuzzeitung* (XVII, 413), and related subject-matter is dealt with in his ballad 'Hastingsfeld' as well as in Heine's 'Schlachtfeld bei Hastings' ('The Battlefield at Hastings'), declared by Fontane in 1889 to be among his favourite poems: see XXI/1, 497). Melusine has to admit that Woldemar's description shows that he possesses imagination, after all: 'Waltham-Abbey kenn ich nun, und an Ihre Phantasie glaub ich von heut an, trotzdem Sie mich mit Traitors-Gate im Stiche gelassen' ('Now I know Waltham Abbey, and from now on I believe in your imagination, even though you let me down over Traitor's Gate'; VIII, 225). There are more applications of the imagination than Melusine was at first prepared to admit; the quiet and contemplative, as well as the sensational. For the Abbey, in contrast to the bloodthirsty Tower, prompts tranquil reflections on the end of a dynasty and the demise of the sovereignty of a race ('Tod und Begräbnis des alten Sachsentums', XVII, 417; the parallel with the approaching end of the Prussian *Junkertum* is not hard to see). Also associated with it is the selfless, anonymous heroism and loyalty of the monks who, according to legend, carried King Harold's body from Hastings to Waltham – rather more appealing to Woldemar, it seems, than the gory associations of punishment for *dis*loyalty or disfavour connected with Traitor's Gate. Waltham Abbey, in Woldemar's description, is suffused with the glow of sunset (which was not the case in the 1857 description mentioned above; XVII, 413), thus contributing to the atmosphere of quiet decline which finds expression in a number of sunset descriptions throughout *Der Stechlin*, culminating in a chapter bearing the title 'Sonnenuntergang'.

Melusine stands for one, romantic version of the poetic – the one that had first attracted Fontane – but her 'firework' quality brings her uncomfortably close to Ebba in *Unwiederbringlich*. In the course of their 'Eierhäuschen' excursion, in chapter 15, Woldemar's party see rockets and fireworks, for which Melusine declares that she has a passion (see the *Unwiederbringlich* chapter, above p. 127). Woldemar reacts unequivocally, in terms of the symbolism of their relationship: 'Ja, unbedingt. Und nur schade, daß alle die, die damit zu tun haben, über kurz oder lang in die Luft fliegen' ('Yes, absolutely. And it is just a pity that all those who have to do with them sooner or later get blown up'; VIII, 143). Melusine's taste for living dangerously has already been demonstrated by her disastrous and short-lived (rocket-like?) marriage to Count Ghiberti; and someone with her temperament, as she comes near to confessing while praising Lorenzen's bachelor-status (VIII, 354), is not really made for marriage at all. The chapter containing the firework discussion is, significantly, one in which an engagement, though 'in the air', fails to take place (VIII, 146) – that between Woldemar and Melusine, which would have been a mistake. She could never have settled for the quiet backwater of Stechlin, which is manifestly Woldemar's destiny. His choice of Armgard is tantamount to a political decision: her quietness and practical good sense can be equated with Lorenzen's path of restraint, his 'stille Weise', and Melusine's passion and fireworks of the imagination with Adolf Stöcker, 'der große Agitator' and chief spokesman of the Christian Socialists, whom Lorenzen admires, but from whom he takes only the good qualities.[10] This is not to detract from Melusine's great charms and her ability to represent the life-spirit itself – as even Adelheid admits (VIII, 234) – but simply to infer that her combination of society lady and full-blooded woman, 'Dame und Frauenzimmer dazu' (Dubslav, VIII, 234) is too strong and too sophisticated for Woldemar.

The engagement that *does* take place, in chapter 25, comes about soon after an account given by Woldemar of his reaction to the tombs of the two Queens, Elizabeth and Mary, near the Chapel of Henry VII in Westminster Abbey. For him they represent universal types, the opposition of 'Leidenschaft und Berechnung, von Schönheit und Klugheit' ('passion and calculation, beauty and shrewdness'; VIII, 226). The two types are, one might say, prosaic and poetic. But the poetic can be understood in senses other than the dramatic, 'Catholic' version represented by Mary Queen of Scots. Armgard puts forward a third model, the saintly Elisabeth of Thuringia, for 'andern leben und der Armut das Brot geben – darin allein ruht das Glück' ('to live for others and to succour poverty with bread – that alone is the source of happiness'; VIII, 226). Armgard's innocence wins against Melusine's sometimes cynically displayed experience, and the engagement that immediately takes place is so little stressed that it almost seems to be the unnoticed but inevitable outcome of some natural process.

The selflessness of Armgard's 'alternative' poetic view of life is very much that of youth, but it has a close affinity with age – with Lorenzen's beliefs and with Dubslav's instinctive style of life. Lorenzen, too, is pure in heart, 'reinen Herzens', possessed of 'Begeisterung und Liebe', love and enthusiasm (VIII, 141). He makes conscious a thought which ripens in the course of Fontane's novel-writing, and was only implied in *Effi Briest* (and *Ellernklipp*): the incompatibility of natural justice with the spirit of the Decalogue: 'Die zehn Gebote, das war der Alte Bund, der Neue Bund aber hat ein andres, ein einziges Gebot, und das klingt aus in: "Und du hättest der Liebe nicht..."' ('The Ten Commandments, that was the Old Covenant, but the New Covenant has a different commandment, just one, and it ends with "And if you have not charity..."'; VIII, 145) – a sentiment with which Dubslav agrees, incidentally, in his own untheological way: 'du sollst, du sollst, und noch öfter "du sollst *nicht*". Und klingt eigentlich alles, wie wenn ein Nürnberger Schultheiß gesprochen hätte' (...'thou shalt, thou shalt, and more often "thou shalt not". And it all sounds like a Nuremberg magistrate talking'; VIII, 340). Lorenzen's views are more poetic than political; he looks for nothing less than the poeticizing of the whole society, in the name of the Portuguese poet João de Deus: '...es gibt dergleichen noch, es muß dergleichen geben oder doch *wieder* geben. [Once again the theme is that of a return to the past in order to make progress, but in a very different sense from that of the Conservative Revolution.] Unsre ganze Gesellschaft – und nun gar erst das, was sich im besonderen so nennt – ist aufgebaut auf dem Ich...' ('...such a thing still exists, must exist or at least must come again. Our whole society – particularly that section which distinguishes itself by the name, Society – is built upon the ego...'; VIII, 145). As Hilde, in *Ellernklipp* (II, 195), had difficulty in remembering certain parts of the Credo, so Lorenzen places charity and hope above creed (VIII, 143).

Dubslav's selflessness can be observed in his actions, more than in his words; as Lorenzen says in his funeral sermon, on the question of Dubslav's faith: 'Er hatte davon weniger das Wort als das Tun' (VIII, 351). But above all his self-conquest is evident in the novel in his refusal to fall completely into the old man's posture of damning the new age as one of unmitigated decline. Not that he does not feel the temptation of age to laud its own time as one of greatness, and view what comes after with jaundiced eyes as a deterioration; for as Dubslav confesses, 'Jeder hält seine Zeit für die beste' ('Everyone thinks his own time is the best'; VIII, 40-1). In a speech in chapter 5, Dubslav expresses the essentials of this view:

Ja, herabgestiegen ist alles, und es steigt immer weiter nach unten. Das ist, was man neue Zeit nennt, immer weiter runter. Und mein Pastor... der behauptet...die aristokratische Welt habe abgewirtschaftet, und nun komme die demokratische...(VIII, 47)

(Yes, it has all slipped into decline, and it's slipping further all the time. That's what they call a new age, things always slipping further. And my Pastor...he maintains...that the aristocrat world is finished, and now it's democracy's turn...)

But, in reply to Rex's shocked reaction to Lorenzen's democratic notions, Dubslav turns a mental somersault as usual, and declares: '...ich muß bekennen, es hat manches für sich, trotzdem es mir nicht recht paßt' ('I must admit there's a lot in it, even though it doesn't suit me particularly well'; ibid.). He enjoys one of the greatest freedoms imaginable: the freedom to 'play' with the idea of the demise of his own class ('das ist alles ja bloß Spielerei', 'that's all just games-playing'; VIII, 192. Graf Barby, his *alter ego*, can even go so far in overcoming his own 'vested interests' as to envisage Europe's dismissal from the centre of world politics: 'Es hat sich überlebt. Und anstaunenswert ist nur das eine, daß es überhaupt noch so weitergeht', 'It has had its day. And the only surprising thing is that we go on at all as before'; VIII, 131). Dubslav knows full well that 'ihm sein geliebter Pastor den Ast absägt, auf dem er sitzt' ('his beloved Pastor is sawing off the branch he's sitting on'; VIII, 42). He does not accept this gladly, for otherwise his renunciation would mean little. But his instinctive morality tells him that what cannot be maintained by a general faith in the institution of aristocracy cannot be maintained in any other way, while his natural religion makes him see any talk of falling off, *Abfall*, as a kind of blasphemy (he makes a confession of this 'natural religion' at the end of his life, when he adopts the young girl Agnes, who is a genuine expression of his belief in youth and renewal).

This question of faith or belief is all-important, as we saw when discussing Prussia's relation to Schleswig-Holstein, and Holk's relationship with his wife, in the chapter on *Unwiederbringlich*. 'Daß man überhaupt so was kann, wie sich opfern, das ist das Große' ('What is great is that people can do such a thing at all as sacrificing themselves'; Dubslav, VIII, 303). At this stage in Prussian history, very few are likely to be willing to give their all for the *Junkertum*. The new passionate cause is Social Democracy, support for which increased at a truly impressive rate in late-nineteenth-century Prussia. However much Dubslav regrets its symptoms, he admits its causes readily enough. If we are to believe Lorenzen, one of the causes is, paradoxically, an *excess* of belief on Prussia's part in its own necessity to continue precisely as it is, although much that was great has now become mediocre: 'Wenn ich zweifle, so gelten diese Zweifel nicht so sehr den Dingen selbst, als dem Hochmaß des Glaubens daran' ('If I am doubtful, my doubts are caused less by things themselves than by the intensity of people's faith in them'; VIII, 252). There are many demonstrations in the course of the novel of this belief in the necessity to preserve all that is, simply because it happens to have had the good fortune to survive. The bourgeois conservatives in particular, for whom Dubslav somewhat misguidedly stands as parliamentary candidate, are fond of seeing all new developments as evidence of further decline in 'dieser Welt des Abfalls' (Oberförster Katzler, VIII, 155). The gulf between Dubslav von Stechlin and the ultra-conservative businessman Gundermann brings out what is organic and natural in Dubslav's view of change, which might be summarized as reluctant acceptance. The conservative camp is at least as strange a mixture as the socialist – which encompasses Lorenzen and Turgelow – containing, as it does, the Junkers as well as Gundermann. The latter, for example, wants to abolish Parliament, while the Junkers are convinced that it represents their only chance of survival (VIII, 180).[11] On the whole, it is the rather less appealing characters in the novel who have most to say about the world's decline: Adelheid (VIII, 79, 327), Cujacius (222), Koseleger (302). So prevalent is this note that it becomes debased almost to a matter of fashion, a *Weltuntergangsstimmung* or *fin de siècle* mood. Dubslav would surely feel obliged to reject this mood, if for no other reason, simply because it *is* a fashion, and one senses this in his reply to Rex, in grudging approval of Lorenzen's reformism: 'ich muß bekennen, es hat manches für sich...' ('I must admit, there's something in it'; VIII, 47).

But a better reason is that it does not accord, in the end, with his instinctive love of life and of youth, nor with his sense of dignity. It is a matter of self-esteem (to be distinguished from arrogance) to accept change with dignity: 'Eigentlich läuft doch alles bloß darauf hinauf, wie hoch man sich selber einschätzt' ('Actually it all comes down to how highly you esteem yourself'; Woldemar, VIII, 198); 'denn wenn der Mensch erst denkt, es ist gar nichts mit ihm, dann ist es auch nichts' ('For if a man begins to think he's useless, then he is'; Dubslav, VIII, 231). We are brought back once again to the power of the imagination to conquer, to effect a self-conquest in the face of death. 'Die Gesinnung entscheidet' ('the state of mind is decisive'), says Lorenzen, in the context of the discussion on heroism in chapter 38 (VIII, 317). And there is something heroic in the way that Dubslav fights off pessimism and retains his equilibrium to the end of his life.

The word *zweideutig* (dubious, suspect) is the key to the doubts which nag at Dubslav's confidence. It originates, significantly (in view of the nature of the late-nineteenth-century Prussian State) from as lowly a source as the policeman, Uncke (VIII, 245), who explains to Dubslav that 'Herr Major denken immer das Gute von 'nem Menschen, weil Sie so viel zu Hause sitzen und selber so sind...', 'You always think well of a man, Herr Major, because you spend so much time at home and you're like that yourself'. By chapter 36, when the sounds of approaching death (apparent throughout the novel in Dubslav's 'Zeitgott mit Hippe', the figure of Father Time with a scythe at Schloß Stechlin, in allusions to diseases and infirmities, in the avoidance of symbols of death like asters (VIII, 58), and in references to the Last Judgment (VIII, 173, 182)) have become more insistent, Dubslav momentarily falls prey to a black mood in which he doubts his fellow men: '. . . Sonderbar, Uncke, mit seinem ewigen "zweideutig", wird am Ende doch recht behalten' ('. . . Strange: Uncke, with his everlasting "dubious", will turn out to be right in the end'; VIII, 294). But in the end, this is not so: the imagination (i.e. poetry) is paramount, or, as Woldemar remarked on an earlier occasion: 'Alles Erlebte wird erst was durch den, der es erlebt' ('Experience is nothing except through him who experiences'; VIII, 200). The same point is made more obliquely in the unobtrusive metaphor of the bees, who know instinctively how to select what is beneficial in nature: 'Sie [die Biene] nimmt nie das Gift, sie nimmt immer bloß die Heilkraft' ('It [the bee] never takes the poison, but only the health-giving properties'; VIII, 334; cf. p. 210 above).

In chapter 38 Dubslav's true poetic nature reasserts itself, in preparation for the final conquest of self, and he rejects Uncke's mistrust by praising trust:

Etwas ganz besonders Schönes im Leben ist doch das Vertrauen, und wenn's auch bloß ein Piepvogel is, der's einem entgegenbringt. Einige haben eine schwarze Milz und sagen: alles sei von Anfang an auf Mord und Totschlag gestellt. Ich kann es aber nicht finden. (VIII, 314)

(Trust is something quite especially fine in life, even if it's only a dicky-bird that bestows it on you. Some people suffer from a black spleen and say that from the beginning murder and violence have been the order of things. But I don't accept that.)

By the time Dubslav has overcome the resentment of old age at change, and has fought off pessimism about humanity at large, he is well prepared for the final battle with his own ego. His conquest of self is in line with these other victories. It is the triumph of life over death: 'Das "Ich" ist nichts – damit muß man sich durchdringen. Ein ewig Gesetzliches vollzieht sich, und dieser Vollzug, auch wenn er "Tod" heißt, darf uns nicht schrecken' ('The ego is nothing – that is the idea one should fill oneself with. An eternal law takes its course, and this course, even when it is called "Death", should not frighten us'; VIII, 346). Because he has lived according to his nature, and in accord with his surroundings, Dubslav is blessed with the facility of dying in harmony with the rules of life, and not in fear, though he would not be human if he were not still subject to bouts of anxiety ('Aber dann kamen doch wieder Anfälle von Angst...', ibid.).

The events that follow Dubslav's death elucidate the victory of life over death and the kind of victory it is. Those most intimately concerned with the news of old Stechlin's passing, Woldemar and Armgard, are still travelling in Italy and unable to receive the message. Instead, with what at a first reading appears to be a cruel irony, we are offered a message from *them*, Armgard's happy letter to Melusine from Rome, which arrives at the Barbys' Berlin apartment simultaneously with a letter from Adelheid informing them of her bereavement. The tone of youth and continuity is immediately caught up again by Fontane, with only one short, seven-line paragraph, the first of chapter 43, giving us a pause for reflection in which to assimilate the knowledge of Dubslav's death (VIII, 347).

Armgard's letter comes from Rome, Eternal City and centre of the classical world, and it underlines the classical, even pagan, atmosphere surrounding Dubslav's end. His death is placed in a context of venerable age combined with continuity, the context of classical antiquity. The Old and the New once again set each other off. That comparatively new-fangled invention, the telegraph (actually invented in 1835, and therefore not so very new) completely fails to convey the message of Dubslav's death to the young couple – who have meanwhile moved on to Capri – in time for them to attend the funeral. We are reminded of

Dubslav's reference in chapter 3 to the wonders of telegraphy. In suggesting, and immediately retracting, the possibility of a frivolous message to the Emperor of China (VIII, 23), Dubslav very lightly puts his finger on a problem of the modern age. With the increasing ease of communication, finding anything worthwhile to communicate becomes the difficulty.[12] And the irony becomes magnified when this apparatus fails although there is, for once, a serious message to communicate. The Old proves its superiority over the New once again, as so often in *Der Stechlin*, for the Prussian Lake Stechlin communicates directly with the classical Vesuvius to 'telegraph' to the young Stechlins: '...aus dem Kegel des Vesuv stieg ein dünner Rauch auf, und von Zeit zu Zeit war es, als vernähme man ein dumpfes Rollen und Grollen' ('...from the cone of Vesuvius there rose a thin column of smoke, and from time to time it was as though one could hear a dull rumble and grumble'; VIII, 357). 'Und dabei', remarks Woldemar, 'komm ich von der eitlen Vorstellung nicht los, daß, wenn's da drüben ernstlich anfängt, unser Stechlin mittut, wenn auch bescheiden' ('Listening to that, I can't shake off the idle notion that if things get serious over there, our Stechlin will join in, however modestly'; ibid.). By symbolic suggestion, it is the *lake* which is 'transmitting' to Woldemar and Armgard, to turn their thoughts towards home at the moment of the old man's death.

The reversal of the normal order of things, which is that Lake Stechlin *receives* important messages from abroad, rather than transmitting them, emphasizes the fact that the news of Dubslav's death has, so to speak, a high order of priority in the classical world, which has lost one of its own. Young Woldemar brings back from Capri to his father's grave a single, very classical memento, a wreath of laurel and olive-branches, to celebrate Dubslav's victory over death and his achievement of peace: 'Den hat er sich verdient' ('He has earned it'; VIII, 358). No doubt Aunt Adelheid would deeply disapprove if she knew: in preparing for Dubslav's lying-in-state, she had arranged for the hall at Schloß Stechlin to be decked out in more Christian fashion with *palm*-leaves and laurel (VIII, 349). Pastor Lorenzen's funeral oration has as much of the free Republican flavour of a classical *ave atque vale* as of a pious Lutheran address, and a central statement in it is the quotation from Terence to which attention was drawn in the chapter on *Frau Jenny Treibel* (p. 150 above) – 'Nichts Menschliches war ihm fremd, weil er sich selbst als Mensch empfand und sich eigner menschlicher Schwäche jederzeit bewußt war' (VIII, 351).

Dubslav's behaviour in summoning the purveyor of simples, 'die Buschen', is another reversion to the pagan, to the Wendish part of his ancestry, and we are reminded of Melusine, a soulmate of Dubslav's, and her love for pagan times (VIII, 268). He is, of course, only half-serious when he enlists the aid of the old witch, and he certainly places no more confidence in her 'Bärlapp und Katzenpfötchen' (club-moss and cat's foot) remedies than he does in the digitalis prescribed by Dr Sponholz and endorsed by the up-to-date, left-wing young locum, Moscheles. Dubslav's consultation of old Buschen is a comic prelude to a much more fruitful and less playful episode with which the novel is rounded out: the introduction of Buschen's granddaughter Agnes into Stechlin's intimate company for the last few weeks of his life. There is something very patriarchal, a stylistic echo of King David, in the old man's summoning the young girl to his side to lighten his last days, and in the mutual enjoyment they derive from the experience. We have heard his confession of lack of faith in conventional religion ('auf dem Sinai hat nun schon lange keiner mehr gestanden...', 'No one has stood on Mount Sinai for a long time now'; VIII, 339), and we are now hearing, or rather seeing, in Agnes a profession of his real faith. The young girl combines so many of the qualities by which he has lived. She is of the people, and he is most comfortable in the company of the simple and uneducated, such as old Engelke, the man-servant. She is youth incarnate, even down to her bright red stockings, in which he takes a positive delight, in contrast to his violent antipathy to all that Dr Moscheles's red tie stands for. The discrepancy is explicable by resort to a quotation from Melusine's conversation with Lorenzen in chapter 29: 'Ich respektiere das Gegebene. Danach freilich auch das Werdende, denn eben dies Werdende wird über kurz oder lang abermals ein Gegebenes sein' ('I respect the given world. Secondly, however, I respect what is in process of becoming, for this will itself sooner or later become a given in its turn'; VIII, 251). It would be too much to expect Dubslav to welcome Dr Moscheles as a herald of change, 'das Werdende' (which Stechlin respects no less than Melusine does), for Moscheles is too deeply implicated in and identified with an attack on the *status quo*, 'das Gegebene', which he does not pay Stechlin the compliment of respecting. But Agnes is a different matter. She expresses 'das Werdende' in its innocent mode, a statement that youth always has an unconscious revolutionary function as the natural vehicle of change.

While Agnes represents youth, she is after all the grand-daughter of 'die Buschen', so that the extremes of old and new meet in her person as they do in Dubslav's. She is associated with the ancient folklore of the region and is half-pagan herself. She may also be thought of as bringing together Dubslav's own age and youth, for there is a strong suggestion from the Domina, which Dubslav does not try to refute, that Dubslav has in the past had a much closer relationship with Karline, Agnes's rather loose-living mother, than the Domina thinks suitable. (It may only be the prurient mind of the old spinster at work, but nonetheless the idea is firmly planted in the reader's consciousness that Agnes is Dubslav's natural daughter, which, symbolically, she is in any case.) 'Und dir trau ich ganz und gar nicht [on his deathbed!], und der Karline natürlich erst recht nicht, wenn es auch vielleicht schon eine Weile her ist' ('And I don't trust you at all, and Karline even less, of course, even if it was perhaps some while ago now'; VIII, 328).

On safer ground is the inference that Agnes is a good example of a typical Fontane/Stechlin reversal. Dubslav's interest in her seems – to the Domina, even to Engelke – like 'nach unten rechnen' (see p. 197 above, and the quotation from VIII, 354), in other words a final display of *unstandesgemäß* (unsuitable), wrong-headed and eccentric behaviour from Dubslav. Yet what she does represent for Stechlin is precisely the reverse, 'nach oben rechnen', a final homage to what is fresh, natural and, in the best sense, *märkisch* (belonging to the Mark). Her employment by Dubslav literally to put to flight all his sister's profoundly prosaic influence, her narrow-mindedness and snobbery, makes Agnes by contrast a symbol of the flower of Dubslav's humanity, imagination, sense of freedom, love of youth and acceptance of change. She is, in short, a perfect poetic symbol of all that is best in old Stechlin. No reader will be surprised that Fontane, the lover of femininity and author of *Effi Briest*, should have chosen a young girl to round out the symbolic import of the novel which completes his life's work.

Appropriately, then, gathering flowers for Dubslav's bedside, Agnes sympathetically experiences the moment of his death as a sensation of shivering, but then immediately enjoys a renewed sense of *life*, which suggests to the reader a correction of any tendency to mourn the old man's passing, for it would be wrong to resist 'the eternal law' when Dubslav himself has made his peace with it (VIII, 346–7). The only tears shed at his funeral, be it noted, spring from Agnes's eyes, are shed almost disinterestedly, and enjoy the poetic value of stemming from a young, innocent outsider, an outcast even, who disappears whence she came, back into the forest.

Der Stechlin is a political novel, and even Dubslav's funeral is a political occasion, at which attention is once again focussed on that ugly, prosaic symbol of politics, Gundermann (VIII, 351). To turn from him, as Fontane does, to the child's spontaneous grief, is to read a final comment on politics. Dubslav's understanding of politics, like Lorenzen's, is pristine, childlike and poetic rather than political, and the elusiveness of his views[13] and what he stands for can best be understood if we do not attempt to reconcile the contradictions, but accept them as his creative offspring, as resistant to final resolution as poetic ambiguity itself.

NOTES

FOREWORD

1. Cf. Werner Hoffmann, who refers to the basic dilemma of the (visual) arts in the nineteenth century as the opposition of 'höhere Wahrheit und gegenständliche Faktentreue': *Das Irdische Paradies* (Munich 1960), p. 21.
2. See Karlheinz Gärtner, *Theodor Fontane: Literatur als Alternative* (Bonn 1978), pp. xvi, xviii.
3. Richard Brinkmann, *Theodor Fontane: Über die Verbindlichkeit des Unverbindlichen*, 2nd edition (Tübingen 1977), p. 188.
4. See Fontane's letter to Friedländer, *Theodor Fontane, Briefe an Georg Friedländer*, ed. Kurt Schreinert (Heidelberg 1954), p. 235.
5. See Heinz Eugen Greter, *Fontanes Poetik* (Bern, Frankfurt a.M. 1973), pp. 131–2.
6. Albert Boime, *The Academy and French Painting in the Nineteenth Century* (London 1971), p. vii, cit. Werner Hoffmann, 'Poesie und Prosa: Rangfragen in der neueren Kunst', *Jahrbuch der Hamburger Kunstsammlungen*, XVIII (1973), 173–92.
7. Gärtner, *Theodor Fontane*, p. 30; Ingrid Mittenzwei, *Die Sprache als Thema: Untersuchungen zu Fontanes Gesellschaftsromanen* (Bad Homburg 1970), p. 22.
8. Katharina Mommsen, *Hofmannsthal und Fontane* (Bern etc. 1978); cf. the parallels drawn by Erika Swales, *passim*, to Thomas Mann's *Buddenbrooks*, in 'Private Mythologies and Public Unease: on Fontane's *Effi Briest*', *The Modern Language Review*, 75 (1980); see also Walter Müller-Seidel, *Theodor Fontane, Soziale Romankunst in Deutschland* (Stuttgart 1975), p. 467: 'Der Stil dieser Nuancenkunst – bis hinein in die Lustspiele Hofmannsthals ist er zu verfolgen – ist wenigstens "spätrealistisch", wenn er überhaupt noch realistisch ist.'
9. Peter Demetz, 'Der Roman der guten Gesellschaft', *Theodor Fontane*, Wege der Forschung, vol. CCCLXXXI, ed. Wolfgang Preisendanz (Darmstadt 1973), p. 259.
10. See Hoffmann, 'Poesie und Prosa', p. 181.
11. Peter Demetz, *Formen des Realismus. Theodor Fontane. Kritische Untersuchungen*, 2nd edition (Frankfurt a.M. 1973), p. 451.
12. Peter-Klaus Schuster, *Theodor Fontane: Effi Briest – Ein Leben nach christlichen Bildern* (Tübingen 1978).
13. *Deutsche Parteiprogramme, eine Auswahl vom Vormärz bis zur Gegenwart*, ed. W. Mommsen (Munich 1960), p. 142; my emphasis.
14. Karl Richter, *Resignation. Eine Studie zum Werk Theodor Fontanes* (Munich 1966), p. 129.
15. Heinrich Spiero, *Fontane* (Wittenberg 1928), p. 270.
16. Richard Brinkmann, *Theodor Fontane*, p. 190. Brinkmann continues:

'... seine Kompromißbereitschaft mildert zuweilen in der Dichtung stärker als plausibel die Dynamik, die seine theoretischen Ansichten über die zeitgenössische Gesellschaft und sein Grundkonzept der Spannung von Alt und Neu bewegt und die auch von einer poetischen Darstellung ausgehen könnte, die nicht im Dienst eines konkreten politischen und gesellschaftlichen Programms steht.'

17. Hugo Aust, *Theodor Fontane: Verklärung. Eine Untersuchung zum Ideengehalt seiner Werke* (Bonn 1974), p. 253. See also p. 255.

18. E.g. Theodor Fontane, *Schriften zur Literatur*, ed. H.-H. Reuter (Berlin 1960), p. 253.

19. Cf. the extreme notion of Joachim Biener, *Fontane als Literaturkritiker* (Rudolstadt 1956), pp. 39 and 62, that 'Verklärung' is 'Abschwächung und Milderung der in der Klassengesellschaft vorhandenen antagonistischen Widersprüche'; quoted by Aust, *Theodor Fontane: Verklärung*, p. 254.

20. Josef Thanner, *Die Stilistik Theodor Fontanes. Untersuchungen zur Erhellung des Begriffes 'Realismus' in der Literatur* (The Hague/Paris 1967), p. 123.

21. Wolfgang Preisendanz, *Humor als dichterische Einbildungskraft* (Munich 1963), p. 217.

22. Letter to Emilie, 24 June 1881, Theodor Fontane, *Briefe*, ed. Kurt Schreinert and Charlotte Jolles (Berlin 1968–), vol. I, pp. 154–5.

23. Norbert Frei, *Theodor Fontane: Die Frau als Paradigma des Humanen* (Königstein/Ts., 1980).

24. Michael Minden, ' "Effi Briest" and "Die historische Stunde des Takts" ', *The Modern Language Review*, 76 (1981), 869–79; p. 872.

25. Swales, 'Private Mythologies and Public Unease', p. 119, quoting in support Müller-Seidel, *Theodor Fontane*, p. 369.

26. H. B. Garland, *The Berlin Novels of Theodor Fontane* (Oxford 1980), pp. 207–8.

27. Theodor Fontane, 'Ein neues Bild Karl Gutzkows', *Aufzeichnungen zur Literatur. Ungedrucktes und Unbekanntes*, ed. H.-H. Reuter (Berlin 1969), p. 356.

28. Letter of 19 July 1886, in *Briefe*, ed. Schreinert and Jolles, vol. I, p. 315. See also *Theodor Fontanes Briefe. Erste Sammlung*, ed. Otto Pniower and Paul Schlenther (Berlin 1910), p. 146.

29. Preisendanz, *Humor als dichterische Einbildungskraft*, p. 217.

30. Letter to Emilie, 24 June 1881, *Briefe*, ed. Schreinert and Jolles, vol. I, p. 154.

31. See the letter to Wilhelm Hertz, 17 June 1866, *Theodor Fontanes Briefe. Zweite Sammlung*, vol. I, ed. Pniower and Schlenther (Berlin 1910), p. 246: 'Man muß nicht alles sagen wollen. Dadurch wird die Phantasie des Lesers in Ruhestand gesetzt, und dadurch wieder wird die Langeweile geboren.' See also R. Geoffrey Leckey, *Some Aspects of Balladesque Art and their Relevance for the Novels of Theodor Fontane* (Bern 1979), p. 48.

32. Theodor Fontane, *Sämtliche Werke* (Munich 1959–) (Nymphenburg edition), vol. XI, p. 418: 'In einer reizvollen Vieldeutigkeit, die man an schönen Liedern mit Recht zu preisen und zu bewundern pflegt, liegt auch der Zauber dieses Bildes. Es ist dies nicht die Unbestimmtheit der künstlerischen Schwäche, die nur unbestimmt ist, weil das Bestimmte jenseits ihrer Kraft liegt, es ist *jene* Unbestimmtheit, die immer da waltet, wo ein reiches inneres Leben sich in seiner Ganzheit vor uns erschließt und, statt einsichtiger Befriedigung, eine vielfache und fruchtbare Anregung gibt.' See Schuster, *Effi Briest – Ein Leben nach christlichen Bildern*, pp. 148–50.
33. Cf. Greter's conclusion, p. 140: 'Das gesamte poetologische Bemühen Fontanes ist in seinem Kern darauf gerichtet, auf immer neue Weise und aus immer anderer Sicht jenen Durchgangsprozeß zu beschreiben und zu begreifen, der aus "Prosa" wirkliche "Poesie" werden läßt.'
34. Vincent J. Günther, *Das Symbol im erzählerischen Werk Fontanes* (Bonn 1967).
35. Kate Millett, *Sexual Politics* (New York 1970), p. 89.
36. Dietrich Weber, '*Effi Briest* – "Auch wie ein Schicksal"; über den Andeutungsstil bei Fontane', *Jahrbuch des freien deutschen Hochstifts* (1966), pp. 457–74. Compare also P. P. Schwartz, ' "Tragische Analysis" und Schicksalsvorausdeutungen in Fontanes Roman *Effi Briest*', *Sprachkunst*, 7 (1976), 247–60.

1. INTRODUCTION

1. Conrad Wandrey, *Theodor Fontane* (Munich 1919), p. 154.
2. William Empson, *Seven Types of Ambiguity*, 3rd edition (London 1956), p. viii.
3. References given in parentheses throughout relate to volume and page numbers of the Nymphenburg edition of the *Sämtliche Werke* (Munich 1959–).
4. See *Balladen und Gedichte*, XX, 70, 73, and *Der Stechlin*, VIII, 208, 236, 253–4; also the letter to Lepel, 10 May 1852, and the *Tagebuch* entry for 18 July 1852, XVII, 528: 'England stirbt an Erwerb und Materialismus.'
5. Basil Willey, *Nineteenth Century Studies* (London 1949), p. 188.
6. Cf. Eda Sagarra, *Tradition and Revolution* (London 1971), pp. 152–3.
7. Willey, *Nineteenth Century Studies*, p. 262.
8. *Friendship's Garland* (London 1871), p. 8.
9. Eda Sagarra, *A Social History of Germany 1648–1914* (London 1977), p. 180.
10. Humphrey House, *All in Due Time* (London 1955), p. 93.
11. See Sagarra, *A Social History of Germany*, pp. 288, 292.
12. Sagarra, *Tradition and Revolution*, p. 296.
13. See Sagarra, *A Social History of Germany*, p. 276.
14. Sagarra, *Tradition and Revolution*, p. 65.

15. Ibid., p. 304.
16. See Willey, *Nineteenth Century Studies*, p. 246.
17. Cit. F. Sengle, 'Der Romanbegriff in der ersten Hälfte des neunzehnten Jahrhunderts', *Arbeiten zur deutschen Literatur 1750–1850* (Stuttgart 1965), p. 178.
18. Cit. Fritz Martini, *Deutsche Literatur im bürgerlichen Realismus, 1848–98* (Stuttgart 1962), p. 116.
19. *Sämtliche Werke*, ed. August Sauer and Reinhold Beckmann, 42 vols (Vienna 1904–48), vol. II, no. 9, p. 156, *Tagebuch* 2137.
20. *Grillparzers Gespräche und die Charakteristiken seiner Persönlichkeit durch die Zeitgenossen*, ed. August Sauer, vol. III, no. 800, p. 274. See W. N. B. Mullan, *Grillparzer's Aesthetic Theory* (Stuttgart 1979), p. 54.
21. See B. A. Rowley, 'Theodor Fontane: A German Novelist in the European Tradition?', *German Life and Letters*, N.S. XV (1961), 75.
22. See *Literatur als Wissenschaft. Eine Einführung für Germanisten*, ed. Dieter Breuer et al. (Frankfurt a.M. 1972), pp. 345, 354.
23. Stuttgart 1955, pp. 445f.
24. Roger Paulin, 'The German Historical Novel 1830–1870', unpublished text of a paper delivered at the Conference of University Teachers of German in Great Britain and Ireland, Manchester 1979.
25. 'The Romances of Walter Scott', *Wiener Jahrbücher*, 22 (1823), 1–75. I am grateful to Roger Paulin for supplying this reference and for allowing access to his unpublished ms.
26. Paulin, 'The German Historical Novel 1830–1870'.
27. 'The Life of George Eliot', first published 1885, reprinted in *John Morley: Nineteenth-Century Essays*, ed. P. Stansky (Chicago 1970), p. 309.
28. Rowley, 'Theodor Fontane', p. 75.
29. A. M. Vogt, *Art of the Nineteenth Century*, transl. A. F. Bance (London 1973), p. 18. Compare a typical statement by Fontane on his attitude to the writing of history, which applies equally well to his novel-writing: 'Mein stolzes Beginnen lief nun darauf hinaus: Allerkleinstes – auch Prosaisches nicht ausgeschlossen – exakt und minutiös zu schildern und durch scheinbar einfachste, aber gerade deshalb schwierigste Mittel: durch Simplizität, Durchsichtigkeit im einzelnen und Übersichtlichkeit im ganzen, auf eine gewisse künstlerische Höhe zu heben ...' (letter of 5 Jan. 1895 to Heinrich Jacobi).
30. *Adel des Geistes* (1910), *Gesammelte Werke*, Aufbau edition (Berlin 1965), vol. 10, pp. 487–8.
31. My findings are corroborated by a recent book, Norbert Frei's *Theodor Fontane, Die Frau als Paradigma des Humanen* (Königstein/Ts., 1980). The author's object is to demonstrate that, through his treatment of females, Fontane seeks and achieves a synthesis of the two forces that determined his development from earliest years: *Romantik* and *Realismus*, or *Poesie* and *Prosa*. Frei supplies valuable additional documentation of this polarity, found equally in Fontane's life and in his works. What Frei

does not do, surprisingly, is to place this polarity historically as a central nineteenth-century preoccupation in the arts.

2. POESIE AND PROSA

1. Letter to Friedländer, 22 Oct. 1890, *Briefe an Friedländer*, ed. Schreinert.
2. Müller-Seidel, *Theodor Fontane*, pp. 44–5: 'In allen solchen Äußerungen, wie befremdlich sie sich zum Teil auch anhören mögen, ist die deutsche Einheit der zentrale Gedanke; und es ist kein schlechthin undemokratisches Denken, das sich mit diesem Gedanken verknüpft.'
3. H.-H. Reuter, *Fontane* (Munich 1968), vol. I, p. 167.
4. See Reuter, *Fontane*, vol. I, p. 164.
5. 'Willibald Alexis', XXI/1, 210–11.
6. Fontane, *Aufzeichnungen zur Literatur*, ed. Reuter, p. 90.
7. Kenneth Attwood, *Fontane und das Preußentum* (Berlin 1970), p. 45.
8. Attwood, *Fontane und das Preußentum*, p. 296.
9. Müller-Seidel, *Theodor Fontane*, p. 318.
10. Frei, *Die Frau als Paradigma des Humanen*, p. 116.
11. See Reuter, *Fontane*, vol. I, p. 288.
12. Ibid., p. 294.
13. Letter to Wilhelm Hertz, 17 May 1866, *Theodor Fontane: Briefe an Wilhelm und Hans Hertz, 1859–1898*, ed. K. Schreinert and G. Hay (Stuttgart 1972).
14. Sagarra, *A Social History of Germany 1648–1914*, p. 206.
15. See Müller-Seidel, *Theodor Fontane*, p. 124.
16. I am summarizing Peter Demetz's general argument in *Formen des Realismus*.
17. Letter to James Morris, 31 Jan. 1896, *Theodor Fontane: von Dreißig bis Achtzig, sein Leben in seinen Briefen*, ed. H.-H. Reuter, 2nd edition (Munich 1970).
18. Erich Heller, 'Fontane and the Novelist's Art', *Times Literary Supplement*, 20 Oct. 1978, p. 1224.
19. Müller-Seidel, *Theodor Fontane*, p. 99.
20. See Müller-Seidel, *Theodor Fontane*, pp. 100 and 165.
21. *Wanderungen*, II/2, 'Das Oderland', p. 102.
22. *Causerien über Theater*, ed. Paul Schlenther (Berlin 1905), p. 293.
23. *Causerien*, pp. 271–2.
24. *Causerien*, 1 Oct. 1889, p. 463.
25. Mario Praz, *The Hero in Eclipse in Victorian Fiction* (London 1956), p. 230.
26. See Raymond Giraud, *The Unheroic Hero in the Novels of Stendhal, Balzac and Flaubert* (New Brunswick NJ 1957), p. 50.
27. See *Causerien*, 31 Oct. 1871, pp. 113–14.
28. Letter to Paul Lindau, 14 June 1872, *Fontanes Briefe in zwei Bänden*, ed. G. Erler (Berlin and Weimar 1968), vol. I.
29. Letter to Mete Fontane, 25 Aug. 1891, *Von Dreißig bis Achtzig*.

30. See Attwood, *Fontane und das Preußentum*, pp. 269 and 276, and the letter to Friedländer, 22 March 1896, *Briefe an Friedländer*. See also *Theodor Fontane, Briefe und Tagebuch*, ed. Mario Krammer, *Die neue Rundschau*, XXX, 12 (1919), 1448.
31. Letter to Friedländer, 22 March 1896, *Briefe an Friedländer*. See Attwood, ' "Examenunsinn", "Examendünkel" und "der sechste preußische Sinn" ', *Fontane und das Preußentum*, pp. 266f.
32. Letter to Friedländer, 27 May 1891, *Briefe an Friedländer*.
33. Letter to Friedländer, 14 May 1894, ibid.
34. Letter to Friedländer, 5 April 1897, ibid.
35. *Reden Kaiser Wilhelms II*, ed. Axel Menthes (Munich 1976), p. 73.
36. Letter to Emilie, 25 June 1884, *Fontanes Briefe in zwei Bänden*, vol. II.
37. *Causerien*, p. 172.
38. Hugo Bieber, *Der Kampf um die Tradition* (Stuttgart 1928), p. 435; cit. Müller-Seidel, *Theodor Fontane*, p. 31.
39. Letter to Friedländer, 5 April 1897, *Briefe an Friedländer*.
40. Letter to James Morris, 31 Jan. 1896, *Theodor Fontanes Briefe. Zweite Sammlung*, ed. Pniower and Schlenther.
41. Werner Oberle, *Der adelige Mensch in der Dichtung* (Basel 1950), p. 112: cit. Attwood, *Fontane und das Preußentum*, p. 214.
42. *Causerien*, 21 Oct. 1888, p. 191.
43. *Causerien*, 1 June 1878, p. 84 (in a review of a performance of Schiller's *Die Jungfrau von Orleans*).
44. *Causerien*, 1 Oct. 1889, p. 435.
45. *Causerien*, 20 Oct. 1889, p. 303.
46. Letter to Friedländer, 8 July 1895, *Briefe an Friedländer*.
47. Frei, *Theodor Fontane: Die Frau als Paradigma des Humanen*, p. 91.
48. Letter to Wilhelm Wolfsohn, 10 Nov. 1847, *Fontanes Briefe in zwei Bänden*, vol. I.
49. *Causerien*, 19 June 1872, p. 347. Fontane goes on, however, to put the Houses of Parliament in the same category of 'flawed but aesthetically attractive'! See pp. 347–8: 'Und vor die neuen englischen Parlamentshäuser gestellt, die sozusagen von Fehlern wimmeln, würd' auch ich mich durch diesen chaotischen, mit allerhand Häßlichem und Ridikülem beklebten Bau immer wieder viel mehr gefesselt und nach oben gezogen fühlen als durch ein halbes Dutzend *Schinkelscher* Schönheitsbauten.'
50. Frei, *Theodor Fontane. Die Frau als Paradigma des Humanen*, p. 79.
51. Cf. Müller-Seidel, *Theodor Fontane*, p. 155: 'Die Frauenfrage ist im letzten Drittel des 19. Jahrhunderts eine Frage der Bildung und der akademischen Bildung nicht zuletzt.' The exception that proves the rule is Melusine in *Der Stechlin*, whose educational level is considerably higher than that of Woldemar von Stechlin. Graf Holk in *Unwiederbringlich* is also somewhat undereducated, certainly compared with the court circles in which he moves. See also, on the question of women's education, Sagarra, *A Social History of Germany 1648–1914*, pp. 415–19.
52. P. U. Hohendahl, 'Theodor Fontane: *Cécile*. Zum Problem der Mehr-

deutigkeit', *Germanisch-Romanische Monatsschrift*, NF 18 (1968), 394; cit. Frei, *Theodor Fontane. Die Frau als Paradigma des Humanen*, p. 110.

53. Hohendahl, 'Theodore Fontane: *Cécile*', p. 398.
54. There was no married women's property act in Germany equivalent to the legislation introduced in England in the late nineteenth century. See Sagarra, *A Social History of Germany 1648–1914*, p. 420.
55. See Müller-Seidel, *Theodor Fontane*, p. 166.
56. Schopenhauer, *Parerga und Paralipomena*, 'Über die Weiber', *Sämtliche Werke* (Wiesbaden 1949), vol. VI, p. 655; cit. Müller-Seidel, *Theodor Fontane*, p. 166.
57. See Müller-Seidel, *Theodor Fontane*, p. 370.
58. N. Schöll, '*Mathilde Möhring*: Ein anderer Fontane?', *Formen realistischer Erzählkunst: Festschrift for Charlotte Jolles*, ed. J. Thunecke (Nottingham 1979), pp. 594–5. See also, for a contrasting view, A. F. Bance, 'Fontane's *Mathilde Möhring*', *The Modern Language Review*, 69:1 (1974), 121–33.
59. Attwood, *Fontane und das Preußentum*, p. 290.

3. *ELLERNKLIPP* AND *EFFI BRIEST*

1. Quoted by Wandrey, *Theodor Fontane*, pp. 146–7.
2. In his reply to criticism of *Ellernklipp*, Fontane stressed his debt, as a novelist, to the ballad-form, and to some extent his words on this occasion can be taken to apply to all his novels: 'Ich war, von meinem 16. Lebensjahre an, Balladenschreiber . . . und kann deshalb . . . von der Ballade nicht los. Dies balladeske Gefühl leitet mich bei allem, was ich schreibe . . .' In the same context (XXI/1, 496) he also refers to all literary production as 'Poesie'.
3. Leckey, *Some Aspects of Balladesque Art*, especially p. 85.
4. See Adelheid Bosshart, *Theodor Fontanes historische Romane* (Winterthur 1957), p. 62: also Renate Schäfer, 'Fontanes Melusine-Motiv', *Euphorion*, 56 (1962), 69–104; and Charlotte Jolles, *Theodor Fontane* (Stuttgart 1972), p. 98.
5. Quoted by Wandrey, *Theodor Fontane*, p. 149.
6. Thomas Carlyle, *On Heroes, Hero-worship and the Heroic in History*. The works of Thomas Carlyle in thirty volumes, vol. V (London 1896), p. 224.
7. But note Effi's discomfiture on account of the heavy Old Testament bias of the sermons in the Berlin church in chapter 32: 'Aber es ist doch alles bloß, wie wenn ich ein Buch lese . . . Er spricht immer so viel vom alten Testament. Und wenn es auch ganz gut ist, es erbaut mich nicht' (VII, 401).
8. Leckey, *Some Aspects of Balladesque Art*, p. 96.
9. *Catachesis Minor D. Martini Lutheri, Germanice et Latine* (Erfurt 1637).
10. Leckey, *Some Aspects of Balladesque Art*, p. 96.

11. Quoted by Bosshart, *Theodor Fontanes historische Romane*, p. 95.

12. I am using the term in the sense promulgated by David Lodge: see 'The Language of Modernist Fiction: Metaphor and Metonymy', *Modernism*, ed. M. Bradbury and J. McFarlane (Harmondsworth 1976), p. 483; and *The Modes of Modern Writing* (London 1977), p. 80: 'Prose, which is "forwarded essentially by contiguity" (Roman Jakobson) tends towards the metonymic pole, while poetry, which in its metrical patterning and use of rhyme and other phonological devices emphasizes similarity, tends towards the metaphoric pole. Romantic and symbolist writing is metaphoric, and realist writing is metonymic: "following the path of contiguous relationships, the realistic author metonymically digresses from the plot to the atmosphere and from the characters to the setting in space and time..." (Jakobson).'

13. Compare Pastor Niemeyer's words on Life, VII, 414: 'Was ich vom Leben halte? Viel und wenig. Mitunter ist es recht viel und mitunter ist es recht wenig.'

14. Note that, before her marriage, when there is a threat that she might have to modify her natural behaviour for the sake of social conventions, she is allowed to avoid the difficulty. During the visit of mother and daughter to Berlin to purchase the trousseau (chapter 3), Frau von Briest allows Effi to evade her social obligations: 'Es waren glückliche Tage gewesen, vor allem auch darin, daß man nicht unter unbequemer und beinahe unstandesgemäßer Verwandschaft gelitten hatte. "Für Tante Therese", so hatte Effi gleich nach der Ankunft gesagt, "müssen wir diesmal inkognito bleiben"' (chapter 4, VII, 186). It is in this very significant sense of a lack of training in social self-discipline, not just in the matter of outer appearances and failure to throw off a tomboyish manner, that Frau von Briest has failed to 'make a lady' out of Effi (cf. Effi's reproach 'Warum machst du keine Dame aus mir?', chapter 1, VII, 172).

15. Quoted by Helmuth Nürnberger, *Der frühe Fontane* (Hamburg 1967), pp. 297–8.

16. Cf. A. J. P. Taylor, *Bismarck* (London 1955), p. 109: 'Like all his contemporaries, [Bismarck] tended to assume that things would run themselves pretty well, once a few adjustments had been made. The political reformers... always supposed that the spate of legislation would sooner or later come to an end when 'the liberal state' had been made; they never foresaw legislation as a continuous, endless process. Even the most radical Socialists, Marx and Engels themselves, imagined that politics would cease for ever once socialism had been created.'

17. E. R. Curtius, *Kritische Essays zur europäischen Literatur*, 3rd edition (Berne 1963), p. 123. See also p. 119: 'Diese geistigsittliche Autorität in Deutschland auszuüben ist bei der Zerklüftung unserer geistig-politischen Welt – diesem wahrhaften bellum omnium contra omnes – nahezu unmöglich.'

18. Bosshart, *Theodor Fontanes historische Romane*, p. 95.

19. Leckey, *Some Aspects of Balladesque Art*, p. 49.
20. For example, in the upbringing of Annie, 'Roswitha hatte das poetische Departement, die Märchen – und Geschichtenerzählung, Johanna dagegen das des Anstands...' (VII, 366).
21. *Luthers Werke in Auswahl*, ed. Otto Clemen (Bonn 1913), *Der große Katechismus* (1529), p. 56: 'Ich gleube an den Heiligen geist/ein heilige Christliche kyrche/die gemeine der heiligen/Vergebung der sunden/aufferstehung des fleischs/und ein ewigs leben/Amen.'
22. E. P. Thompson, *The Making of the English Working Class* (London 1963), p. 12.
23. These are not, therefore, in one of the best-known phrases of Fontane criticism, merely 'bric-à-brac left over from Poetic Realism'. See J. P. Stern, '*Effi Briest: Madame Bovary: Anna Karenina*', first published in *The Modern Language Review*, LII (1957), 374, n.4.
24. Flaubert, in a celebrated letter to Louise Colet of 1852, wrote: 'Ce qui me semble beau, ce que je voudrais faire, c'est un livre sur rien, un livre sans attache extérieure, qui se tiendrait lui-même par la force interne de son style, comme la terre sans être soutenue se tient en l'air, un livre qui n'aurait presque pas de sujet ou, du moins, où le sujet serait presque invisible, si cela se peut.' (Above all this would serve as an excellent description of *Der Stechlin*.) *Correspondance*, II, 354–6, cit. Damian Grant, *Realism*, Critical Idiom (London 1970), p. 17. Compare Müller-Seidel, *Theodor Fontane*, pp. 425–6, and Fontane in a letter to Siegmund Schott, 14 Feb. 1897: 'Das Buch [*Die Poggenpuhls*] ist ein Roman und hat keinen Inhalt, das "Wie" muß für das "Was" eintreten – mir kann nichts Lieberes gesagt werden.'
25. To talk of the duel as in some sense offering a trial of authenticity for Innstetten is surely to give it more significance than it deserves. See Swales, 'Private Mythologies and Public Unease: on Fontane's *Effi Briest*', pp. 114–23: 'By fighting the duel and facing the consequences he hopes to wrest some kind of experiential authenticity from his confusion and uncertainty' (p. 119). This seems to be something of a leap to make from the quotation the author gives to support her conclusion: 'He feels that if he does not go through with the duel he will always appear to his friend (Wüllersdorf) (and, by implication, to himself) as an invulnerable person, who is "noch nie an einer Sache erstickt" (VII, 375).' Surely there is no need for terms such as 'experiential' and 'authenticity' where Innstetten is apparently simply saying that, by analysing the reasons why he should not fight the duel, he would appear both to himself and to Wüllersdorf to be rationalizing his own cowardice or, at the very least, his indecision. This seems to be the import if one places the quotation in context: 'in ihrer Seele klingt es [says Innstetten to Wüllersdorf]: "der gute Innstetten, er hat doch eine wahre Passion, alle Beleidigungen auf ihren Beleidigungsgehalt chemisch zu untersuchen, und das richtige Quantum Stickstoff findet er *nie*. Er ist noch nie an einer Sache erstickt"... Habe ich recht, Wüllersdorf, oder nicht?'. In other words, if he,

Innstetten, is not capable of choking over *this* insult (the adultery) then he is simply not capable of choking over any: his rationality and tolerance are merely an excuse.

26. Otto Rank, *The Don Juan Legend*, transl. David G. Winter (Princeton 1975), p. 88.

27. Cf. Hugo Aust, 'Theodor Fontane: "Die Poggenpuhls"', *Fontane aus heutiger Sicht*, ed. Hugo Aust (Munich 1980), pp. 215–18.

28. Cf. the letter to James Morris, 5 Feb. 1898, and compare some comments from a much earlier period of his life, the letter to Emilie written in Aachen, en route to England on 12 April 1852: he speaks of Catholicism as 'eine große Volksverdummungs –, im günstigsten Falle eine klug eingerichtete Volksbeherrschungs-Anstalt'. Admittedly, this attitude was modified by contact with a fine Catholic family in Berlin, the Wangenheims, for whom Fontane acted as a private tutor. See Nürnberger, *Der frühe Fontane*, p. 193.

29. Joe McCarney, *The Real World of Ideology* (Hassocks 1980), p. 124.

30. Cp. Müller-Seidel, *Theodor Fontane*, p. 115: 'Das Fremde – wir kennen es aus den vorweggenommenen Betrachtungen der Chroniknovellen – hat im Mit- und Gegeneinander der Lebenskreise seine deutlich wahrnehmbare Funktion. Im realistischen Roman Fontanes bedeutet es vielfach das Poetische schlechthin.'

31. Innstetten does, on one occasion after the duel, imply that he regards himself as no better than a *Totschläger*: 'Wie soll ich einen Totschläger an seiner Seele packen? Dazu muß man selber intakt sein' (VII, 420).

32. Old Pastor Siebenhaar in *Quitt* is the mouthpiece for Fontane's deep suspicion of all pharisaic insistence on duty and the voice of conscience for the good of others' souls: 'Es ist eine Täuschung, wenn wir uns immer und ewig auf unser Amt und unsere Pflicht oder gar auf unseren Schwur und unser Gewissen berufen. Das meiste, was wir tun, tun wir doch aus unserer Natur heraus, aus Neigung und Willen' (VI, 46–7).

33. Geoffrey Gorer, *The Life and Ideas of the Marquis de Sade* (London 1964), p. 156.

34. This character-trait of Innstetten's is unmistakeably borrowed from an anecdote about Walter Scott, reported as a footnote in *Jenseit des Tweed*, describing 'das halb gläubige, halb ironische Verhältnis, in dem Walter Scott zu seinen Gespenstergeschichten stand. Er erzählte eine derselben mit dem größtmöglichsten Aufwand seiner Darstellungsgabe und hielt einen kurzen Augenblick die Gemüter seiner Zuhörer wie in einem Bann des Schreckens. Aber auf Augenblicke nur; Rogers selbst (the host) erholte sich zuerst und rief seinen Gästen zu: "Nein, Scott, das ist zu arg; Unsinn von Anfang bis zu Ende"; worauf dieser lebhaft und selbst noch aufgeregt erwiderte: "Aber ich hab' es von meiner Großmutter", rasch dann und unter lautem Lachen hinzufügend: "Freilich, die alte Frau log entsetzlich"' (XVII, 252).

35. It may not only be for reasons of poetic economy that Fontane endows

the Innstettens with only one child, conceived, as the dates indicate, during their very first days together as man and wife, the honeymoon period.

36. Müller-Seidel, *Theodor Fontane*, p. 84. See also p. 260.
37. Müller-Seidel, *Theodor Fontane*, p. 221.
38. See Una Maclean, *Magical Medicine* (Harmondsworth 1974), p. 147.
39. Compare Frau von Carayon's words to Victoire in chapter 4 of *Schach von Wuthenow*: 'Aber das laß dir sagen, es liegt alles vorgezeichnet in uns, und was Ursach' scheint, ist meist schon wieder Wirkung und Folge' (II, 292).
40. I am using these terms in an anthropological sense, as defined by Ian Hogbin, *Social Change* (London 1958), p. 35: 'Equilibrium implies balance, perhaps momentary, between opposing forces, stability that the thing in question is firmly established and unlikely to suffer sudden change. But if we say that a society is stable, we do not necessarily mean that its institutions are static; they may be adjustable and hence able to continue developing new stages of equilibrium.'
41. I am indebted to Roger Paulin for access to his stimulating, as yet unpublished paper on the historical novel, 'The German Historical Novel 1830–1870', delivered at the Conference of University Teachers of German in Great Britain and Ireland, Manchester 1979.
42. Claude Lévi-Strauss, *The Savage Mind* (London 1966), p. 255, translation of *La Pensée Sauvage* (Paris 1962), p. 338.

4. IRRUNGEN, WIRRUNGEN

1. M. A. McHaffie, no doubt partly for alliteration's sake, translates the title as *Errors, Entanglements*. It is difficult to see where the text bears out the first term of the pair. See 'Fontane's *Irrungen, Wirrungen* and the novel of Realism', *Periods in German Literature*, vol. II, ed. J. M. Ritchie (London 1969), p. 167.
2. McHaffie, 'Fontane's *Irrungen, Wirrungen*', p. 187.
3. See Theodor Fontane, *Aus dem Nachlaß, Gesammelte Werke II*, vol. IX (Berlin 1905–11), p. 270.
4. 'Bis vor kurzem hab ich auf Andreas geschworen; aber wenn ich so was sehe, wie das hier, so weiß ich nicht, ob ihm der Oswald nicht gleichkommt oder ihn überholt... All dergleichen aber ist mir bloß zu denken erlaubt, vor den Leuten es aussprechen hieße meinen "Seesturm" ohne Not auf den halben Preis herabsetzen' (III, 122–3). For Fontane, with his love of conversation, any inhibition of this kind imposed upon self-expression (even if self-imposed) is a dehumanizing agent.
5. Fontane clearly has a concept of the 'natural aristocrat', whose chief characteristics are simplicity, spiritual generosity, and noble restraint. These are the qualities demonstrated by Frau von Poggenpuhl, for example, especially in her long climactic speech at the end of *Die Poggenpuhls* (IV, 372).

6. McHaffie, 'Fontane's *Irrungen, Wirrungen*', p. 183, quoting from Fr. Hegel, *Sämtliche Werke*, ed. Hermann Glockner (1928), vol. 14, p. 395.

7. The reception of *Irrungen, Wirrungen* indicates how explosive this material was for contemporaries: 'Das Bürgertum empörte sich über den Roman... allein aufgrund der Tatsache des "freien" Liebesverhältnisses, der Adel hingegen reagierte einzig empfindlich auf das Faktum der "Mésalliance"' (Carin Leisenhoff, *Fontane und das literarische Leben seiner Zeit. Eine literatursoziologische Studie*, Bonn 1976, p. 69). See also Frederick Betz, 'Fontanes "Irrungen, Wirrungen". Eine Analyse der zeitgenössischen Rezeption des Romans', *Fontane aus heutiger Sicht*, ed. Aust, pp. 261–2.

8. Frau Dörr remarks in chapter 9 that 'hier alles Sumpf is und bloß so tut, als ob es Wiese wäre' (III, 135). The party take a rest on an *Unkrauthaufen*: 'Dieser Pedenhaufen war ein prächtiger Ruheplatz' (III, 136). Earlier in the walk they had passed another refuse-heap, in this case the lumber of a monumental mason's yard: 'allerhand Stuckornamente, namentlich Engelsköpfe, lagen herum' (III, 134).

9. On the subject of the combination of *Vernunft* and *Leidenschaft*, compare my remarks on the same topic in chapter 6, on *Frau Jenny Treibel*, p. 156 above.

10. The resonance here is, of course, that of *La Dame aux Camélias*, the title of a tale of *mésalliance* by Alexandre Dumas Fils which appeared first as a novel in 1848, and then in a stage version whose première in 1852 marked the beginning of the realistic theatre.

11. Cf. Dirk Mende, 'Frauenleben. Bemerkungen zu Fontanes "L'Adultera" nebst Exkursen zu "Cécile" und "Effi Briest"', *Fontane aus heutiger Sicht*, ed. Aust, p. 198. Mende quotes from, and declares equally relevant to the Wilhelmine Reich, a book which analyses 'hysterical' ailments among female members of the American upper-middle class in the nineteenth century: 'Krankheit beherrschte das Leben der Frau der Oberschicht. Badekurorte und Frauenspezialisten gab es plötzlich überall, und die Damen der Gesellschaft suchten sie regelmäßig auf.' Quoted from Barbara Ehrenreich und Deirdre English, *Zur Krankheit gezwungen. Eine schichtenspezifische Untersuchung der Krankheitsideologie als Instrument zur Unterdrückung der Frau im 19. und 20. Jahrhundert am Beispiel der USA* (Munich 1976), p. 19.

12. Fontane was appalled by what he saw as the hypocritical response to, and the scandal surrounding, the publication of *Irrungen, Wirrungen*. See the letter to his son Theodor of 8 Sept. 1887.

13. Demetz, *Formen des Realismus*, p. 150.

14. The order and unquestioning purposefulness of working-class lives are often glimpsed by middle- and upper-class characters in Fontane's fiction, provoking a twinge of envy and unease: there is the girl scouring pots at Hankels Ablage in *Irrungen, Wirrungen*; the servant whom Jenny observes absorbed in her ironing in *Frau Jenny Treibel*; and the

woodcutters whose steady application attracts the attention of Graf Holk's daughter Asta in *Unwiederbringlich*.

15. Whereas Lene has the simplicity of a character in a ballad, Botho's cultural conditioning leads him to *project* balladesque qualities onto Lene's milieu. So, for example, he associates Frau Nimptsch with a ballad by Adalbert von Chamisso praising his washer-woman (III, 108).
16. Peter Quennell, 'Mayhew's London', *Casanova in London and Other Essays* (London 1971), p. 152.
17. See H. W. Koch, *A History of Prussia* (London 1978), p. 280.
18. McHaffie, 'Fontane's *Irrungen, Wirrungen*', p. 187.

5. UNWIEDERBRINGLICH

1. Cf. Leckey, *Some Aspects of Balladesque Art*, p. 163.
2. 8 Sept. 1887, on the subject of *Irrungen, Wirrungen*; Reuter (ed.), *Fontane von Dreißig bis Achtzig*, p. 301.
3. Cf. Jolles, *Theodor Fontane*, p. 73: 'Die erste Niederschrift fällt in die zweite Hälfte des Jahres 1887.'
4. See L. D. Steefel, *The Schleswig-Holstein Question* (Cambridge, Mass., 1932), p. 3.
5. Cf. Frances M. Subiotto, 'The function of letters in Fontane's *Unwiederbringlich*', *The Modern Language Review*, 65 (1970), 306–18.
6. See Steefel, *The Schleswig-Holstein Question*, p. 6.
7. Frei, *Die Frau als Paradigma des Humanen*, p. 59, brings out the connexion between the 'false-poetic' appeal of the Hansen women and that of the court: 'Der Versuch des Grafen Holk, sich von der übertriebenen Prinzipienstrenge seiner Frau Christine zu emanzipieren, mißlingt; die Flucht in die pikante Romantik des Kopenhagener Hoflebens scheitert. Dabei scheint alles Poesie schlechthin zu sein. Bereits Frau und Tochter Hansen ... sind nichts "Alltägliches und Triviales", alles ist so "mysteriös verschleiert". Da gibt es "Goldleisten und türkische Teppiche", "Märchengrusel" und vor allem "eine wundervolle Geschichte von dem Kaiser von Siam". Holk aber wird beruhigt – "das war hier immer so".'
8. The phrase 'etwas Geheimnisvolles, Mystisches' was not used of Ebba, in fact, but is employed by Holk to enthuse about the homeopathic medicine practised by a veterinary surgeon new to the neighbourhood (V, 14).
9. Fontane picks out the motif of adolescent attraction again when, at the first Danish National Exhibition, the two teenage great-nieces of the Princess are described as being 'Feuer und Flamme'; but not because of a patriotic interest in history, for '... auf die Dauer entging es doch niemandem, daß das ganze Interesse für Admiräle nur Schein und Komödie war, und daß die Prinzessinnen immer nur andächtig vor den Bildnissen solcher Personen verweilten, die, gleichviel ob Männer oder Frauen, mit irgendeiner *romantisch-mysteriösen* Liebesgeschichte verknüpft war' (V, 109; my italics).
10. Reuter, *Fontane*, vol. II, p. 713.

234

11. Compare the Princess's observation, alluding to Schloß Fredericksborg, that not even museums, apparently sedate repositories of the past, are as innocent as they appear (V, 127).

12. The area is also rich in *Opferstätten*. One is reminded of the sacrifice-motif in *Ellernklipp* and *Effi Briest*. The theme acquires an ironic, anti-heroic twist here, for Graf Holk, the manly hunter, is sacrificed upon the altar of Ebba's vanity. She is a headhunter for whom a victim with Holk's impeccable pedigree perhaps offers a sweet revenge for the humiliation she frequently suffers because of her semitic descent.

13. The whole setting is highly picturesque and 'poetic', a Walter Scott-ish and balladesque backdrop to the highly *un*poetic reality of decadent court life, whose keynote is (V, 127) 'alles kann entheiligt werden'. (*À propos* Walter Scott, note that when Holk first sets off for the court at Copenhagen he takes with him some volumes by Scott – 'man kann nie wissen, und der paßt immer', V, 49). The setting mercilessly reveals the barrenness of the Princess's existence and the court trappings that support it, the wastefulness of its idle pastimes and its divorce from productive activity: 'Alles nur, pour passer le temps', as Holk belatedly realizes (V, 203). The hollowness of court life is present throughout the novel in the cumulative effect of the adjective 'gnädig', applied to almost any utterance of the Princess, although her remarks rarely rise above the level of malicious gossip. The court is sterile, its chief pillars ageing bachelors and spinsters, its major domo (as the text hints more than once: see V, 65, 125) homosexual. The premature Yuletide feast at Fredericksborg, celebrated in what is essentially a summer residence, pathetically exemplifies the hermetic artificiality of an inward-looking society thrown back upon its own resources, casting into stark relief the spiritual affliction (the decadence, the *mal du siècle*) already apparent in Holk's reaction to his first encounter with the court in chapter 12: 'Ein Gefühl von Einöde und Verlassenheit überkam Holk ...' (V, 75). That feeling presages his *Verlassenheit* at the end of the novel, after the court has done its work upon his life and reduced him to its own condition: barren, wifeless, effectively childless, his house, like the various royal residences, no longer a home but a shell, a museum dedicated to earlier days.

14. Compare Christine, V, 19, 'Ich habe kein Interesse für Kriegsgeschichten', and Ebba, V, 135: 'Ich sehe nicht ein, warum wir uns immer um die Männer oder gar um ihre Schlachten kümmern sollen; die Geschichte der Frauen ist meist viel interessanter.'

15. The Don Juan theme, whose ironic relevance to Holk is obvious, is referred to by the Graf in conversation with Ebba, V, 143 (the irony is that she is a kind of female Don Juan and he is her victim); and also in a passing allusion to one of the courtiers whom Holk is to replace when he is called to Copenhagen, Baron Steen. Fontane's subtlety is once more in evidence here, for in an ironic sense Holk substitutes very adequately for both the courtiers he is called to replace. Thuresen Bille has measles, in other words an inappropriate childish affliction, parallel to Holk's

infatuation with Ebba (and compare note 9, above). Baron Steen, according to the malicious gossip of Pentz, has gone off to Etna to enjoy vicariously a tumescence of which he is himself no longer capable: 'Seitdem Steen allerpersönlichst sein eruptives Leben nicht mehr fortsetzen kann, hat er sich den Eruptionen der feuerspeienden Berge zugekehrt ... Er war trotz aller Anstrengungen, ein Don Juan zu sein, im wesentlichen immer nur ein Junker Bleichenwang, also, gemessen an seinen Ansprüchen, so ziemlich das Lächerlichste, was man sein kann' (V, 38).

16. Compare the metaphor of 'new wine in old bottles' applied to Wilhelm II's attempt 'das Neue mit ganz Altem besorgen zu können', quoted in chapter 2 above, p. 23.

17. See M. Unamuno y Jugo, *The Tragic Sense of Life*, transl. J. E. Crawford Flitch (New York 1954), p. 20.

18. Norman O. Brown, *Life against Death. The Psychoanalytical Meaning of History* (London 1959), p. 109.

19. The rocket-motif is taken up again in *Der Stechlin* with reference to Melusine (VIII, 143).

20. The reader will be inclined to wonder why Fontane chose this particular novel. We know that, along with *The Pickwick Papers, David Copperfield* was Fontane's favourite Dickens work (cf. his list of outstanding books, supplied in 1889 in answer to an enquiry: XXI/1, 498). The subject – the education of an initially naive hero towards a better understanding of women – is not unrelated to that of *Unwiederbringlich*.

21. This complex of ignorance is summed up in the motif of Don Quixote. As Ebba says, Holk is not 'der Held der Liebe', as he imagines, but its Don Quixote. The Don tried to adhere to outmoded ideals, and such an adherence to what cannot and should not be preserved forms part of Holk's divided make-up and ignorance of himself and others. He is on the one hand an *Augenblicksmensch* (V, 30), an instinctive lover of life, free of anxiety about consequences: but, on the other hand, he wants to *build* (cf. his *Baupassion*) upon the momentary satisfaction of Eros he has enjoyed with Ebba and, like a kind of anti-Faust, perpetuate the moment, 'den Augenblick verewigen' (Ebba, V, 202). He is caught in the unanalysed internal contradictions of his own nature: having given free rein to the part of himself which is determined to take life lightly, he now insists on taking his relationship with Ebba (of all people) seriously; whereas she is a living symbol of surrender to the transient emotions and enjoyment of the moment. So much is made clear in a vivid image in chapter 14, during the excursion to the *Eremitage*, where deer stream in their hundreds past the royal party, to Ebba's genuine and innocent delight: 'Aber diese Stimmung Ebbas verflog, wie gewöhnlich, rasch wieder' – as swiftly as the deer themselves (V, 92).

6. *FRAU JENNY TREIBEL*

1. The opening sentence of *Frau Jenny Treibel* is highly reminiscent of that of another satirical novel of manners much admired by Fontane, *Vanity Fair*: 'An einem der letzten Maitage, das Wetter war schon sommerlich, bog ein zurückgeschlagener Landauer vom Spittelmarkt her in die Kur- und dann in die Adlerstraße und hielt gleich danach vor einem... ziemlich ansehnlichen, im übrigen altmodischen Hause' (VII, 7). Compare Thackeray: 'While the present century was in its teens, and on one sunshiny morning in June, there drove up to the great iron gate of Miss Pinkerton's academy for young ladies, on Chiswick Mall, a large family coach, with two fat horses in blazing harness, driven by a fat coachman in a three-cornered hat and wig, at the rate of four miles an hour.'

2. Mr Nelson, as an Englishman, has a central role to play in Fontane's allusions to sartorial standards, for 'London was undoubtedly the arbiter of correct masculine costume, as even fashionable foreigners realized' (James Laver, *Dandies*, London 1968, p. 96). Hence the exaggerated, and disappointed, expectations of sartorial revelations from Mr Nelson (VII, 19).

3. See W. Gordon East, *An Historical Geography of Europe* (London 1966), p. 263.

4. This 'rückläufige Bewegung' to which Lorenzen refers is undoubtedly the cult of monumental Germanicness, of self-conscious awareness of the 'great' German past, the 'deliberate grafting of the new Reich on to fictitious traditions' (see Sagarra, *Tradition and Revolution*, p. 296, and also Fontane's reference to the 'Volk der Dichter und Denker' theme, quoted in Attwood, *Fontane und das Preußentum*, p. 271).

5. *Das Unterrichtswesen im deutschen Reich*, ed. W. Lexis; 'Geschichtlicher Rückblick', Dr R. Lehmann, vol. II (Berlin 1904), p. 71.

6. *Das Unterrichtswesen im deutschen Reich*, p. 76.

7. Heller, 'Fontane and the Novelist's Art', p. 1224.

8. On this question of reconciling the voices of reason and the heart, see E. Kohn-Bramstedt's observations on Thackeray and *Effi Briest*, 'Marriage and Misalliance in Thackeray and Fontane', *German Life and Letters*, III (July 1939), 285–97; p. 296.

9. This is not, of course, a new observation, but was made as long ago as the late 1920s by H. Spiero, *Fontane* (Wittenberg 1928), p. 269: 'Was für die einen der Holzhof, der Kommerzienratstitel und eine Meißner Vase, ist für die andern die amtliche Versorgung, der Professortitel und der Zeus.'

10. Although, as circumstances dictate, this Schmidt territory (the 'Englisches Haus') is only hired for the evening.

11. Compare the letter to Fontane's daughter Mete, 13 March 1888: 'Wir haben nur das bißchen Kunst und Wissenschaft, das uns, in ehrlicher Arbeit, über uns erhebt und haben als Bestes – die Natur.' For Professor Schmidt, too, 'Natur ist Sittlichkeit und überhaupt die Hauptsache'

(VII, 167). Note that the first draft of *Frau Jenny Treibel* was completed in the spring of 1888.

7. *DIE POGGENPUHLS*

1. Hugo Aust points out that the Poggenpuhls belong, as they always have, to this distinct sub-species of the Junker class, and not to the landed core of the *Junkertum*: 'Historisch gesehen, gehören die Poggenpuhls dem "Schwertadel" an; nicht der Grundbesitz, sondern die militärische Leistung bildete die Grundlage für seinen gesellschaftlichen Führungsanspruch' ('Theodor Fontane: "Die Poggenpuhls". Zu Gehalt und Funktion einer Romanform', *Fontane aus heutiger Sicht*, ed. Aust, p. 218).

2. Aust suggests that the Poggenpuhls represent a different case from the Junkers in general. Whereas the landed Junker class was in a state of unprecedented decline by the end of the nineteenth century, as contemporary observers such as Friedrich Engels and Max Weber frequently noted, the Poggenpuhls have *never* done more than subsist and cling desperately to their aristocratic status. 'Die Familiengeschichte der Poggenpuhls versiegt nicht, sondern sie dauert an' (Aust, p. 222). Yet they have surely survived intact, with their quaint aristocratic code of honour, only because of the prestige enjoyed by the aristocracy in general. That prestige constituted a large part of their identity, so that once the Junker class comes under critical scrutiny and is no longer accepted unquestioningly as a natural ruling élite, the Poggenpuhls too are faced with a decline which is new even to them. City life inescapably presents them with the unpalatable truth which the rural Junker can more easily evade.

3. Koch, *A History of Prussia*, p. 273.

4. Fontane asserts once again his admiration of independence, in a letter of 24 Nov. 1880 to Graf Philipp zu Eulenburg: 'Jeder Mensch, der den Mut hat, anders zu empfinden als der große Haufe, auch selbst in Mutsachen *mutig* anders zu empfinden, als die lederne Tapferkeitsschablone vorschreibt, erweckt mein Interesse.'

5. His criticism is aimed at the new 'heroic' cult of the Second Reich, the bombastic style and would-be 'greatness' of parvenu Prussia.

6. But this particular opposition of poetic and prosaic, summoned up by the invocation of contrasting names, has a long history in Fontane. See the contrast of 'Cromwell' and 'James Watt' (both names of locomotives) in the 'Waltham-Abbey' essay (XVII, 413).

7. The Quitzows, Dietrich and Johann, were Junkers who rebelled, in the early fifteenth century, against usurping Hohenzollern power. See Fontane's letter of 6 June 1893 to Friedrich Stephany, and also Reuter, *Fontane*, vol. 1, pp. 470–1.

8. *DER STECHLIN*

1. As Charlotte Jolles has pointed out, in raising this topic (as in many other ways) *Der Stechlin* pre-empts Thomas Mann's *Der Zauberberg*, where Naphta is a more demonic counterpart to Professor Cujacius. See ' "Der Stechlin": Fontanes Zaubersee', *Fontane aus heutiger Sicht*, ed. Aust, pp. 239–57.

2. Vogt, *Art of the Nineteenth Century*, p. 142. On the subject of Fontane's attitudes to the art of his time, a question which naturally arises in response to the discussions of art movements in *Der Stechlin*, information may be found in 'Zu kunstkritischen Schriften Fontanes', *Fontane Blätter* 4, part 3, part 27 of series (1978), 174–200; Charlotte Jolles, 'Fontanes Studien über England' in *Fontanes Realismus, Wissenschaftliche Konferenz zum 150. Geburtstag Theodor Fontanes in Potsdam* (Berlin 1972), pp. 99f.; Schuster, *Theodor Fontane: Effi Briest – Ein Leben nach christlichen Bildern*; Wilhelm Vogt, 'Fontane und die bildende Kunst' in *Sämtliche Werke*, Nymphenburg edition, XXIII/2, 188. What we can glean is that Fontane was greatly attracted to Turner (XXIII/1, 28) although he did not approve of the later, more extreme canvasses, where colour and light become the entire content of the painting (XXXIII/1, 139). His attitude to the Impressionists, too, was very positive (XXXIII/2, 171, 1883). Curiously (in the light of the discussions between Cujacius and Woldemar in *Der Stechlin*), Fontane in 1883 *equates* Impressionism and Pre-Raphaelite art, along with Realism and Naturalism, as currents productive of new insights. On the evidence of *Der Stechlin*, fifteen years later Fontane appears to have modified his preference for the Pre-Raphaelites (recorded as early as 1874, letter to the Zöllners of 3 Nov.) and he now contrasts the Impressionists to them. In short, however, both movements (Impressionists *and* Pre-Raphaelites) at various times served their turn for him as antithetical to 'hierarchical' art.

3. It must be added, though, that Fontane does not extend his admiration for the middle way to include the middle *class*. His view is fairly accurately conveyed by Wrschowitz in *Der Stechlin* in conversation with Melusine: 'Oberklasse gutt, Unterklasse serr gutt; Mittelklasse *nicht* serr gutt' (VIII, 216). The appealing quality of Fontane's Junkers lies in their combination of upper-class unselfconsciousness and their ability to remain in touch with the common clay ('Es heißt immer, der Adel gehöre auf seine Scholle, und je mehr er mit der verwachse, desto besser sei es. Das ist auch richtig': Stechlin to Graf Barby, VIII, 283). This gives the Junkers, in Fontane's no doubt idealized version, great symbolic value as mediators between the aristocracy proper and the lower classes, but without being *middle* class. The latter class is incapable of mediating anything, so busy is it copying its betters, so entirely pleased with itself. As Wrschowitz goes on to say, 'Mittelklassberliner findet gutt, was *er* sagt, aber findet *nicht* gutt, was sagt ein anderer.'

239

4. This phrase was used by Fontane in describing Morven, in 'Oban', *Jenseit des Tweed*, XVII, 364.
5. Charlotte Jolles points out that *Der Stechlin* is the reverse of a *Bildungsroman*, and belongs to another German literary tradition: 'Der "Stechlin" gehört eher zur deutschen literarischen Tradition der Darstellung des Lebensabends. Wir brauchen nur an Storm und Raabe zu denken. Stifters "Nachsommer" vereint beide Elemente...', ' "Der Stechlin": Fontanes Zaubersee', *Fontane aus heutiger Sicht*, ed. Aust, p. 247.
6. On the question of Fontane's knowledge of Nietzsche, see J. Thunecke, 'Lebensphilosophische Anklänge in Fontanes *Stine*', *Formen realistischer Erzählkunst*, pp. 505–25.
7. There is in the novel a play with 'hoch' and its comparative form, and with the prefix 'ober-', which is reminiscent of *Frau Jenny Treibel*. Lorenzen, for example, remarks that 'In unserer Obersphäre herrscht außerdem auch eine naive Neigung, alles "Preußische" für eine höhere Kulturform zu halten' (VIII, 251). Of Lorenzen himself however it is said by Woldemar that he is 'einer aus der wirklichen Obersphäre, genau von daher, wo alles Hohe zu Haus ist, die Hoffnung und sogar die Liebe' (VIII, 143).
8. Cf. McHaffie, 'Fontane's *Irrungen, Wirrungen*', p. 172: 'Fontane's fictional world reverses the values of the real world to ensure that the reader, like the gossiping officers, will find the problems of Botho more engrossing than the policies of Bismarck.' Cf. also p. 260 of *Der Stechlin*, where Dubslav's speech of welcome to his new daughter-in-law refers to past battles and celebrates a new *Siegesbotschaft*: 'Nicht die von Königgrätz und nicht die von Mars-la-Tour, aber die von einem gleich gewichtigem Siege.'
9. To quote Brian Rowley, 'It is a favourite device of the Romantic story to embody the hero's choice between two worlds in a choice between two women, but gradually, as the *Märchen* gives way to the *Novelle*, the embodiment of the supernatural is seen less as an ideal and more as a temptation, while that of the natural appears less shallowly conventional and more solidly real' (*The Romantic Period in Germany*, ed. S. Prawer, London 1970, p. 127; see also Introduction, pp. 6–7).
10. See E. Sagarra, ' "Eingepökeltes Rindfleisch oder Spargel und junges Gemüse?". The Christian Social Background to Fontane's *Stechlin*', *Formen realistischer Erzählkunst*, ed. Thunecke, p. 582.
11. Gundermann plays heavily on Prussian history, while the Junkers, the direct heirs to that history, seem historically unaware, to the point of stupidity. (Cf. 'Die Natur ist dumm', VIII, 25.) Fontane, for all his love of history, may well see their historical ignorance as a positive quality, in contrast to Gundermann's fashionable and chauvinistic over-enthusiasm for a certain interpretation of history. Fontane's social criticism, then, moves into the area of Nietzsche's *Unzeitgemäße Betrachtungen*. Cf. J. P. Stern, *Nietzsche* (Hassocks 1978), p. 49: 'When, in the second of his *Thoughts out of Season* (1874), Nietzsche enquires into "The Use and

Disadvantage of History for Life", the very title of his essay questions one of the cultural axioms of the day – that a knowledge of its own past necessarily strengthens the life of a given society.'

12. Marshall McLuhan quotes (with disapproval, of course) John Crosby writing from Paris to the *New York Herald Tribune* about the installation of the first Telstar communications satellite: 'The fundamental flaw in this communications miracle', observes Crosby, as does Dubslav von Stechlin in his own way, 'is the same one that has bugged every communications miracle since they started carving hieroglyphics on stone tablets. What do you say on it?' *Understanding Media* (London 1964), p. 251.

13. The allusiveness and ambiguity of political implications is not confined to Dubslav, however, but characterizes the novel throughout and is apparent, for the sake of example, in two related anecdotes which are open to variant interpretations. The stories in question are those of the Siamese princess abducted and misused by a neighbouring potentate – after her repatriation her virgin purity is 'restored' by means of solemn ritual and ceremony – and of the ageing English duchess who has had her facial beauty restored, but objects at law to the high fee claimed by the beautician: the court finds against the duchess. E. F. George ('einer der wenigen, die sich mit der möglichen Funktion der Siam-Geschichte auseinandersetzen', according to Hugo Aust, who endorses George's interpretation) holds that both these stories are cautionary tales warning us not to reject change, since 'to ignore or resist it is to ignore or resist life itself'; for 'what is demanded here in each case is a reversal of the natural order, and this is only possible in a world of grotesque unreality'. I would suggest, somewhat to the contrary, that both these elusive symbolic stories of 'reversal' (be it noted, however, that in the English story the central focus is the existence of the court case at all, rather than the 'reversal') are connected with the power of the imagination to accommodate facts in stable societies which have achieved a high cultural level. Both Siam and nineteenth-century England possess the necessary sophisticated mechanism to deal with 'the scandal of change'. The context of the London anecdote is the expression of Prussian envy of the comparatively progressive English court's ability to handle a modern type of litigation. In the case of the Siamese princess, the key concept once more is surely that of belief, *Vorstellung* or *Gesinnung*, so common and emphatic a theme throughout Fontane. The fact of the Siamese princess's virginity – itself a fetish object whose significance depends on a consensus of belief – is re-created by a collective belief dictated by the culture and laid down in certain ritual gestures enabling the imagination to triumph over factualness. Contrast Prussia's difficulty, as Fontane sees it, in coming to terms with its own abrupt changes in the last third of the nineteenth century, in 'living down' its military successes and evolving social structures (progressive and yet in the best sense regressive, i.e. 'altpreußisch', at the same time) commensurate with the dynamic forces

of its modernization and industrialization. (See E. F. George, 'The Symbol of the Lake and Related Themes in Fontane's *Der Stechlin*', *Forum for Modern Language Studies*, 9 (1973), 150; and Reclam's 'Erläuterungen und Dokumente' volume on *Der Stechlin*, ed. H. Aust (Stuttgart 1978), p. 41.)

SELECT BIBLIOGRAPHY

Unless otherwise indicated, all references to Fontane's writings relate to the Nymphenburg edition of the *Sämtliche Werke* (Munich 1959–). Titles represented here are primarily those to which reference has been made in the text. For a full Fontane bibliography see Charlotte Jolles, *Theodor Fontane*, Sammlung Metzler, vol. 114, 2nd edition (Stuttgart 1976). It is not possible to list all the works on Fontane which I have consulted at some time and from which I have benefited.

Arnold, Matthew: *Friendship's Garland*, London 1871
Attwood, Kenneth: *Fontane und das Preußentum*, Berlin 1970
Aust, Hugo: *Theodor Fontane: Verklärung. Eine Untersuchung zum Ideengehalt seiner Werke*, Bonn 1974
 (ed.) *Fontane aus heutiger Sicht*, Munich 1980
Bance, A. F.: 'Fontane's *Mathilde Möhring*', *The Modern Language Review*, 69 (1974), 121–33
Bange, Pierre: *Ironie et dialogisme dans les Romans de Theodor Fontane*, Grenoble 1974
Bieber, Hugo: *Der Kampf um die Tradition*, Stuttgart 1928
Boime, Albert: *The Academy and French Painting in the Nineteenth Century*, London 1971
Bosshart, Adelheid: *Theodor Fontanes historische Romane*, Winterthur 1957
Breuer, Dieter (et al., ed.): *Literatur als Wissenschaft. Eine Einführung für Germanisten*, Frankfurt a.M. 1972
Brinkmann, Richard: *Theodor Fontane: über die Verbindlichkeit des Unverbindlichen*, 2nd edition, Tübingen 1977
Brown, Norman O.: *Life against Death. The Psychoanalytical Meaning of History*, London 1959
Demetz, Peter: *Formen des Realismus. Theodor Fontane. Kritische Untersuchungen*, 2nd edition, Frankfurt a.M. 1973
'Der Roman der guten Gesellschaft', *Theodor Fontane* (Wege der Forschung, vol. CCCLXXXI), ed. Wolfgang Preisendanz, Darmstadt 1973
East, W. Gordon: *An Historical Geography of Europe*, London 1966
Empson, William: *Seven Types of Ambiguity*, 3rd edition, London 1956
Fontane, Theodor: *Aus dem Nachlaß, Gesammelte Werke II*, vol. IX, Berlin 1905–11
 Causerien über Theater, ed. Paul Schlenther, Berlin 1905
 Schriften zur Literatur, ed. H.-H. Reuter, Berlin 1960
 Theodor Fontanes Briefe. Erste Sammlung, Zweite Sammlung, ed. Otto Pniower and Paul Schlenther, Berlin 1910
 Briefe an Georg Friedländer, ed. Kurt Schreinert, Heidelberg 1954
 Briefe, ed. Kurt Schreinert and Charlotte Jolles, Berlin 1968–
 Fontanes Briefe in zwei Bänden, ed. G. Erler, Berlin and Weimar 1968

SELECT BIBLIOGRAPHY

Aufzeichnungen zur Literatur. Ungedrucktes und Unbekanntes, ed. H.-H. Reuter, Berlin 1969

Theodor Fontane: von Dreißig bis Achtzig, sein Leben in seinen Briefen, ed. H.-H. Reuter, 2nd edition, Munich 1970

Theodor Fontane: Briefe an Wilhelm und Hans Hertz, 1859–1898, ed. K. Schreinert and G. Hay, Stuttgart 1972

Frei, Norbert: *Theodor Fontane: Die Frau als Paradigma des Humanen*, Königstein/Ts. 1980

Garland, H. B.: *The Berlin Novels of Theodor Fontane*, Oxford 1980

Gärtner, Karlheinz: *Theodor Fontane: Literatur als Alternative*, Bonn 1978

Giraud, Raymond: *The Unheroic Hero in the Novels of Stendhal, Balzac and Flaubert*, New Brunswick NJ 1957

Greter, Heinz Eugen: *Fontanes Poetik*, Bern, Frankfurt a.M. 1973

Günther, Vincent J.: *Das Symbol im erzählerischen Werk Fontanes*, Bonn 1967

Heller, Erich: 'Fontane and the Novelist's Art', *Times Literary Supplement*, 20 Oct. 1978

Hoffmann, Werner: *Das Irdische Paradies*, Munich 1960

'Poesie und Prosa: Rangfragen in der neueren Kunst', *Jahrbuch der Hamburger Kunstsammlungen*, XVIII (1973), 173–92

Hohendahl, P. U.: 'Theodor Fontane: *Cécile*. Zum Problem der Mehrdeutigkeit', *Germanisch-Romanische Monatsschrift*, n.s. 18 (1968), 381–405

Jolles, Charlotte: *Theodor Fontane*, Sammlung Metzler, 2nd edition, Stuttgart 1976 (1st edition 1972)

Koch, H. W.: *A History of Prussia*, London 1978

Kohn-Bramstedt, E.: 'Marriage and Misalliance in Thackeray and Fontane', *German Life and Letters*, III (July 1939), 285–97

Leckey, R. Geoffrey: *Some Aspects of Balladesque Art and their Relevance for the Novels of Theodor Fontane*, Bern 1979

Leisenhoff, Carin: *Fontane und das literarische Leben seiner Zeit. Eine literatursoziologische Studie*, Bonn 1976

Lexis, W. (ed.): *Das Unterrichtswesen im deutschen Reich*, Berlin 1904

Lodge, David: *The Modes of Modern Writing*, London 1977

McHaffie, M. A.: 'Fontane's *Irrungen, Wirrungen* and the novel of Realism', *Periods in German Literature*, vol. II, ed. J. M. Ritchie, London 1969

Mann, Thomas: 'Der alte Fontane', *Adel des Geistes*, 1910, reproduced in *Gesammelte Werke*, Aufbau edition, vol. 10, Berlin 1965

Martini, Fritz: *Deutsche Literatur im bürgerlichen Realismus, 1848–98*, Stuttgart 1962

Menthes, Axel (ed.): *Reden Kaiser Wilhelms II*, Munich 1976

Millett, Kate: *Sexual Politics*, New York 1970

Minden, Michael: '"Effi Briest" and "Die historische Stunde des Takts"', *The Modern Language Review*, 76 (1981), 869–79

Mittenzwei, Ingrid: *Die Sprache als Thema: Untersuchungen zu Fontanes Gesellschaftsromanen*, Bad Homburg 1970

Mommsen, Katharina: *Hofmannsthal und Fontane*, Bern etc. 1978

SELECT BIBLIOGRAPHY

Mommsen, W. (ed.): *Deutsche Parteiprogramme, eine Auswahl vom Vormärz bis zur Gegenwart,* Munich 1960

Morley, John: *John Morley: Nineteenth-Century Essays,* ed. P. Stansky, Chicago 1970

Mullan, W. N. B.: *Grillparzer's Aesthetic Theory,* Stuttgart 1979

Müller-Seidel, Walter: *Theodor Fontane. Soziale Romankunst in Deutschland,* Stuttgart 1975

Nürnberger, Helmut: *Der frühe Fontane,* Hamburg 1967

Oberle, Werner: *Der adelige Mensch in der Dichtung,* Basel 1950

Paulin, Roger: 'The German Historical Novel 1830–1870', unpublished text of paper delivered at Conference of University Teachers of German in Great Britain and Ireland, Manchester 1979

Praz, Mario: *The Hero in Eclipse in Victorian Fiction,* London 1956

Preisendanz, Wolfgang: *Humor als dichterische Einbildungskraft,* Munich 1963

Rank, Otto: *The Don Juan Legend,* transl. David G. Winter, Princeton 1975

Reuter, H.-H.: *Fontane,* vols. I and II, Munich 1968

Richter, Karl: *Resignation. Eine Studie zum Werk Theodor Fontanes,* Munich 1966

Rowley, B. A.: 'Theodor Fontane: A German Novelist in the European Tradition?', *German Life and Letters,* n.s. XV (1961), 72–88

Sagarra, Eda: *Tradition and Revolution,* London 1971

A Social History of Germany 1648–1914, London 1977

Schäfer, Renate: 'Fontanes Melusine-Motive', *Euphorion,* 56 (1962), 69–104

Schobess, J. and Teitge, H.-E. (eds): *Fontanes Realismus: Wissenschaftliche Konferenz zum 150 Geburtstag Theodor Fontanes in Potsdam: Vorträge und Berichte,* Berlin 1972

Schöll, N.: '*Mathilde Möhring*: Ein anderer Fontane?', *Formen realistischer Erzählkunst: Festschrift for Charlotte Jolles,* ed. J. Thunecke, Nottingham 1979

Schuster, Peter-Klaus: *Theodor Fontane: Effi Briest – Ein Leben nach christlichen Bildern,* Tübingen 1978

Schwartz, P. P.: ' "Tragische Analysis" und Schicksalsvorausdeutungen in Fontanes Roman *Effi Briest*', *Sprachkunst,* 7 (1976), 247–60

Sengle, F.: 'Der Romanbegriff in der ersten Hälfte des neunzehnten Jahrhunderts', *Arbeiten zur deutschen Literatur 1750–1850,* Stuttgart 1965

Spiero, Heinrich: *Fontane,* Wittenberg 1928

Stern, J. P.: *Re-Interpretations,* London 1964

Subiotto, Frances M.: 'The function of letters in Fontane's *Unwiederbringlich*', *The Modern Language Review,* 65 (1970), 306–18

Swales, Erika: 'Private Mythologies and Public Unease: on Fontane's *Effi Briest*', *The Modern Language Review,* 75 (1980), 114–23

Thanner, Josef: *Die Stilistik Theodor Fontanes. Untersuchungen zur Erhellung des Begriffes 'Realismus' in der Literatur,* The Hague/Paris 1967

Thunecke, J. (ed.): *Formen realistischer Erzählkunst. Festschrift for Charlotte Jolles,* Nottingham 1979

SELECT BIBLIOGRAPHY

Unamuno Y Jugo, M.: *The Tragic Sense of Life*, transl. J. E. Crawford Flitch, New York 1954

Vogt, A. M.: *Art of the Nineteenth Century*, transl. A. F. Bance, London 1973

Wandrey, Conrad: *Theodor Fontane*, Munich 1919

Weber, Dietrich: *'Effi Briest* − "Auch wie ein Schicksal"; über den Andeutungsstil bei Fontane', *Jahrbuch des freien deutschen Hochstifts* (1966), pp. 457–74

Willey, Basil: *Nineteenth Century Studies*, London 1949

INDEX

INDEX

1608437R0

Printed in Great Britain
by Amazon.co.uk, Ltd.,
Marston Gate.